Explore

NELLES

CANADA

PACIFIC COAST, THE ROCKIES, PRAIRIE PROVINCES, AND THE TERRITORIES

Authors:
Nicola Förg, Katrain Habermann, Arno Bindl, Astrid Filzek-Schwab, Jürgen Scheunemann, Michael Werner, Bernhard Mogge, Dionys Zink

An Up-to-date travel guide with 143 color photos and 17 maps

First Edition
1998

Dear Reader,

Being up-to-date is the main goal of the Nelles series. To achieve it, we have a net-work of far-flung correspondents who keep us abreast of the latest developments in the travel scene, and our cartographers always make sure that maps and texts are adjusted to each other.

Each travel chapter ends with its own list of useful tips, accommodations, restaurants, tourist offices, sights. At the end of the book you will find practical information from A to Z. But the travel world is fast moving, and we cannot guarantee that all the contents are always valid. Should you come across a discrepancy, please write us at: Nelles Verlag GmbH, Schleissheimer Str. 371 b, D-80935 München, Germany, Tel: (089) 3571940, Fax: (089) 35719430.

LEGEND

	Public or Significant Building		National Border		Interstate
	Hotel		Provincial Border		Toll Expressway
	Shopping Center	Kapuskasing	Place mentioned in Text		Expressway
o	Market				Principal Highway
✝	Church	✳	Place of Interest		Main Road
●	Underground Station	♣	National Park, Provincial Park		Other Road
⊁	International Airport	\ 25 /	Distance in Kilometers		Railway
⊰	National Airport	Mt. Otish 1135	Mountain Summit (Height in Meters)		Trans-Canada Highway
					U.S. Highway
					Route Number

CANADA
Pacific Coast, the Rockies,
Prairie Provinces, and the Territories
© Nelles Verlag GmbH, D-80935 München
All rights reserved

First edition 1998
ISBN 3-88618-368-8
Printed in Slovenia

Publisher:	Günter Nelles	**English Editor:**	Anne Midgette
Editor in Chief:	Berthold Schwarz	**Translations:**	Lesley Booth, Kent Lyon
Project Editor:	Nicola Förg	**Maps:**	Nelles Verlag GmbH
Editors:	Andrea Russ	**Color Separations:**	Priegnitz,
	Susanne Braun		München
Photo Editor:	K. Bärmann-Thümmel	**Printed by:**	Gorenjski Tisk

- X03 -

TABLE OF CONTENTS

GUIDELINES

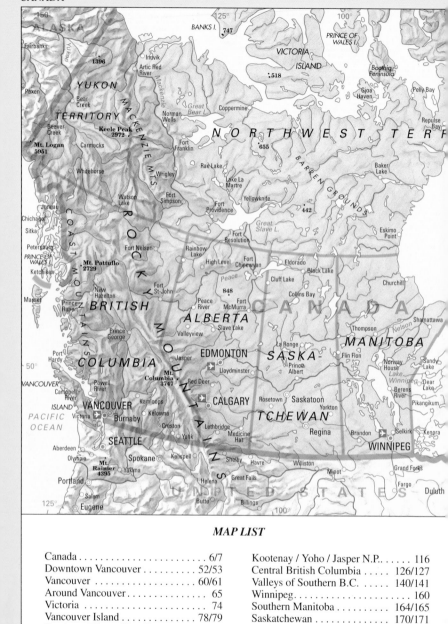

MAP LIST

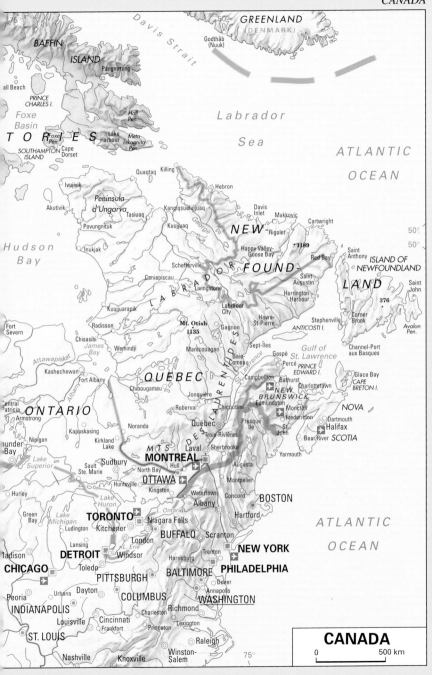

Davis Strait

GREENLAND
(DENMARK)

Godthåb
(Nuuk)

BAFFIN

ISLAND

Pangnirtung

all Beach

PRINCE
CHARLES I.

Foxe
Basin

Hall
Pen.

Labrador

Sea

ATLANTIC

OCEAN

T O R I E S

Foxe
Pen.

Lake
Harbour

Meta
Inkognita
Pen.

SOUTHAMPTON
ISLAND

Cape
Dorset

Quaqtaq   Killing

Hebron

Ivujivik

Peninsula
d'Ungarva

Tasiuaq

Kangiqsualujjuaq

Davis
Inlet

Makkovic

Cartwright

Akutivik

Povungnituk

Kuujjuaq

NEW

Rigolet

50°
50°

Hudson

Bay

Inukjak

George

Happy-Valley-
Goose Bay

•1189

Red Bay

Saint
Anthony

ISLAND OF
NEWFOUNDLAND

Scheffferville

FOUND-

Saint-
Augustin

Saint
John

Caniapiscau

Livingstone

Harrington
Harbour

LAND

Kuujjuarapik

L A B R A D O R

Labrador
City

Gagnon

Havre-
St-Pierre

Stephenville

ANTICOSTI I.

Corner
Brook

376

Fort
Severn

Radisson

Mt. Otish
1135

Sept-Îles

Channel-Port
aux Basques

Avalon
Pen.

Chisasibi

Wemindji

James
Bay

Manicouagan

Gulf of
St. Lawrence

Attawapiskat

Albany

Kashechewan

Baie-
Comeau

Gaspé

Percé

PRINCE
EDWARD I.

Glace Bay

CAPE
BRETON I.

Fort Albany

QUEBEC

Chibougamau

Campbellton

Bathurst

Charlottetown

entral
atricia

Armstrong

ONTARIO

Noranda

Jonquière

Roberval

Chicoutimi

NEW
BRUNSWICK

Edmundston

Moncton

Fredericton

St.
John

NOVA

Dartmouth

Halifax

Nipigon

Kapuskasing

Kirkland
Lake

Québec

Presque
Île

Bear River

SCOTIA

under
Bay

Lake
Superior

M T S

Trois-Rivières

Laval

Sherbrooke

Yarmouth

Sudbury

North Bay

Hull

MONTREAL

Augusta

Sault
Ste. Marie

Huntsville

OTTAWA

Montpelier

Hurley

Lake
Huron

Kingston

Watertown

Concord

BOSTON

ATLANTIC

Green
Bay

Lake
Michigan

Ludington

Albany

Hartford

OCEAN

TORONTO

Niagara Falls

Madison

Lansing

Kitchener

BUFFALO

Scranton

London

DETROIT

Windsor

L. Erie

Trenton

NEW YORK

Toledo

Harrisburg

CHICAGO

PITTSBURGH

BALTIMORE

PHILADELPHIA

Peoria

Urbana

Dayton

COLUMBUS

Dover

INDIANAPOLIS

Louisville

Cincinnati

Annapolis

WASHINGTON

Charleston

Richmond

ST. LOUIS

Frankfort

Princeton

Lexington

Nashville

Knoxville

Winston-
Salem

Raleigh

75°

CANADA

0   500 km

DES LAURENTIDES

St. Lawrence

L. Ontario

7

THE COUNTRY AND ITS PEOPLE

Nearly everyone, at one time or another, has dreamed of outdoor adventures, of complete solitude in gorgeous scenic surroundings, where the constraints and concerns of modern life fade into unimportance. In Canada, you can rediscover your sense of wonder. In the Prairie Provinces of Manitoba, Saskatchewan and Alberta there are grasslands and wheat fields stretching as far as the eye can see; in British Columbia, fishermen experience moments of greatness on the shores of crystal-clear lakes, and in the Arctic zone, the midnight sun shines upon the drifting ice floes. Motorists are ecstatic when they can drive miles on end without encountering another vehicle – ecstatic, at least, until they find themselves stranded on the roadside with a flat tire for the first time. While herds of bison graze in the vast national and provincial parks, campers accustomed to all the comforts of home test their stamina as they pitch tents in the wilderness far from civilization, flip through their books to see what to do when face to face with a bear or moose, trudge along overgrown trails or wade through torrents while carrying heavy backpacks. Those who find the Rocky Mountains too monotonous can head for the Pacific coast and enjoy the British way of life and culture in Vancouver, journey back into bygone days in the nostalgic atmosphere of old gold rush towns, or simply savor Canadian hospitality and its people's easygoing lifestyle.

Preceding pages: Maligne Lake – one among many watery jewels. Inuit – a native people in the throes of cultural change. Left: A perfect recreation: Barkerville evokes the days of the Gold Rush.

Although maple forests are rather rare in western Canada, no visitor to the country in autumn will soon forget the memorable spectacle of their foliage, drenched in hues of bright yellow and flaming red. After such a sight, it becomes clear why the Canadians chose a red maple leaf to adorn their national flag as a symbol of the country.

Canada was colonized by the French in the 17th century, fell to England in 1763 in the French and Indian War, and is today an autonomous member of the British Commonwealth. Although some factions feel close ties to their British "motherland," disputes and rivalries continually flare up between English- and French-speaking Canadians in this officially bilingual country. Another sensitive issue is the native population's struggle to regain their ancestral lands. After decades of effort, the government finally granted 18,000 Inuit their own territory in 1993. Now, other Indian tribes are demanding their own land, as well.

GEOGRAPHY

The Northwest Territories, Yukon Territory, British Columbia and Alberta comprise the western half of Canada; this guide also describes the country's central reaches, the provinces of Saskatchewan and Manitoba. Canada measures nearly 4 million square miles (9,997,000 sq. km) in area, making it, after Russia, the second-largest nation on Earth. From the Atlantic to the Pacific, Canada measures 3,400 miles (5,500 km), and nearly 3,000 miles (4,600 km) from north to south. With roughly 300,000 square miles (755,000 sq. km) of inland water, Canada enjoys one-third of the world's fresh water. Water also forms its natural borders: the Arctic Sea to the north, the Atlantic to the east, and the Pacific to the west. The United States shares with Canada three of the "Great Lakes" – Superior, Huron and Erie – while from the

province of Manitoba to British Columbia, the 49th parallel, a straight line, forms the U.S.-Canadian border. On the Pacific coast, the Coast Mountains – with elevations of up to nearly 10,000 feet (3,000 m) – stretch from north to south, running parallel to the Rocky Mountains.

The Canadian Shield wraps around Hudson Bay like a horseshoe. This geological plate in the Canadian northeast consists of Precambrian volcanic rock estimated to be 3.5 billion years old. Today it forms a rocky, hilly landscape with scattered lakes. The prairies of the U.S. continue into the large Interior Plains of Canada; the fertile, sedimentary soil here is a result of huge lakes formed during the Ice Age which disappeared over the centuries. Lake Manitoba and Lake Winnipeg, for instance, are remains of the gigantic Ice Age lake known as Agassiz. In three levels, the so-called prairie steps,

the Lowlands rise from 980 to 4,900 feet (300 - 1,500 m). The Cordillera or Coast Mountains on the Pacific coast, with their characteristic steep faults, were formed during the continental drift as tremendous geologic forces pushed tectonic plates along the North American continental plate. At nearly 20,000 feet (5,950 m), Mount Logan in the Yukon Territory is Canada's highest point. Offshore by the Northwest Territories lies the Arctic archipelago, measuring a total 507,000 square miles (1.3 mill. sq. km).

Climate

"Ten months of good sledding, two months of bad," quipped a manager of Hudson's Bay Northern Stores, asked to define Canada's climate. And when describing a colony that was, in his day, known as La Nouvelle France, Voltaire, the sharp-tongued French philosopher and writer, had only the disparaging observation, "Nothing more than a few fields covered with snow."

Above: Canadian winters are darn cold! Right: Low scrub and lichen are characteristic of the Canadian tundra.

14

In Canada, summers are dry and, by European standards, more warm than hot: average temperatures in July and August run around 77°F/25°C. Winters in the north are severe, with temperatures sinking to -40°F (-40°C). In the winter of 1989/90 temperatures dropped to as low as -58°F (-50°C). The closer you get to the Arctic Circle, the longer they last; and parts of the Canadian Shield are literally frozen solid the whole year round.

Due to the mountains running north-south, there are, however, exceptions: cold Arctic air flows into the United States, while tropical warm air from the Gulf of Mexico brings hot days to central Canada. According to statistics, rainy days outweigh sunny days by 200:160.

Hurricanes rage across the country several times a year, ushering in long periods of rain that often result in flooding. Tornadoes are less frequent; but when they do come they can cause casualties and immense destruction. One curious weather phenomenon is the chinook, especially in Alberta; this warm wind can create temperature increases of as much as 65°F (20°C) within an hour.

Flora and Fauna

The vast, sparsely populated country consists of glaciers, forests, treeless tundra, green, wooded taiga and fertile plains where grain is cultivated. In western Canada there are three dozen national and provincial parks; one of these alone, the Wood Buffalo Park, is larger than Switzerland. The permafrost of the Arctic region allows mosses, lichens, small bushes and berries to flourish on what is otherwise barren ground; these plants form a dietary staple for musk ox and caribou.

To the south, there is a band of forest tundra 300-500 miles wide (500-800 km), sprinkled with lakes and coniferous trees such as spruce, white and jackpine; this provides an ideal habitat for black bears, beaver, deer and moose. Farther south, near Edmonton, the forest turns into parkland. Aspens, berry and hazelnut

15

bushes add color to the autumn foliage, particularly on the clear sunny days of an "Indian summer."

Towering cedars and spruce are characteristic of the coastal rain forest. South of Alberta, Saskatchewan and Manitoba, grasslands and farmland dominate: this was the grazing land of the immense bison and buffalo herds back in 1830 when they numbered 40 million head. Just 70 years later, their population had shrunk to 1,000 head. Today, large herds of these animals have come back to graze, but only in protected areas.

HISTORY

The original inhabitants of present-day Canada were Indians and Inuit who migrated from northern Asia across the Bering Strait. According to Icelandic sagas, Vikings sailed to the shores of North America as early as the 10th century; archaeologists have indeed found remains of a Viking colony in Newfoundland.

In 1497, Giovanni Cabato (John Cabot), an Italian from Genoa in the service of Henry VII of England, attempted to reach China via the fabled Northwest Passage – his voyage, however, ended on the eastern shores of Newfoundland. The Frenchman Jacques Cartier discovered the St. Lawrence River and laid claim to the surrounding land on behalf of France. The immensely rich fishing grounds attracted English and French fishermen, while trappers and fur traders made contact with the Huron and Algonquin Indians and exchanged valuable furs for knives, axes and European goods.

The fur trade was soon booming, and the French government offered traders the exclusive rights to trade furs providing they establish settlements in the "New World." In 1604 the French seaman Samuel de Champlain, who had received this monopoly, took a group of

Above: Leif Eriksson discovers America.
Right: Trading firewater for furs – a dubious bargain.

16

settlers to Canada to found the colony of Acadia. Unfortunately, the colony was plagued by famine, illness and conflicts with the Indians. Port Royal in Nova Scotia, present-day Annapolis, became the center of "New France." New trading posts sprang up in the surrounding area and the French pioneers, *coureurs de bois*, explored vast areas of North America. Champlain founded a trading post on the banks of the St. Lawrence River in 1608, on the site of present-day Quebec City.

The English attempted to assert their territorial claims by attacking the French settlements. Two decisive events occurred to further their efforts. First, Champlain had soon became involved in tribal fighting between the Algonquin and Iroquois Indians. When he sided with the Algonquin, the Iroquois immediately became his bitter enemies; and they took their revenge, when England appeared on the scene to challenge France's power, by fighting on the side of the English. And then two French fur traders, angry with

their governor because of exorbitant trade taxes and road tolls and frustrated by English competition, founded the Hudson's Bay Company (HBC) in 1670, further weakening France's influence. Before long, the HBC controlled extensive parts of the French territories, and it continued to expand its influence.

In 1713, England took Newfoundland, which had thereto been inhabited by both nations, and France was left only with the tiny islands of St. Pierre and Miquelon. This defeat was followed by a number of attacks over the next few decades, which finally culminated in the French and Indian War (1756-63), from which the English emerged as victors. At the beginning of the English colonial period (1763-1867) there were 60,000 French settlers in Canada, but only 3,000 English ones. England, however, managed to deal with this difficult situation with the Quebec Act of 1774, under which the Catholic French-Canadians were granted the right to their own language, private ownership, French civil law and freedom

17

of religion. The next year saw the outbreak of the Revolutionary War (1775-1783), the struggle between the 13 English colonies to the south and their former "mother country" which led to the founding of the United States of America.

Canada remained neutral, but some 50,000 loyalist English settlers who found themselves on the "wrong" side of the newly-drawn American border migrated to Nova Scotia, New Brunswick and Ontario. Thus, England's French colony was gradually transformed into a region dominated by English speakers. French influence was steadily eroded further, until the mid-19th century, with a continuing influx of hundreds of thousands of immigrants from Ireland, Scotland, England and Germany. After a lot of backing and forthing between the two nations, the 49th parallel was finally recognized as the border between Ontario, Canada and the USA in 1846.

Above: Canadian paper factories can grow to enormous dimensions.

1867 marked the beginning of a new era: in this year, the present-day provinces of Quebec (Lower Canada) and Ontario (Upper Canada) united with New Brunswick and Nova Scotia to form a new federal state, the Dominion of Canada, and proclaimed its own constitution based on those of England and the United States. The massive territory of the Hudson's Bay Company was integrated two years later; 1870 saw the addition of the province of Manitoba, followed by British Columbia in 1871, and, after some years had passed, Alberta, Saskatchewan and the Northwest Territories in 1904 and 1905.

In the 20th century, Canada supported Great Britain during the Boer War and participated in both World Wars. The World Wars also set off a new wave of immigration to Canada. The young nation was caught up in the turbulence of international economic crises; workers and farmers demanded improvements to their material situation. Canada became a member of the United Nations in 1945 and a member of NATO in 1949. In the same year, Newfoundland joined the confederation. In 1969, under Prime Minister Pierre Trudeau, the Official Languages Act went into effect: the country pledged to support French language and culture, and recognized both French and English as official languages with equal status and equal use in administration and civil services. In 1988, Canada became the first country in the world to pass a law supporting multiculturalism.

Although Queen Elizabeth proclaimed Canada's independence with the Constitution Act on April 17, 1982, the nation remains a member of the Commonwealth. The Queen of England is sovereign of Canada and is represented as head of state by a Governor General, an official nominated by the Cabinet in Ottawa and appointed by the Queen. The Governor General appoints and dismisses ministers, signs bills into law and generally represents the country. The federal parliamentary monarchy of Canada consists of ten provinces and two territories with their own constitutions. Each region is governed by a provincial governor.

There are approximately 150 ethnic groups living in Canada. Of these, 67% speak English and 26% speak French. Among the remaining 7% are descendants of practically every other nation in the world, many of whom are Germans who continue to cultivate their mother tongue. Most of these groups get along well with one another; it's only between the English- and French-speaking Canadians that tensions still frequently arise.

Many French-Canadians long for their own state within the confederation. In 1980, when the issue came to a referendum, 60% of the French-Canadians living in Quebec voted against it. In the independence referendum in October, 1995, the separatists were defeated by a mere 27,000 votes. British Columbia, Alberta and Newfoundland have also expressed a wish for independence.

THE PROVINCES

British Columbia

Before the first Europeans began to explore the shores of what is now British Columbia, nearly 80,000 Indians were living in the region. Aside from being excellent fishermen, they traded on "intertribal routes" in copper, furs, mussels, fish oil and blankets made from the wool of wild goats.

In 1778, James Cook landed on the island that would later be named Vancouver Island in honor of Captain George Vancouver, who surveyed the coastline and the island in the service of the British Crown. James Cook's reports of the abundance of furs attracted many traders who came to buy the highly prized otter pelts from the Indians.

In 1793, Alexander Mackenzie of the North West Company was the first to travel overland across the North American continent and reach the Pacific coast. In 1805, on McLeod Lake, Simon Fraser founded the area's first trading post. In their search for valuable furs, the fur traders penetrated deeper and deeper into the wilderness, establishing an entire chain of trading posts as they did so. After 1843, Fort Victoria was the most important trading post and the western headquarters of the Hudson's Bay Company.

Vancouver Island was declared a British colony in 1849; in 1858, the government proclaimed the mainland as the colony of British Columbia (B.C.) and in 1871, both colonies were united to form the province of British Columbia, with Victoria as the capital.

British Columbia is rich in minerals and natural resources, and its per capita income is among the highest in all of Canada. Thanks to the extensive forests on Vancouver Island and along the coast, with Douglas and hemlock fir, cedars and pines, Port Alberni, Nanaimo, Prince George, Powell River and Quesnel have

Sullivan Mine at Kimberley is among the most productive lead and zinc mines in the world. Kitimat's aluminum factory secures Canada's position as the world's third-largest producer of aluminum. Aircraft and shipbuilding, food processing, and the chemicals and electronics fields are other industries that contribute greatly to the province's prosperity.

Alberta

The first European to roam the territory of the nomadic Prairie Indians was the Frenchman Pierre Gaultier de La Vérendrye, in 1740. A few white settlers and fur traders soon followed. At the end of the 18th century, the two rivals Hudson's Bay Company and North West Company established trading posts along the rivers; after 1870, settlers began farming. The number of Indians had been drastically reduced: the white man had slaughtered their main dietary staple, the bison, and many Indians died of illnesses brought in by the settlers, such as influenza and tuberculosis. In addition, traveling traders from Montana stirred up trouble by offering Indians cheap whiskey in exchange for their furs. Ultimately, the North West Mounted Police intervened and established a post at Fort McLeod in 1874. As the years passed, the Indians were pushed farther and farther westward.

become centers for processing lumber, especially the manufacture of paper and cellulose.

Today, tourism has blossomed into the region's second-largest industry; fishing (salmon and halibut) is another major source of revenue. And various agricultural specializations have developed in the predominately mountainous areas of B.C.: agriculture in the Fraser Valley; fruit and vegetable farming, and even wine, in Okanagan Valley. In the northeast, on the border with Alberta, wheat and oats are cultivated. The regions around William's Lake and Kamloops have developed into major centers for raising beef cattle.

Mining is one of Canada's oldest industries. Copper, lead, zinc, sliver and gold are mined near Prince George, Kamloops and Trail; one of the largest smelters in the country operates at Trail. The

The Canadian Pacific Railway reached Calgary in 1883, and an increasing number of settlers poured into Alberta, which became a Canadian province in 1905, and by 1911 already had a population of 374,000.

Due to its petroleum and gas reserves, as well as its fertile soils, Alberta is one of the richest provinces in Canada. Wheat, barley, oats, and forage cereals are the main crops on its area of more than 49,000,000 acres (20 million ha). Livestock also plays an important role. Its agricultural surplus is exported to more than 40 countries.

Above: An oil pump in Alberta. Right: In 1774, Samuel Hearne founded the first village in Saskatchewan.

The first oil well in the province was tapped near Calgary in 1914. Today, there are more than 10,000 oil and gas wells in central and northern Alberta. In addition, huge coal deposits help keep the unemployment rate the lowest in Canada. Edmonton, the capital of Alberta, has risen to become the country's third-largest financial center, after Toronto and Montreal.

Saskatchewan

Before the first farmers broke the soil with their ploughs, herds of bison ranged the vast grassy plains of this broad province. After 1750, when French pioneers began making their way through the wilds, the Hudson's Bay Company and North West Company set up trading posts along the Saskatchewan River.

The first permanent settlement, Cumberland House, was established by the British explorer Samual Hearne in 1774. The year 1873 saw the founding of the North West Mounted Police. When the railroad reached Saskatchewan, rampant land speculation and the accompanying change in living standards led to an open rebellion of the Métis (half-breeds descended from the unions of European settlers and Indian women). In 1885, the Métis joined forces with the Blackfoot and Cree Indians to demand rights to the land; but with the help of North West Mounted Police, their rebellion was put down. In 1882, the government of the territories established its headquarters in Regina. The first election took place in 1897, and Regina has been the capital ever since Saskatchewan became a province in 1905.

The primary source of income is agriculture: a full one-third of the province's area is used for grain. Saskatchewan produces more than 60% of Canada's entire wheat crop. Next in importance is livestock (chickens, turkeys, pigs and sheep), particularly in the southern part of the

province. Natural energy sources are also being developed – Saskatchewan is the second-largest producer of petroleum in Canada. Natural gas has been discovered in the southwestern part of the country, and 40% of the world's potash deposits are found in Saskatchewan. As for mineral resources, uranium, copper, zinc, silver, gold, and selenium are all mined here. Tourism is also growing in importance; hunters and fishermen, in particular, enjoy visiting Saskatchewan.

Manitoba

The first seafarers reached Hudson Bay in 1610. Sixty years later, King Charles II of England granted a charter with rights to the land to the Hudson's Bay Company. This company, however, had its hands full competing with the French trading company Radisson and de Grosseilliers, who held their own trade monopoly in the area. Together with his sons, the Frenchman Pierre Gaultier de La Vérendrye opened trading posts in the

Red River region in the early 1730s, and, in 1737, founded what is now Winnipeg. Some years later, Lord Selkirk arrived with Scottish settlers, who established an agricultural colony in the middle of the prairie. After the Hudson's Bay Company sold its land holdings to the new nation of Canada in 1869, Manitoba was declared the fifth Canadian province in 1870. The railroad reached Manitoba at the end of the 19th century, and brought a flood of immigrants into the region.

In this easternmost of the three Prairie Provinces, agriculture provides the main source of income. Grain cultivation and cattle breeding yield high profits. The forest belt in the north forms the basis for the lumber industry, with paper and cellulose factories; fishing and fur-trapping also remain important sectors of the economy. Mineral resources, such as copper, nickel, gold and zinc, are also

Above: Temporarily thawed – tundra in the Northwest Territories. Right: On the trail of gold (the Chilkoot Pass in 1896-97).

mined here. Manitoba has massive oil resources and maintains large hydroelectric power stations on the Saskatchewan and Nelson Rivers. The province is sparsely populated: only 1 million people live in an area of more than 390,000 square miles (1 million sq. km), and 50% of that population lives in the capital, Winnipeg.

Northwest Territories

Seeking the Northwest Passage to the Orient in 1576, Martin Frobisher, an English navigator, was the first European to explore the Arctic waters of what is now called the Northwest Territories. He founded the settlement Frobisher Bay on Baffin Island, today Iqualuit. The first European to describe the interior of the country was Samuel Hearne, who traveled from Hudson Bay to the mouth of the Coppermine River on the northern coast in 1770. In 1779, Alexander Mackenzie of the Hudson's Bay Company discovered the Great Slave Lake. A 19th-century explorer, Sir John Franklin, surveyed the Mackenzie District and a large part of the northern coastline. Most of the settlements in this region were founded for whalers and missionaries. Back then, the northern part of today's Prairie Provinces and the whole area up to the Alaskan border were part of the Northwest Territories; the province's present borders were not drawn up until 1912.

The Territories cover an area of 1,337,700 square miles (3.34 million sq. km). Half of the estimated 55,000 inhabitants are Indians and Inuit; the other half are Métis and Canadians of European descent. Oil has been extracted here since 1920; a couple of years ago, additional reserves of oil and natural gas were discovered in the Mackenzie River delta. Around 1930, the discovery of gold drew people from every nation to Yellowknife to try their luck at prospecting; today, the Giant and Con Mines are still among Canada's largest producers of gold. Mining, in fact, is the province's most important industry: in addition to gold, the mines yield zinc, lead, silver, copper, tungsten, cadmium and bismuth. Fur trapping, as well as the artisan work of the Dene Indians and the Inuit, are also notable sources of revenue.

Yukon and the Gold Rush

Yukon is an Indian word meaning "great river," and the place was destined to live up to the promise of its name. On August 17, 1896, George Carmack, "Shookum Jim" Mason and Tagish Charlie stumbled upon some large gold nuggets in the scree and gravel of Bonanza Creek, a tributary of the Klondike River at its confluence with the Yukon. This sparked off a nearly inconceivable rush to the gold fields: in May 1898 alone, 4,735 ships, boats and barges made their up the Yukon to Dawson City, bearing a total of 28,000 prospectors. It was a dangerous journey: hundreds of boats foundered in the turbulent waters of Miles

Canyon. The whirlpools and underwater rocks claimed so many lives that eventually local guides had to be employed to guide the various vessels through the infamous White Horse Rapids. Just a year later, 60 steamers, 8 river tugs and 20 freight barges capsized on the river.

And yet most of the prospectors poured in over the Inside Passage and the Coast Mountains. The Canadian historian Pierre Berton has made a list of provisions a man needed to sustain him on the trail over the steep Chilkoot Pass into the Yukon: 400 pounds of wheat flour, 50 pounds each of corn and oatmeal, 35 pounds of rice, 100 pounds of beans, 100 pounds of sugar, 8 pounds of baking powder, 200 pounds of ham, 2 pounds of soda, 36 yeast cakes, 15 pounds of salt, 1 pounds of pepper, 16 ounces of mustard, 8 ounces of ginger, 25 pounds each of dried apples, peaches and apricots, 25 pounds of fish, 10 pounds of dried plums, 50 pounds each of dried onions and potatoes, 24 pounds of coffee, 5 pounds of tea, 4 dozen cans of condensed milk, 15

pounds of vegetables for soup and 25 cans of butter. And he also needed the following "household supplies": 40 pounds of candles, 60 boxes of matches, 5 bars of washing soap, coffee pot, plates, cutlery, 2 frying pans, cooking stove, an ax, saws, 200 feet of rope, 15 pounds of tar, a canvas tent, 2 pairs of shoes, two blankets, four towels, rainwear, 12 pairs of wool socks and 5 yards of mosquito netting. If a man could not afford mules or a porter, it would take him 40 trips across the pass to transport everything.

Before long, organized gangs had sprung up and started robbing the prospectors of their possessions, and the Mounted Police had their hands full. In 1897, Archie Burns from Fortymile opened a cable car operation which, running only on horsepower, hoisted everything over the pass, basket by basket and sack

Above: Fortune-hunters laden with heavy luggage on their way to the Yukon (collectors' card, circa 1900). Right: Can-can line in Dawson City.

by sack. A few months later, there were five such goods cable cars in operation – one of them steam-powered, with two baskets – which could transport all of a prospector's equipment, weighing more than a ton.

Thousands of men followed the call of gold. Within only three years (1896-1899) the population of Dawson City increased to 25,000, making it the largest city in Canada west of Winnipeg. The new arrivals were a motley crew: English, Irish, Scandinavian, German, French, Scottish, Métis, Salvation Army soldiers and bored ne'er-do-wells, prisoners and intellectuals. Enduring unspeakable hardships, they panned and dredged the sludge of the riverbanks. A mere 200 miles (300 km) from the Arctic Circle, they thawed the frozen ground with open fires. Dawson City's wooden houses often burned down, so the location looked more like a permanent construction site than a settlement. In 1899, however, a telephone line was installed on muddy Front Street; and there were al-

ready cinemas, three daily newspapers, Turkish baths, electric light, a theater and even steam heating.

Naturally, there were other establishments as well: stories were told of a shipload of English widows and Belgian madams who "enriched" the scene. The wooden huts of Paradise Alley soon housed some 70 brothels, standing cheek by jowl. In fact, the gold miners brought many of the girls in with them over the Chilkoot Pass so that they could work for them "on site." The Mounties, backed up by government soldiers, kept law and order: no one was permitted to carry firearms, and even theft remained within reasonable bounds. In 1898, the new province of Yukon was separated from the Northwest Territories.

During the gold rush, miners extracted some 500 million dollars in gold. Although large corporations succeeded in taking over mining rights from most of the miners, some of them actually did become millionaires. Only a few, however, were able to enjoy their wealth –

there are many anecdotes and stories telling of how money and possessions literally ran through their fingers.

When in August 1899, rumors started flying of enormous gold discoveries in Nome, Alaska, 800 miles (1,300 km) away, 8,000 thereto luckless miners pulled out within a week and went off to try their luck there. Companies bought up their Yukon claims; large-scale diggers moved earth and gravel in areas where, until then, only pickaxes had been used; and the people who did stay ended up working for one of the mining companies. Dawson City became a quiet town again. Even today, however, there are still a few hardy dreamers who scour the muddy banks of the Klondike and even comb the piles of mining slag in search of nuggets. In conjunction with the construction of the Alaska Highway, Whitehorse replaced Dawson City as capital of the Yukon in 1953, although today the town has only 800 inhabitants.

In the annual "Klondike Days," held in July and August, Dawson City recaptures

the flavor of its past, mainly for the benefit of tourists. Its little houses have been restored. Behind the museum stands the log cabin where Robert W. Service, a Scottish banker, wrote his *Best Tales Of The Yukon*, telling of the arduous 1898 Trail, the magical lure of gold, and the men who risked everything to get it. Jack London, whose adventure novels include *Burning Daylight*, *White Fang* and *The Call of the Wild*, also lived in Dawson City for a few years.

To this day, mining remains the most important branch of industry in the Yukon Territory. The mineral resources – gold, silver, lead, zinc, copper and cadmium – have only partly been explored. The vast forests sustain active logging and lumbering industries. In addition, tourism has become an important source of revenue.

Above: Jack London memorialized his Yukon experiences in his novel Burning Daylight. Right: Sir Martin Frobisher's third expedition in 1578.

EXPLORERS AND HEROES

The Northwest Passage

After the days of Columbus, many seafarers were joined by a common goal – to discover the Northwest Passage. The hypothetical Passage represented a shortcut from Europe to China and to the spice countries of India and Ceylon, which as it was could only be reached by sailing around the tip of Africa. Such a sea passage through North America was indeed finally found in 1850, by almost pure coincidence, by Captain Robert Le Mesurier McClure of the British Royal Navy, who was in the Arctic searching for the missing Captain John Franklin.

The Vikings were probably the first Europeans to sail westward (around the year 1000) and set foot on North American soil. There is historical documentation of the fact that the Viking Eric Rauda (Eric the Red) ventured as far as Greenland in 982 and founded two settlements there; these, however, totally disappeared at some point during the 14th century.

In the summer of 1576 Martin Frobisher, an adventurous English ship's lieutenant, set sail from London with two ships, hoping to find the Northwest Passage. However, after he had lost one of the ships and its crew in a storm, he was forced to turn back. In a second attempt, he managed to reach the 63rd parallel, within the Canadian archipelago, and discovered an inlet penentrating deep into the rocky, cliff-lined shore. For a few days, he sailed westward through this narrow bay (now known as Frobisher Bay, on Baffin Island), completely convinced he was the first to find the Northwest Passage to Asia.

After having been knighted by Elizabeth I and promoted to the rank of Admiral in Command, he wanted to provide proof that he had indeed discovered the Northwest Passage. To this end, he once again sailed northwest with 17 ships and

140 crew members. The intended triumph ended in tragedy; after long meanderings, only a few of the ships returned, and the Northwest Passage remained obstinately undiscovered.

Explorations in the Northeast

The Dutch also hearkened to the call of the north. They already had trade relations with China and the Spice Islands of Indonesia, and were also looking for a shorter alternative to the long journey around Africa. They equipped three expeditions in 1594, 1595 and 1596 to find a passage; their plan, however, was to reach China via a northeastern route. The ships of the first polar expedition, under the command of Admiral Cornelius Naij and his navigator Willem Barents, circumnavigated Lapland and sailed as far as the island Novaya Zemlya in northern Russia, the western coast of which they explored in July 1594. The body of water between Lapland and Novaya Zemlya was later named the Barents Sea.

In Holland, meanwhile, preparations for the next expedition were already underway: 16 ships, loaded with fine cloths to exchange for Chinese and East Indian valuables, set off in 1595. No one doubted that they would reach their exotic destinations in this next attempt via the northeastern route. The fleet was, however, surprised by the northern winter and they were forced to abandon all ideas of sailing any farther: rather than taking any further risks, Barents, who was also commander of this expedition, chose to turn back with all of his ships. The sparkling stones which he brought back from this trip proved to be worthless rock crystal. After Barents' failure, the Dutch government lost interest in further expeditions, although they did offer a prize to anyone who discovered a northeast passage.

But the merchant *Mijnhers* had a burning desire to shorten their trade routes to

the Orient. They financed two ships under the command of Willem Barents – this time together with Jacob van Heemskerk – and Jan Cornelius Rijp. They set off in May 1596. On July 9, 1596 they landed on Bjornoy (Bear Island, south of Spitsbergen), from where they continued to sail north. A few days later they discovered a wholly unknown group of islands, which they believed were at the eastern tip of Greenland. "We named the land Spitsbergen (pointed mountains) because of the many high and pointed peaks on it," Rijp later told the magistrate in Delft, Holland for the official record. Since they had failed to sail around Spitsbergen, they turned back for Bjornoy. There, the two commanders had a decisive falling-out: Rijp wanted to continue farther north; Barents felt drawn eastward.

Barents headed straight for the island of Novaya Zemlya. By now, the first walls of ice were already closing in, putting an end to any thoughts of turning back. The crew found refuge in a bay at

27

the east of the island. Ice floes demolished their ship, and they had to build a shelter from driftwood on land; the discovery of reindeer tracks and a freshwater stream on the island, however, refueled their hopes. By early October 1596, they were able to move into a solid wooden hut, complete with a fireplace, a chimney, and even a steam bath fashioned from the wood of winebarrels. An additional source of furnishings and food was the ship, which they had pulled up on shore.

In the spring they repaired their ship, built a second one, and loaded both with everything they would need for their next voyage. Barents wrote down the story of their experiences over the last few months and left these papers in a powder horn hanging above the fireplace. On June 14, 1597, the men boarded the ships

Above: Dutch merchants financed the search for a Northeast Passage to China and India. Right: Sir John Franklin died in the Arctic archipelago in 1848.

and set their course for the northern tip of Novaya Zemlya.

The journey was arduous and horrific, and Barents, who was already ailing, died en route. In the end, only 12 men reached the coast of Russia alive. Nearly 300 years later, in 1871, a Norwegian captain arrived in the bay on Novaya Zemlya and found the Barents house, covered with ice, but extremely well preserved. He brought away with him a number of objects, including the powder horn with Barents' journal.

Peregrenations in Hudson Bay

William Baffin and Henry Hudson are two names closely associated with the history of the Northwest Territories. The northwestern travels of Hudson and his ship, the *Discovery*, are documented in the ship's logbooks from 1607 to 1611. The man who made it beyond the 82nd parallel, but ultimately failed to discover the long-sought passage, was the first to document his observations concerning

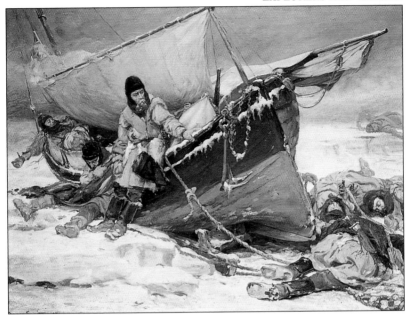

the deviations of the compass needle – the difference, that is, between the magnetic and geographic North Poles. This deviation was first localized on Boothia Island in 1831; today, the official site of the magnetic pole is Bathurst Island, more than 800 miles (1,400 km) from the North Pole itself.

In 1610, Henry Hudson explored the east coast of a huge bay, which now bears his name as Hudson Bay. Despite his discoveries, his travels were not a financial success; the English merchants therefore released him from their service, whereupon he began working for the Dutch Company. With them, too, he had bad luck: his crew had thereto only sailed the South Seas, and these fair-weather sailors were not prepared for the harsh conditions in the north. They mutinied, and Hudson was forced to turn back.

Subsequently, however, three English businessmen proved themselves willing to finance a voyage for the exploration of the waterways in the north – on the condition that Hudson be accompanied by an English seaman named Coleburn. Hudson, however, shook off this "supervisor" before he had even left the Thames estuary, and sailed off alone. He ended up following in Frobisher's footsteps to Meta Incognita, finally reaching Charles Island. When he saw a seemingly endless expanse of water extending to the south and southwest, he thought he had found his goal. The last entry in his logbook is dated August 3, 1611.

As his sailors later testified before the maritime court, they sailed on through Hudson Bay to James Bay, where their winter camp was to be set up. The crew worked reluctantly; finally, most of them took sides with Maat Green against Captain Hudson. When the bay thawed early the following summer, the mutineers left Hudson and his son, a few of his trusty men, a rifle and a bit of food in a boat, then sailed away. No trace of them was ever seen again.

In 1615-16, William Baffin came via the John Davis Strait to explore Hudson Bay, and began doubting that a north-

western passage existed at all. In the course of his voyage, his doubts developed into firm convictions, which he later emphasized before the British admiralty with such vigor that Northwest Passage "case" was deemed "closed" for the next 200 years.

Not until 1818 did the expedition of James Ross, a compatriot of Baffin, reawaken interest in the race to find the Northwest Passage. As a result, the British government commissioned Captain John Franklin in 1819 to find a sea route from Hudson Bay to the Arctic Ocean. Franklin explored a large portion of the Mackenzie district and mapped the northern coastline. But on his next expedition (1845-48), he and his crew disappeared. In the summer of 1850, 14 ships participated in the search of Franklin. Finally, his winter camp was found on Beechey Island, and in 1859 explorers located his

Above: Icebergs put an effective end to the first expeditions. Right: Guns for bear pelts: the Hudson's Bay Company.

grave on King William's Island, with a note from spring of 1848. His ships *Erebus* and *Terror* had been icebound; his crew wanted to continue on foot. Examination of the tin cans found on site revealed that the men had all died of lead poisoning. As a final ironic twist of fate, it was on this search for Franklin that Royal Navy finally discovered the actual Northwest Passage.

Cook and Vancouver, Mackenzie, Fraser and Hearne

In the late 18th century, many seafarers were drawn to the coast of British Columbia. Spanish ships sailed these waters in 1774, followed, in 1778, by James Cook in search of the Northwest Passage. Cook sent back detailed reports of the abundance of furs in the coastal region, which sparked England's interest in exploring the area more extensively. Captain George Vancouver set out in 1791; he mapped the coastline and circumnavigated a huge island, later named Vancouver Island in his honor. In his travel journal, *A Voyage of Discovery To The North Pacific*, Vancouver described, among other things, the rich fishing grounds in these waters, with the result that fishermen started casting their nets around the islands in ever-increasing numbers. Ultimately, so many hunters and trap setters converged there that the sea otter nearly became extinct.

Alexander Mackenzie, a Scotsman, is yet another famous name in the annals of Canadian exploration. When the North West Company was looking for men to develop the fur trading routes to the west, he acted quickly, becoming the first man to navigate the 2,500-mile (4,120 km) Mackenzie River in 1789. Three years later, in 1792, he set out again in search of the Northwest Passage. When he reached the Pacific the following year, he had set a record; he was the first European known to have traversed the entire North American continent.

The Letters And Journals Of Simon Fraser 1806-1808 have lost none of their fascination. In them, the fur trader and explorer describes his voyages of exploration on the Fraser River, which he originally took to be the Columbia River. Fraser set up the first trading post in Fort McLeod, and, later, additional ones in St. James and Fort George. When gold was discovered in this area in 1858, it set off a run of settlers and trappers to Fraser River. In 1808, Fraser followed the river to its mouth, the present site of Vancouver.

Englishman Samuel Hearne, working in the service of the Hudson's Bay Company, performed a similarly trail-blazing pioneering feat: the first explorer of Barren Grounds, between the Mackenzie and Hudson Bays, he traversed this wilderness region between 1769 and 1772. Hearne learned from the Indians how to travel using dog sleds, canoes and snowshoes; together with Chief Matonabee, he walked the length of the Coppermine River on foot.

The Hudson's Bay Company

When a Canadian needs something from the department store, he simply says that he is "going to the Bay." Any 5-year-old knows that he means one of the department stores that has descended from the legendary trading establishments of the Hudson's Bay Company. And since the HBC is more than 300 years old, people have jokingly dubbed it "Here Before Christ." Today, the company's 500-odd branches, scattered throughout the country and employing more than 38,000 people, are a part of everyday life.

The company's story begins with two French trappers: Pierre Esprit de Radisson and Médart Chouart, Sieur de Groseilliers. Radisson had reached Hudson Bay overland from "New France" in 1662. He and his fellow countryman were self-employed, delivering their furs to the French governor, who gave them recompense. One day, however, there was a disagreement with the governor regarding the price of the furs. Rather than

appealing to the responsible monarch, Louis XIV of France, the irate trappers decided to go over to the competition, King Charles II of England. He referred them to his cousin, Prince Rupert of Bohemia. The Prince soon realized that fur trading in the New World could be quite a lucrative proposition, and he and the king granted the two trappers a charter that gave them sole rights to the fur trade for England.

Upon returning to Hudson Bay, the two men named the surrounding area Rupert's Land and, in 1668, at the mouth of the Rupert River, founded the first branch of the Hudson's Bay Company (HBC) with headquarters in Fort Simpson. There, trappers and traders could exchange their furs for food, clothing, equipment or even money.

On their expeditions, the trappers were happy to work with the Indians: not only

Above: Typical 18th-century trapper ("Leatherstocking" model Daniel Boone).
Right: Fur-trader's traditional transportation.

did the Indians know the best trails, but also the best places for catching otter and beaver. However, the Indians' initial infatuation with the glittering glass beads the Europeans had to offer them soon wore off; they quickly recognized the superiority of the white man's tools and weapons, and sought more substantial forms of compensation.

In the following years, trading posts sprang up out of the ground like mushrooms. Business flourished to the satisfaction of all trading partners, helped along by the whims of fashion in far-off Europe: the men and women of the upper classes had begun wearing beaver hats, and there was plenty of beaver to be had in Canada, while supplies from Scandinavia or Russia were far scarcer, and horrendously overpriced.

Meanwhile, the neighboring territory of America was caught up in a revolution that amounted to civil war. Deserters, homeless people and adventurers traipsed through the country, and, hearing that they could make a fortune with furs, had no qualms about paying off the Indians exclusively in whisky. In faraway Ottawa, the established merchants began to feel the sting of competition. For this reason, a few of them joined forces to found the North West Company, whose trappers were to lay their traps farther west and develop new trade routes. The company worked on the same principles as the HBC, so that both companies were soon engaged in a bitter struggle to show the most profit and to have the more courageous men. At first, the rival's bid for supremacy got off to a good start: demonstrating the truth of the motto that "competition is good for business," the North West Company was able to register substantial revenues around the turn of the century. Soon, however, the overhead costs were outstripping the profits, and the HBC was able to take over the North West Company in 1821. Yet the passing years left their mark on

the HBC, as well: the economic, political, and even the sociopolitical conditions had changed. The vast territory had been unified into the new Dominion of Canada, and in 1868 roughly 3,000,000 square miles (8 million sq. km) of land that had once belonged to the HBC were transferred to the Confederation in exchange for 300,000 pounds sterling.

The Canadian National Railway

In 1876, the eastern part of Canada's Intercolonial Railway was completed, running from Halifax and St. John to Montreal, Toronto and Lake Huron. This led politician Joseph Howe to state optimistically, "I believe that many people here today will live to hear the steam train's whistle in the Rocky Mountains and will be able to travel from Halifax to the Pacific in five or six days' time."

To the less idealistic, Howe's dream seemed completely far-fetched, given the difficulties that had been encountered in developing the west. Western Canada was explored less on horseback than by canoe. Indians and trappers followed the course of the rivers, and the first prospectors from the trade companies also used waterways to penetrate into the interior of the the country. The notion of building a railroad through the vast forests, across deep river valleys and over icy mountains seemed fanciful. Railroad construction became a political issue when, in 1871, British Columbia joined the Dominion of Canada only on the condition that the railroad be extended to the Pacific. Two companies applied for the job, one by legal means, the other – the Canadian Pacific Railway – with bribery: the company was owned by businessman Hugh Allan, who had promised Prime Minister Macdonald enormous funding for his election campaign and for the Conservative Party. The bribery scandal became public, which toppled Macdonald and the Conservatives: the Liberals won the election. They only managed to remain in power for five years, however, and Macdonald was reelected in 1878.

Now, he was finally in a position to realize the dream of the transcontinental railroad; he commissioned the engineer Sir Stanford Fleming to plan the route. The only condition was that it had to be laid solely on Canadian soil. Fleming devised a route running at the latitude of Edmonton, but it was rejected. The proposed solution of his colleague Major A. Rogers, through the Selkirk Mountains and over Roger's Pass – named for him – met with more approval. Not until later, however, when a few local railroad companies joined to form the Canadian National Railway, was Fleming's proposal made reality.

The construction of the railway required tremendous effort. Landslides and avalanches covered stretches that had already been completed, while the extreme

Above: A technical masterpiece that claimed many lives in the making – the construction of the railway line through the Rocky Mountains. Right: Mounties – members of the Royal Canadian Mounted Police.

differences in temperature had such adverse affects on the materials that they splintered or broke. Time again, soldiers and the RCMP had to force their way through Indian blockades. But necessity is the mother of invention, as the saying goes, and the Canadian railway builders created revolutionary constructions, such as the Spiral Tunnels near Lake Louise. They also invented special technical support equipment, such as a snowplow with rotating blades and a new brake system that was soon in use worldwide.

The Royal Canadian Mounted Police

The West was wild, its customs and traditions rough. The borders weren't even exactly defined; American trappers and hunters crossed over without the least problem. Goods were smuggled back and forth; gangs of horse thieves crisscrossed the country. Anyone looking for justice had to fend for himself.

In 1873, after a dramatic shoot-out between white wolf hunters and Assini-

boines Indians on Cypress Hill, the government realized that something had to be done. Prime Minister John A. Macdonald sent out civilian troops to enforce order among the lawless, keep the Indians quiet and collect tolls at the United States border. An active police station, staffed with 300 men, was established at Fort Walsh. This force of riders was called the North West Mounted Police. In 1876, an additional unit was set up at Fort Calgary. The "Mounties" managed to keep peace with the Indians in the region without any bloodshed. Their tenacity in tracking down criminals in the wilderness became legendary and won them enormous respect. The Mounties developed great skills in mediating between the whites and the Indians. Unlike the U.S. Marshalls, they were rarely if ever involved in bloody conflicts. Sole exception was the brutal put-down of the rebellion led by Louis Riel and the French-Indian Métis in 1885 (see p. 41).

When gold was discovered on the Klondike River in 1896, prospectors from all over the world streamed into the province by the thousands. The Mounties kept a watchful eye on all those who entered the territory to try their luck with only their shirts on their backs. They stood watch at the Chilkoot Pass, checking to see whether the gold-seekers – often inexperienced city dwellers – were equipped for survival in the wilderness. Mounties were present when claims were made, mines opened or even when a horse was to be sold. Occasionally, the Mounties also acted as strike-breakers when this was in the best interests of the Canadian Pacific Railway. In 1882, for instance, a Mountie broke a blockade of the Cree Indians at Maple Creek, and the Mounties intervened again the following year when Blackfoot Indians fought vehemently against the track that was to be laid through their territory.

In 1904, the Mounties were granted the honorary title of "Royal" as a reward for fighting on the side of the British during the Boer War (1899-1902). Subsequently, in 1920, the Royal Canadian

Mounted Police was legally declared the country's national police force. The elite troop, consisting today of approximately 20,000 men and women, continues to represent the "long arm of the law" for the government in Ottawa, acting as police force, administration, rescue service and internal security corps rolled into one.

The Bush Pilots

In the north, where the roads end and there is practically no other means of transportation, the bush pilots are indispensable. In the pioneer days, rivers and lakes represented the most important travel routes. Canoes and boats took the trappers and settlers into the wild interior of the country. Today, these waterways form ideal landing sites for the bush pilots. The pilots of these heavily-laden fly-

Above: Seaplanes are an essential means of transportation in the Far North. Right: Traditional Inuit summer hunting camp.

ing machines have even been known to tie a pool table or a piano onto a plane. There is hardly a destination too difficult: in summer they land on pontoons; in winter, on skis; and wheels are mounted for conventional landing strips. Their standard emergency gear includes a rifle, a distress transmitter, maps, fishing gear, dehydrated food and a sleeping bag on board.

The cooperation between man and machine, ongoing since 1924, has conferred upon the Canadian bush pilots a quasi-legendary status. Their territory, comprising around one-third of the area of Canada, is dubbed "north of sixty," north, that is, of the 60th parallel. There, too, are their hangars – in places such as Tuktoyaktuk, Fort Good Hope or Yellowknife on Great Slave Lake, some 300 miles (450 km) south of the Arctic Circle. Anyone with a special interest in this icy region, particularly if he's already read *Northern Survival* or *Down But Not Out*, will be eager to see an area of which it's been said that "anyone traveling in the

Arctic or through any cold and barren region by land should be capable of building an igloo single-handedly." The next recommendation reads, "Mice and lemmings are edible and should not be scorned by accident survivors."

After February, 1924, when pioneer aviator Ben Eielson started flying regularly from Fairbanks, Alaska to McGrath, he brought food and clothing to the gold diggers there. From then on, the so-called Beavers and Otters began taking over postal, transport and taxi services; their pilots provided assistance, represented rescue in case of emergency, and often formed the only link to civilization. These virtues remain intact today: they are excellent navigators, flying on instinct and with an incredible ability to keep on course despite the seemingly unchanging vista of endless forests and water below.

At the bar, you can still here locals recounting tales of pilots such as Darryl, who drinks whiskey while standing on his head; or Dunc, who can find any destination with the sun or the stars and a string; or Wop May, who, in his Bellanca, hunted down the crazy trapper Albert Johnson, who had killed two people.

THE PEOPLE OF CANADA

The Inuit

The native Canadians call themselves *Inuit*, which means "the people." It was their enemies, the Algonquin Indians, who disparagingly called them "Eskimo" which translates as "eaters of raw meat." The Inuit reached Alaska from Asia around 10,000 years ago; about 4,000 years later, they migrated farther and settled in the Canadian Arctic region. The oldest known Inuit culture is the Pre-Dorset culture (c. 2000-1000 BC), which created artfully worked stone tools. The Inuit of the Dorset culture (c. 1000 BC) were already building sleds and stone

houses, and their shamans created totemic figures from stone and bones. Another wave of immigration brought the Thule people from Alaska.

The Inuit homeland is an expanse of treeless tundra extending to the ice-covered coasts of the Arctic archipelago. Nature plays a leading role in their religion; in a kind of séance, the shaman (*angakok*) contacts the spirit world. The Inuit live in a harmonious relationship with nature: an animal is only killed to provide a family with food or clothing, and when it is, nothing goes to waste: sleds are built from the animal's bones, while its sinews serve as cord or thongs.

Contact with the white man quickly taught the Inuit new things – not necessarily to their advantage. Gradually, they abandoned their traditional nomadic life and moved into permanent settlements. They paid a high price for such modern comforts as electricity, snowmobiles and canned food: it took only a few decades for a culture thousands of years old to collapse. Today, every second Inuit is un-

employed; families are destroyed by alcoholism, and extended families are falling apart.

Inuit politicians have, however, recently pushed through their demands for rights in Ottowa. On April 1, 1999, the 18,000 Inuit will be granted their own territory: *Nunavut*, "our land," comprising 741,000 square miles (1.9 m. sq. km). Nunavut encompasses the Arctic archipelago as far as Greenland, all of Hudson Bay and roughly half of the Northwest Territories – approximately one-fifth of Canada. Ottawa is paying a settlement of 580 million dollars divided over a 14-year period, but is estimating the actual total costs at up to 1.1 billion dollars. In the long run, the plentiful mineral deposits and other natural resources in the area should secure the Inuit's economic future.

Above: Modern life encroaches as community members settle down. Right: Living quarters and traditional dress of the Vancouver Indians (woodcut from 1890).

The Dene

Other Native Canadians also giving the politicians something to worry about: like the Inuit, they are also demanding their own territory. Rather than "Indians," this group prefers to be called "natives," "first people" or "Dene," which means "person" in many Indian dialects.

"The eagle saved a girl from the great flood and set her down on the ground so that she could establish a large nation" – thus runs the creation myth of the Dakota Indians. The Siksika say that the god Napi bade the clay figures of a woman and a child, "Arise and go forth; you shall become people," while the Nakota version is that Inktome took a piece of clay from the paw of a muskrat and rolled it into a ball which then became the Earth.

These three Indian creation myths demonstrate a strong belief in nature, a world in which animals, plants and other natural objects have souls. The first Europeans who came here, however, saw the

land in rather different terms: as something to be bought, sold, or speculated with, a commercial commodity.

When the white man began negotiating with tribal chiefs, there were a few tribes that allowed their lands to be taken away in exchange for "firewater" and weapons. Yet there were others who refused to sign any bills of sale, as they held the deeply ingrained belief that people, animals and land belong to no one, and therefore cannot be bought or sold. Undaunted, the Europeans built their railroads and farms anyway.

It is ironic that post-war Indian politics granted money and reservations to those very tribes that could present bills of sale (450,000 *status Indians*). Those without such treaties, whose ancestors had resisted the earliest European advances, were initially left empty-handed (500,000 to 1,000,000 *non-status Indians*). Today, anyone recognized as a status Indian has to be purely of Indian descent. At present, there are around 390,000 registered status Indians.

One result of this criterion is that Indians are reluctant to marry Caucasians, fearing loss of their privileged status. One of the "privileges" involved in being Indian is receiving regular payments of money from the government. Many people call this "guilt money," money to pay off the guilt of having destroyed an entire culture. Canada, it is true, can and does boast of never having had the kind of bloody Indian wars that occurred in the United States; but on the other hand, there was no need for such conflicts: as the buffalo was nearly exterminated, the traditional Indian way of life, which centered around this animal, also met its demise.

Today, people's positions have become more entrenched, which leads to highly emotional discussions predicated on the dichotomy of evil white man and defenseless Indian victim. More and more often, Indian groups test their strength by blockading farms or forcing the suspension of construction projects such as the power station on James Bay.

Sometimes this leads to additional problems. When, in the summer of 1995, the coastal Indians fought vehemently for the reinstatement of their whaling rights, the environmental protection agencies had to deal with a dilemma: they were caught between the argument, on the one hand, that whaling is a part of the Indian heritage, even if it's no longer done from a dugout canoe, and, on the other hand, their responsibility to protect endangered species.

Now the native peoples' goal is to maintain their cultural identity and free themselves from dependency on government benefits. The first steps toward this goal are visible in tourist initiatives, such as the Indian-planned and Indian-run museums in Wanuskewin, Saskatchewan and Head Smashed Buffalo Jump, Alberta; in private lumbering initiatives; and even in an Indian airline, Air Creebec, which belongs to the Cree.

Above: An Osage, an Iroquois and a Dawnee. Right: Métis descendants.

The Métis

Another ethnic minority is the Métis. These descendants of the unions of European settlers and Canadian Indians originally lived as buffalo hunters and produced *pemmican*, a type of jerky made of dried and ground buffalo meat combined with mosses and lichen. They sold this "delicacy" to the trappers, traders and so-called "voyagers," a term for the men who came thousands of miles in their canoes to transport food and ammunition into the wilderness and bring valuable furs back out with them.

In the 18th century, however, hundreds of thousands of immigrants, streaming in with the government's permission to settle in the vast lands of Saskatchewan and Manitoba, started to encroach on Métis territory. The battle for land rights has continued down to the present day: Indians and Métis are still negotiating with the government about their historic claims, as well as ownership and extraction of the land's natural resources.

One notable figure in the annals of the Métis was Louis Riel. Today, more than a century after his execution, there is still disagreement as to the justice of his sentence. Riel was born in the settlement of Red River, near Fort Garry. Living there in 1869 were administrators of the Hudson's Bay Company, as well as English, Canadian and American traders, Scottish and English settlers, and French and English Métis. That year saw the passing of the Rupert's Land Act, by which the lands of the HBC went over to the British Crown to be integrated into the Dominion of Canada; a process which was duly completed in 1870.

The Métis, who had already been forced to stand by helplessly as the bison herds were slaughtered, reacted strongly against this "sell-out." They feared that they would be unable to maintain their semi-nomadic lifestyle in the face of the incoming wave of even more white set-

tlers. Louis Riel took the lead in the rebellion, captured the governor, occupied Fort Garry and demanded land rights for his people.The government in Ottawa sent in troops, who put down the uprising in a bloody struggle. Riel managed to flee to Montana, and the contested district was declared the province of Manitoba in the Canadian Confederation. The Métis of Red River emigrated to Saskatchewan in search of a new home.

Meanwhile, the iron tracks of the Canadian Pacific Railway were making their way westward through the provinces, and the Métis feared yet another invasion of settlers. In their hour of need, they called on Louis Riel, who was supporting himself with a teaching job on the other side of the border.

Riel's course of action was confrontation: late in March, 1885, the Métis were facing off against the troops of the North West Mounted Police at snow-covered Duck Lake on the Saskatchewan River. This open rebellion shook the country. Regular troops of soldiers were sent in on the new railway to reinforce the Mounties. With Louis Riel and his Métis on one side, the superior forces of the government of the other, the battle began at Batoche on May 12, 1885: the Métis were defeated. Louis Riel was arrested, tried in Regina for high treason, convicted, and hanged.

Immigrants

In the wake of the catastrophic famine that struck Ireland in 1847, hundreds of thousands of Irish people poured into the country. From 1857 on, children from English slum areas were also shipped off to Canada. But the largest wave of immigrants came between 1880 and 1914. The West was still scarcely populated, there was fertile land to be had, the advent of the railway represented the start of a working infrastructure, and, most importantly, there was room to breathe freely. People who had only been able to eke out a meager existence as sharecroppers in their own countries suddenly found themselves, in the New World, masters of their own lands. People who had been persecuted for their beliefs found freedom of religion. As a result, immigrants streamed in from Germany, the Netherlands, Scandinavia, Poland, and Hungary, later followed by Romanians, Ukrainians and Russians. Around the turn of the century, Asians represented approximately 11% of British Columbia's population: they had been brought in to lay track for the railroads, and were later employed in fish canneries.

During World War I, in the years of the Great Depression, and after World War II, the government drastically cut down on immigration quotas and began to follow a restrictive immigration policy. Only qualified applicants employed in certain fields where there was a lack of manpower had a chance of getting in. The specialized knowledge and skills of such arrivals played an integral role in the country's rapid postwar development in the areas of economics, research and science.

Today, the country's multinational mixture is rounded out with people from Asia, Africa, Central and Latin America, India, Vietnam and the Philippines, who have begun new lives in the large metropolitan areas.

Canada is the largest multicultural nation in the world. But despite a general willingness to assimilate, people devotedly maintain the customs and traditions of their native countries, and pass them on from generation to generation.

Religious Minorities

A classic immigrants' country, Canada historically offered refuge to many persecuted religious groups from the Old World. One of these sects is the Hutterites, who reject the doctrine of infant

Right: Inconceivable, inhuman crowding was the rule on emigration ships sailing from Europe.

baptism. The followers of Jakob Hutter came to America around 100 years ago and founded 300 collective farms. Today, the main Hutterite centers lie south and east of Calgary. Although their lifestyle is based for the most part on the precepts and customs of their ancestors, they are making increasing use of modern technology to cultivate their fields and help raise the poultry they sell at markets in the surrounding area.

The Mennonites have an equally oldfashioned lifestyle. The group is named for Menno Simons, a Catholic priest born in Friesland in 1496. He began preaching around the North Sea and the Baltic in the 16th century, and had soon attracted a large following. Simons rejected the ideas of infant baptism and military service, oaths, marriage, and any kind of national interference in questions of religion – and the Mennonites continue to adhere to his beliefs.

The German Mennonites were persecuted by both Roman Catholic and Protestant rulers. Many of them emigrated to Canada as early as the end of the Thirty Years' War (1618-48); others moved to the Netherlands, or accepted Frederick I's offer of refuge in Lithuania. But as Frederick actually wanted soldiers, and their faith forbade military service, the Mennonites moved on when Catherine II of Russia was looking for settlers for the Ukrainian steppe in the 18th century. There, too, however, they were again confronted with the specter of military service after 1850.

An attractive offer from Canada couldn't have come at a better time, and 200,000 Mennonites responded accordingly. Each head of the family was promised 160 acres (64 ha) of land, freedom of religion, exemption from military service and even the right to his own language and school system. Kitchener, Ontario (which was named Berlin until 1914) became the new center for the Mennonites; but in Steinbach, Manitoba

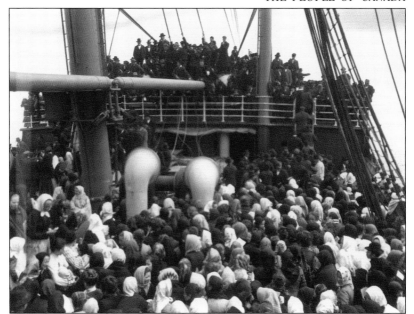

or St. Jacobs, Alberta you can also still see them in their traditional black garb, tilling their fields or driving, in their horses and carts, their agricultural products to market. For the most part, they still do live without electricity, telephones or automobiles.

An extremely conservative splinter group of the Mennonites are the Amish. In 1693, under the Alsatian bishop Jakob Amman, they split off from their Mennonite brothers in faith and emigrated to the U.S.A. They reject all modern conveniences, including radios, zippers, refrigerators and freezers, and attempt to keep their society untainted by the influences of the modern world. They are excellent farmers. In spite of the high birth rate, however, many young people do not want to follow in their fathers' footsteps, and one-third of the Amish youth leave their communities before the ceremony of adult baptism.

Another minority group are the Mormons, who in Cardston, in southern Ontario, have the only Mormon temple in the nation. In 1887, Charles Ora Card led a group of believers from their base in Utah to the promised land of Canada.

Cowboy Country

Important articles of clothing in the Prairie Provinces are cowboy boots and cowboy hats, and the local radio stations issue a diet of almost exclusively country-western music. American radio stations in neighboring Montana also broadcast western music with a Christian message.

Attending a rodeo is an absolute must for anyone visiting western Canada. The most famous one is the Calgary Stampede, but even the smaller local rodeos offer a colorful panoply of horse dealers, weathered rodeo riders, a wide range of headgear from sun hats to baseball caps, and breathtaking performances. In addition to bronco busting, there are such attractions as cow wrestling, which involves a daredevil rider's galloping alongside a cow and, in full gallop, jump-

43

ing atop it and wrestling it to the ground. Another variant is lassoing: a rider lassoes a calf, wraps the end of the rope around his saddlehorn, dismounts and sprints over to the bucking calf, which he pulls to the ground, tying up its forelegs with his lasso. Clouds of dust everywhere, people cheering – whether it's your first or your twentieth rodeo, it remains an unforgettable spectacle. And God's protection is abundantly invoked: each rodeo opens with a prayer for the riders and the animals, after which, without even a moment's pause, the emcee howls into the microphone, "Let's have a rodeo!" and the show begins.

One exceptional event is the Pincher Creek Stampede, held over three days in mid-June. This festival has less to do with a rodeo than with cowboy music, saddle-makers, arts and crafts, and story-

Above: The world-famous Canadian pianist Glenn Gould in 1955. Right: The maple leaf – national symbol of the country of Canada.

tellers; and it attracts spectators from all over western Canada. Then there are powwows, which feature traditional dances of the Prairie Indians. You can get information about events and performances from any local tourist office.

Famous Canadians

Less ostentatious than its flamboyant neighbor to the south, Canada has nonetheless produced a goodly number of famous sons and daughters.

The artist and writer Emily Carr (1871-1945) painted the forests and native dwellers of the Pacific coast. Better known today is the author Margaret Atwood (born in 1939), who brings a critical, feminist view to her novels about society and the roles people inhabit in it. Her *The Handmaid's Tale* was made into a film featuring international stars. Other notable Canadian writers include Mordecai Richler, Michael Ondaatje (*The English Patient*), Alice Munro, Mavis Gallant, and Margaret Laurence.

Musically, Canadian folk and folk-rock artists have made an especially strong contribution: among them are Neil Young, Gordon Lightfoot, Buffy Ste Marie and the inimitable Joni Mitchell, a great influence on a number of other singers, who later switched to jazz. And jazz pianist Oscar Peterson is a veritable legend. Leonard Cohen, born in Montreal in 1934, became world-renowned as composer, singer and poet. His melancholy songs and poems tell of love and betrayal, loneliness and pain. His novel *Beautiful Losers* was published in 1966. But perhaps none of Canada's musicians is as well-known as the eccentric pianist Glenn Gould, who died in 1982. Increasingly shy of public performance, preferring to work in the recording studio, he made music history with his provocative, idiosyncratic recordings of, for example, Bach's *Goldberg Variations*.

Canadian physician Sir Frederick Grant Banting (1891-1941) and his team discovered insulin, a substance which is used to control diabetes. In 1923, Banting and his colleague Macleod were awarded the Nobel Prize in Medicine.

Less sober, but no less profound in its effect, was the advent of the Skidoo snowmobile, a 1959 invention of Jean Armand Bombardier, which touched the lives of everyone in the Arctic archipelago.

After overcoming tremendous obstacles, the Métis architect Douglas Joseph Cardinal has become the most famous architect in Canada. His unconventional buildings blend his Indian heritage with Western technology.

The lawyer and liberal politician Pierre Elliott Trudeau has twice served as Prime Minister, in 1968-79 and 1980-84. A staunch opponent of separatism, Trudeau aimed to achieve a bilingual and bicultural nation. His terms of office saw the passing of the Official Languages Bill (1968), declaring English and French to be official languages of equal standing; the Canada Act (1982), confirming Canada's independence; and the Charter of Rights, which granted individual rights to ethnic minorities.

45

VANCOUVER

THE CITY
NORTH AND WEST
VANCOUVER
EXCURSION THROUGH
WHISTLER & FRASER VALLEY

VANCOUVER

Long before the arrival of the Europeans, the Salish Indians, a highly civilized people living mainly from fishing, inhabited the area of present-day Vancouver. James Cook landed near Vancouver in 1778, but he found little of interest in the rainy and densely wooded area, and sailed on. Yet one of Cook's young officers, George Vancouver, could not understand why his captain ignored the area. In 1792, Vancouver came back and claimed the land for the British Empire. In 1793, the explorer Alexander Mackenzie became the first white man to reach the Pacific Ocean overland.

After that, little changed in this region until the middle of the 19th century. Who wanted to settle in a remote, inaccessible forest, anyway? But then the first businessmen came along and recognized the great economic potential in the area's timber. In 1867, the West End of Vancouver – today some of the most expensive real estate in North America – was sold for 114 pounds, 11 shillings and 8 pence.

Preceding pages: Signature trademark of a leisure-oriented city – the runner in Stanley Park. Weekend captains ply the waters between Vancouver and Vancouver Island. Left: Totem pole in Stanley Park.

Life in the sawmills was rough, and alcohol was scarce until John Deighton showed up with a barrel of whiskey and saved the day. He opened up a saloon the same year which became *the* meeting place on the West Coast for loggers and gold-diggers. Because of his verbosity, Deighton was soon dubbed "Gassy Jack." Many of the adventurers, unwilling to attempt the arduous journey overland, set out northwards from Vancouver under sail, their gaze fixed on the gold fields along the Klondike. The name "Gassy Jack" lives on in Vancouver's Gastown district, where attractive boutiques and bars surround the statue of its eponymous founder.

In 1887, the first passenger train steamed into town from Montreal. The arrival of the railway spurred the town to new and rapid growth. Above all, the new railroad made it possible to transport grain from Manitoba and Saskatchewan to Vancouver, from where it could be shipped further. Vancouver's first skyscraper was built in 1909; from then on, the local architecture reflected Vancouver's changing status as it transformed itself from a town into a major international city.

The Great Depression of the 1930s reached Vancouver, as well. Although this city has long been considered a

51

model example of multiculturalism in practice, it has, in its history, seen several periods of conflict between the native peoples and various groups of immigrants. As early as the 19th century, thousands of Chinese immigrants came into the region, mainly to work on laying the railway line workers or as gold-diggers; due to their vastly different culture and to the fact that they represented competition in the market for cheap labor, they experienced considerable discrimination. During World War II, Vancouver's Japanese population was rounded up and interned in concentration camps. In the late 1960s and early 1970s, immigrants from Pakistan had their own share of difficulties.

Exploiting nature is also a hot topic around Vancouver; even before it became widely fashionable, groups of progressively-minded ecologists were forming here. They were instrumental in changing people's outlook, and were able to force through a few political solutions. The environmental organization Greenpeace has its roots here.

All in all, Vancouver has relatively few dark spots on its generally clean slate. In 1986, therefore, it was able proudly and honestly to present itself to the world as a city of tolerance with the Expo. This event was a tremendous success, both financially, in terms of urban planning, and with regard to the fusion and cohesiveness of the city's multicultural society. The year of the Expo also marked Vancouver's 100-year anniversary. The opening of the Dr. Sun Yat-Sen Gardens served to symbolize Canadian-Chinese friendship, just one tile in a veritable mosaic creating an image of solidarity and allegiance to all those who have helped make Vancouver one of the best places in the world to live.

Vancouver is expanding at a rapid rate; the population is growing by a steady 3% per year. Greater Vancouver encompasses 18 communities on nearly 1,200 square miles (2,930 sq. km) and has 1.7

million inhabitants, 100,000 of whom are Chinese. Economically speaking, the city is striving to become a hub for the entire Pacific area. The first phase in the expansion of the Vancouver International Airport was completed in October 1996; it's projected that by the year 2000, it should be handling some 14 million passengers a year, and 17 million by 2005.

For many Canadians from the eastern part of the country, Vancouver, the "Beauty on the Pacific," represents a kind of Promised Land: a place to go when you want to change you life or just feel better. Most people so prefer life in Vancouver so much that after living there for a few years they wouldn't dream of going back to the hustle and bustle of eastern

Lighthouse Brockton Point
Totem Poles
DEADMAN ISLAND
Vancouver
Coal Harbour
Harbour
Canada Place, Vancouver Trade & Convention Centre, CN Imax Theatre
Ferry
West Commisioner St.
Hastings St. W
ific sades
Vancouver Centre, Tourist Inform.
Waterfront Centre
Sea Bus Terminal (Canadian Pacific Waterfront Station)
Burrard Centre
Canadian Craft
Alberi
Museum
Vancouver Library
Waterfront Lookout
Harbour Centre
Steam Clock
Commisioner St.
Railway St.
Stewart St.
Howe St.
Horbly St.
Stock Exchange
Granville
Cordova
Gassy Jack Statue
GASTOWN
Alexander St.
Dunlevy Ave.
JAPANTOWN
Powell St.
Franklin St.
Gore Ave.
Cordova
Georgia
Main Post Office
Hastings
St.
Hastings St.
Reymur Ave.
Glen Drive
Vernon Drive
Clarke Drive
Vancouver Arts Gallery
Robson Square
Robson St.
Queen Elisabeth Theatre
Pender
CHINA-
Pender St.
Dr. Sun Yat-Sen Gardens
Pender
Ave.
Campbell Ave.
Reymur Ave.
St.
Smithe St.
Sam Kee Building
Keefer St.
Vancouver Library Square
Stadium
TOWN
STRATHCONA
Georgia
Hawks St.
St.
Sandman Inn
Union
Gore Ave.
Nelson St.
Cambie St.
North
Georgian Court
South
Prior
Venables St.
Richards St.
Homer St.
Hamilton St.
Pacific Blvd.
Blvd.
Strathcona Park
Malkin
Napier St.
Vernon Dr.
Clarke Dr.
Odlum Drive
YALETOWN
Pacific Blvd.
Pacific
Science World British Columbia
Main St.
Ave.
David Lam Park
Spyglass Pl.
Main Street
Terminal
Ave.
Industrial Ave.
Quebec St.
False Creek
1 Ave.
2 Ave.

DOWNTOWN VANCOUVER
0   250   500 m

Canada. In this city, the proverbial "laid-back" quality of the western part of North America is particularly pronounced. Statistics show that Vancouver's residents drink more wine, eat out more often, take longer coffee breaks and spend more money on sporting goods than people in the rest of Canada. Small wonder, in a city boasting so many leisure activities: Vancouver can offer fantastic beaches in the heart of downtown, yacht clubs and boat docks, a city park with enchanting paths leading through rain forests and giant ferns, and even three ski areas not far from the city center. In addition, there is an active art and culture scene as well as a respectable television and movie industry.

Vancouver has charming neighborhoods, sometimes only a few blocks in area: intimate microcosms that represent warm, personal residential districts without the anonymity that characterizes many large cities.

Competing with San Francisco and Sydney, Vancouver is often cited as a candidate for the title of "World's Most Beautiful City." Canada fans have no problem giving Vancouver the crown, less because of individual buildings than its spectacular location. "Downtown," the old city center, is located on a peninsula, and other city districts stretch along the fjord-like coast. In the foreground, you have boats with brightly-colored sails and beaches of golden sand, with,

53

behind them, the city skyline, and the Coast Mountains forming a picturesque backdrop to the whole. If the city has any drawback, it's the frequency of rain; winters, however, are mild.

For all the hymns of praise you hear about Vancouver, the city does, of course, have some problems. Cut off from eastern Canada throughout its history, Vancouver tends to feel that it's politically underrepresented. Not a single Canadian Prime Minister has been from Vancouver.

In its short history, the city has done well to concentrate its economic energies on the Pacific region. Vancouver boasts one of the most important Pacific ports of North America. The city's close links with Asia are reflected in the size of Vancouver's Chinatown – the second-largest in North America, after San Francisco. In addition, for some years now Vancouver

Above and right: Sailboats inspired the architects of Canada Place, completed for the Expo in 1986.

has been receiving a tremendous influx of Chinese from Hong Kong, so much so that ironic observers have started dubbing the city "Hongcouver" or "Vankong." Wealthy Chinese from Hong Kong have virtually taken over the suburb of Richmond; the shopping malls there are frequented almost exclusively by Asians. Many real estate agents tell the same stories about showing prospective Asian buyers a range of villas in the exclusive residential area of British Properties, in the north of Vancouver, and then asking the client which house he would like to buy; the succinct reply was, "All of them!"

Since Asian multi-millionaires have started buying up entire districts, downtown properties have become too expensive for many Canadians, which has led to dissatisfaction at all levels of society. One of the reasons Vancouver has hitherto been such a great place to live has been the virtual absence of poverty. The city administration will have to take steps if it doesn't want the city center to

degenerate into an exclusively business district as is found in so many other North American cities. For one source of Vancouver's charm is the vibrant life of downtown, with shops, apartments, bars and offices side by side. Even at night the city is alive, and it's perfectly safe to stroll through the streets or make use of the very efficient public transportation system.

THE CITY

Eastward through Downtown

It's easy to explore Vancouver's main attractions **downtown** on foot. That way, you can see not only the gleaming facades but also the narrow, dark back streets running behind the buildings, crisscrossed with a snarl of electric cables and telephone lines installed in such a way that it makes you wonder how the power supply works at all.

The best place to start out on a walk around the city is the **Waterfront Centre** with the **Tourist Information Centre**. Diagonally opposite the Waterfront Centre, at the "British Columbia" pier, you'll immediately spot the eye-catching roof of one of the city's landmarks: the five "sails" of **Canada Place** – originally the Canadian pavilion for Expo '86 – are to Vancouver what the opera house is to Sydney. The pavilion is part of the **Vancouver Trade & Convention Centre**, which houses, in addition to conference rooms of the Pan Pacific luxury hotel – stretch limousines and liveried personnel provide good photo ops – a ship terminal and the **CN IMAX Theatre**. If you stroll along the sidewalks and steps around the complex, you'll come across a number of information plaques with facts about the history of the city and the development of the harbor. The view from the east side of the complex across the harbor is impressive. Right on the water is the beautifully restored **CP Station** (Cordova Street), a relic of the last century which today serves as the Seabus and Skytrain (elevated railway) terminal.

Another wonderful view of Vancouver's skyline can be had on the 15-minute ferry ride to the northern part of the city.

Towering over Hastings Street is the 40-story **Harbour Centre**, which houses, among other things, a large department store. Elevators whizz up the outside of the building to the **Lookout**, a 546-foot (167 m) observation deck. Atop it, there are telescopes for viewing the city and a dramatic audio-visual show about Vancouver.

Once you're back on firm ground, Homer Street will lead you to the old quarter of **Gastown** with its landmark attraction, which claims to be the world's first **steam-powered clock**. A favorite with visitors, the clock still reliably issues a cloud of steam every hour on the hour; every fifteen minutes, it plays a

Above: A unique historic feature of Vancouver – the world's first steam-operated clock. Right: Chinatown – nutmeg oil, bamboo shoots, and Peking duck.

melody that echoes the bells of Big Ben in London. Here, on **Maple Tree Square**, you can also see a **statue** of the eponymous saloon-keeper **Gassy Jack**, who is portrayed standing on a whiskey barrel. Looking at Gastown today, it's hard to believe that in the 1960s it consisted of crumbling warehouses and run-down tenements. Since then, the area has flowered anew into the entertainment district it originally was, filled with bars and shops – just as Gassy Jack would have wanted it. However, now that the tourists have taken over, many residents are moving out of the neighborhood into newer, trendier districts.

Bounded by Carrall and Gore Avenues, Keefer and Cordova Streets, **Chinatown** is just a few blocks away. Its liveliest streets are Pender and Main, lined with shop after shop offering a range of exotic fruits and vegetables, dubious-looking aphrodisiacs and mysterious sea creatures. Although the neighborhood is fairly small, it plunges visitors into another world.

On Carrall Street is the beautiful **Dr. Sun Yat-Sen Garden**, a classical garden that was laid out for the 1986 Expo – the first garden done by Chinese landscape gardeners outside of China. The garden honors the Chinese statesman Sun Yat-Sen, the revolutionary and founder of the Kuomintang, who died in Beijing in 1925. The layout of limestone, flowers and trees was not only designed to please the eye, but also to tell stories. The best way to learn more about this is to take a guided tour.

On the corner of Pendler and Carral stands an architectural curiosity: the **Sam Kee Building**, the world's narrowest office building, just over 4 feet wide (1.3 m).

On its east side, Chinatown borders on **Strathcona**, a neighborhood boasting old wooden houses and defiant inhabitants who managed to avert the construction of a planned freeway through their romantic neighborhood. Northeast of Chinatown is **Japan Town**, running along Powell Street between Gore and Dunlevy Streets. Although the Japanese community never completely recovered from its uprooting in World War II, this quarter remains a focal point for the city's Japanese population and their visitors. You can buy Japanese groceries at the **Sunrise Market**, and the **Japanese Deli House** offers excellent sushi at reasonable prices.

South of Chinatown on Quebec Street lies another legacy of the '86 Expo. The glass sphere of **Science World** houses not a boring array of display cases, but an exciting exhibition about the sciences: amazingly simple models suddenly give new clarity to natural phenomena, and even newcomers to physics can have a few "aha" experiences, pulling on levers and pushing buttons and thereby finding solutions to a number of formerly inexplicable conundrums of physics.

If you're too tired to continue, just take the Skytrain back to Waterfront Centre. If you'd rather continue walking, stroll along **False Creek** towards Granville Bridge.

Yaletown and Library Square

The quarter between Cambie and Hamilton Streets, Smithe and Davie Streets is one of the up-and-coming trendy quarters of the city. Once-abandoned warehouses in **Yaletown** have now become restaurants, bars, boutiques and designer furniture stores. Although the neighboring area is still a red-light district, the borders of this new, trendy quarter delineate an area teeming with Vancouver's beautiful people and yuppies. Designers and successful young businesspeople live in chicly decorated lofts. By day, the neighborhood is less attractive; there aren't any individual buildings that are really worth seeing. At night, however, you can brush shoulders with the young and beautiful.

If you follow Homer Street back toward town, you'll hit West Georgia

Above: Futuristic architecture – the Science Centre. Right: Robson Street, the busy center of downtown.

Street and **Vancouver Library Square**. This new building complex was built by the Canadian top architect Moshe Safdie, who attained world renown by the age of 30 with his cubistic residential complex *L'Habitat* in Montreal. Library Square houses more than 1 million books and electronic media. The library building is a first step in making this neighborhood more attractive – especially important in light of the fact that the population downtown is expected to increase by 40,000 over the next 20 years.

Opposite the library you can marvel at Moshe Safdie's second stroke of genius: the **Ford Centre for the Performing Arts** has 1,824 seats and a gigantic stage, which can support new and elaborate productions with huge crowd scenes.

Walking Westward Downtown

Howe Street runs from Waterfront Centre to **Robson Square**, where there are the Courts of Justice, some governmental buildings, and a multitude of restaurants. The street is a popular venue for street performers, skateboard acrobats and rollerbladers. The most important building, though, is the **Vancouver Art Gallery**. This neoclassical edifice was built in 1907 by Francis Rattenbury, one of the leading architects of his time. In its permanent exhibits, the four-level gallery shows Canadian, American and European paintings; and there is a separate Children's Gallery on the ground floor. The main focus is Canadian artists. Especially well represented is the British Columbian Emily Carr, whose paintings skillfully capture the atmosphere of the rain forests.

If you have shopping in mind, you can detour from Robson Square over to **Granville Street** between West Georgia and Nelson Streets. This area is a center for backpackers, young people who flock to the cinemas and concert halls in the evenings, and the so-called hard'n'heavy

scene. Anyone looking for plastic fashion accessories or leather jackets has come to the right place.

Robson Square marks the start of the most interesting stretch of **Robson Street**. Most of this quarter was inhabited by Germans at the beginning of the 20th century. Today the street, lined with cafes and boutiques, is a promenade with a European flair that could almost be located in Milan or Paris. Little of the German influence remains today, but there are still a few German shopkeepers, among them a baker and the owner of a restaurant.

You should walk up the intersection of Denman Street to get acquainted with yet another neighborhood. **Denman Street** is the center of the **West End**, one of the liveliest parts of the city. The buildings are a mixture of real architectural jewels and newer apartment buildings. Some of the most beautiful Victorian-style buildings in the city stand around **Barcley Heritage Square**. The **Roedde House Museum** has preserved the furnishings of a

typical Victorian house. In this neighborhood, between Coal Harbour and English Bay, the streets are lined with cafés, bars, shops and theaters. The West End is also the gay quarter – tolerant and lively. The beach promenade **English Bay** is a paradise for joggers, rollerbladers, mountain bikers and even people who just want to hang out.

Proceeding along **Lost Lagoon**, you come to **Stanley Park**, which the state gave to the city as a recreation area as early as 1888. Stanley Park is unquestionably one of the most beautiful and varied city parks in the world. Extending over an area of more than 1,000 acres (405 hectares) the park is partly covered with forests and is crisscrossed with nearly 50 miles (80 km) of paths and roads. Only in the eastern part of the park are there gravel paths to stroll on; in the western part, however, you can make use of one of the park's legion beaches or venture deeply into the rain forest – and maybe even get lost. A word of caution: note that the map of the park's paths in the brochure *Visitor's Choice* contains a few inaccuracies.

To get the most out of the park, renting a bicycle is one of the best ways to explore (on foot, the excursion can take on the character of a forced march). Take off along the Seawall Promenade. Near Lost Lagoon there's a par-3 **golf course**; while the paths along the shore offer a succession of beautiful beaches, picnic areas, and magnificent views such as the one from **Fergueson Point** across to Vancouver Island. From **Prospect Point**, where there's a souvenir shop and café, you have the best view of the **Lions Gate Bridge**, built by the Guinness brewery in 1938, which connects the city center to North and West Vancouver. The two towers of this impressive feat of engineering are some 330 feet high (100 m), and the surface of the road is nearly 230 feet (70 m) above the water.

In the southern part of the park, there's a little **zoo** with a bear enclosure; children can ride ponies in the nearby **Children's Zoo**. The adjacent **Vancouver Aquarium** is also worth a visit; it displays interesting underwater flora and fauna of the northwest coast. Its tanks are home to killer whales and white whales, among other creatures; watching these behemoths swim by you through underwater windows is a memorable experience.

Following the Seawall Promenade, you will come upon a replica of the **figurehead** of the *S.S. Empress of Japan*, one of the trade ships of the Pacific fleet that transported goods to Japan around the turn of the century. A little farther south is Vancouver's modern take on Copenhagen's "Little Mermaid," called *Girl in a Wetsuit*. From the lighthouse on Brockton Point, it's not far to the **Totem Poles**, which were brought here from various places on the West Coast and have been delightfully restored: a public sign of the city's attempts to remember and properly honor its Indian heritage. The small peninsula of **Deadman Island**

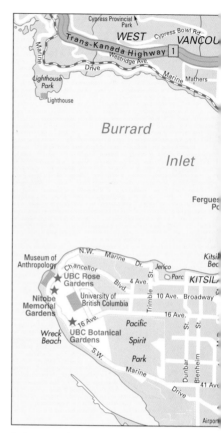

belongs to the navy. And finally, there's the **Royal Yacht Club**, Vancouver's most exclusive sailing club.

Granville Island and Vanier Park

To get to **Granville Island** from downtown, you can either go across the Granville Bridge or take the small, colorful mini-ferry called the Aquabus. In the 1960s, squalid warehouses dominated the scene here, but the 1970s saw the arrival of culture and cuisine, and Granville Island is today a wonderful neighborhood that appeals to locals and visitors alike. A weekend just wouldn't be a weekend without a visit to Granville Island: how can anyone pass up on the attractions of

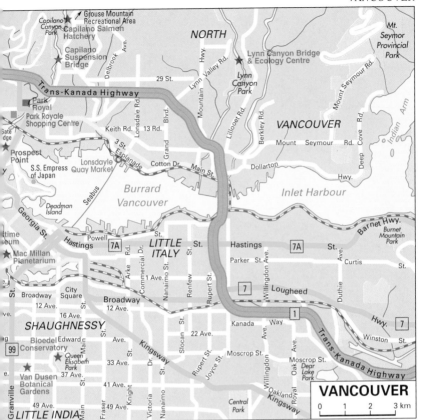

seeing and being seen, listening to spontaneous musical offerings or watching street performers, going to galleries and dining out? The **Public Market** is considered a gastronomic jewel: in its halls, you can sample a range of snacks from all over the world, and its delicatessens and wine dealers prove that Canadians are not a bit averse to culinary pleasures and refinements. The **Granville Island Brewery** (1441 Cartwright Street) brings out the more sophisticated side of a normally rather pedestrian beverage, beer.

The west side of the island is a recreational paradise for sailors and other water sports enthusiasts: the specialty shops here stock a full array of shackles, rope ends, clamps, books on sailing, nautical clothing, and other essential items. Children also love Granville Island, especially for its **Kids Only Market**.

Passing idyllically situated apartment buildings and yacht clubs, you can stroll under the **Burrard Bridge** to **Vanier Park**; the view of the West End skyline from here is enchanting. Vanier Park is also the locus of several city attractions. You can't miss the **Vancouver Museum**; the unusual shape of its roof was inspired by the ceremonial headdress of the West Coast Indians. This is Canada's largest municipal museum; its displays range from Indian art and artisan work to the Pullman wagon of the first train to arrive in Vancouver, from period furniture to a reconstructed trading post, and many other facets of Vancouver's colorful history. The **Maritime Museum** is devoted to the region's seafaring past. The museum's pride is the two-masted schooner *St. Roch*, the first ship to sail through the Northwest Passage. If you want an even closer look at the city's history, or are simply interested in old documents and photographs, the **City of Vancouver Archives** is just the place. Also located in Vanier Park is the **H.R. MacMillan Planetarium**. In the afternoon and evening, visitors can learn all about the Pacific sky; and there are also special shows for the more serious astronomy fan. In the **Gordon Southam Observatory**, stargazers can peer through a telescope with an experienced astronomer on hand to answer questions.

University of British Columbia

Located in the western part of Vancouver, the university campus is a city in itself, complete with green parks and an extremely interesting museum, the **U.B.C. Museum of Anthropology**. Even if you're only staying briefly in Vancouver, this ethnological museum should be at the top of your list, for several reasons. First of all, there is the unique architecture. The famous local architect Arthur Erickson based his designs for this museum on the traditional longhouses of the Indians of the Pacific Northwest. Perched on a rock high above Point Grey, the building commands an extraordinary view across to the north through its huge windows. Displayed inside is the most important collection of Indian art and everyday artifacts from various West Coast tribes, notably the Haida, Kwakiutl and Salish, whose works are fully equal to those of the advanced civilizations of Mexico or Ecuador. Also on display are artifacts of ear-

Right: Remarkable exhibit in the remarkable U.B.C. Museum of Anthropology.

lier Asian, Latin-American and Pacific cultures. Even people who don't normally like museums can't help but be impressed by the presentation of the objects and the power of this art.

Directly behind the museum, a path leads through the trees to **Wreck Beach**, which is popular with local nudists. Back on Marine Drive, there are a number of gardens worth seeing as you move from north to south. The university parks consist of the **Asian** and the **Botanical Garden**; the latter is modeled on gardens of the 16th century and contains a wide variety of herbs and medicinal plants. The **Nitobe Memorial Garden**, one of the most peaceful spots in all Vancouver, displays classical Japanese gardening with a stone pagoda, a tea house, and harmonious landscaping. It is dedicated to Inazo Nitobe, a man remembered for his subtle, diplomatic efforts to link Asian and North American interests. And finally, there's the **Rose Garden**, where visitors are engulfed in an aromatic sea of roses.

Kitsilano, Shaughnessy, Little India and Little Italy

If a trendy part of town exists for the thirty-something crowd, it's **Kitsilano**. Lying between the city's most popular beach, **Kitsilano Beach** (with a heated salt-water pool), and Broadway (9th Avenue), this neighborhood offers wonderful side streets with quaint wooden houses, colorful gardens and lovely promenades. "Hippest" residential areas are the stretch of 5th Avenue between Balaclava and Bayswater Streets or the old workers' houses from the 1920s (along 5th, 6th, Avenues between Stephens and MacDonald Streets). 4th Avenue is a shopping artery which combines the flair of the 1960s with modern 90s elegance. It's also worth browsing the boutiques on Broadway Avenue; along here, too, there are several Greek restaurants.

Bordering this neighborhood to the east is **Shaughnessy**. The oldest part of this district, between 16th and 28th Avenues, was built by the railway company in 1907 as an exclusive residential neighborhood. The area is still expensive today, and, despite its central location, wonderfully quiet – a veritable oasis. Renting a bike may afford you the best means of exploring the park-like streets between 16th and 41st Avenues, allowing you to marvel at the lawns and the monumental villas and finally bearing you through the **Van Dusen Botanical Gardens**, where there are lush rhododendrons, bushes and trees; a pleasant restaurant; and **MacMillan Bloedel Place**, an exhibition devoted to the history of the wood processing industry.

Just one block away, and well worth a visit, is **Queen Elizabeth Park**. From Little Mountain, 490 feet (150 m) high and crowned with the **Bloedel Conservatory**, there's a magnificent view across to downtown. The conservatory's greenhouse dome shelters a flourishing collection of plants from around the world, from rain forests to desert habitats. Tropical birds fly overhead, capping the illusion that you've been transported into a new Eden. And when people are doing their *tai chi* exercises in the park outside, and the sun plays harmonies of light and shadow on the Henry Moore statue in front of the conservatory, there could be no better image of a true urban idyll.

Directly south of Shaughnessy is **Little India**, which centers around Main Street between 49th and 51st Avenues. This is an important hub for Canadians of East Indian origin – and not only for those who live in Vancouver. If a wedding is being planned, any self-respecting East Indian family in this part of Canada has to come to the city to make the necessary purchases, which can run up to $50,000. To the east of this center, the architect Arthur Erickson created another Vancouver highlight: the **Sikh Temple** on Ross Street.

Continuing northwards along **Commercial Drive**, you'll soon reach **Little**

Italy, which centers around that thoroughfare and 1st Avenue. At the moment, Commercial Drive is one of the city's hot spots, and it's a great place for a stroll, offering an array of health food stores, avant-garde record shops, Italian espresso bars and, of course, **The Cultch**, or to be more exact, the **Vancouver East Cultural Centre**, a converted church that has become the most popular culture center in the city.

NORTH VANCOUVER AND WEST VANCOUVER

The easiest way to reach the shore side of **North Vancouver** is to take the **Seabus**, which docks at the **Lonsdale Quay Market**, a busy complex on the waterfront with shops and restaurants and a good spot for a coffee break.

The most important attraction in North Vancouver is the **Capilano Suspension**

Above: Beach volleyball on the "trendy" beach of Kitsilano.

Bridge (3735 Capilano Road) in Capilano Canyon. Nearly 460 feet (140 m) long, this turn-of-the-century bridge swings some 220 feet (70 m) over the turbulent gorge – anyone with a fear of heights should probably stay home. The bridge has been quite commercialized; the adjacent amusement park with Indian wood carvings is rather on the kitschy side and has little relation to genuine Indian art.

Capilano Park Road brings you to the **Capilano Salmon Hatchery**, which is open to visitors; exhibits here provide information about the life cycle of the salmon. Further up the canyon you come to the **Grouse Mountain Recreational Area**, where the so-called *Skyride* takes passengers up to the 4,000-foot (1,250 m) peak in just 8 minutes; in winter, this peak, not far from downtown, becomes Vancouver's local ski area. One of the city's enviable assets is the fact that residents and visitors can ski in the morning and sail in the afternoon, or even go for a quick ski after work, as the slopes are il-

WHISTLER – FRASER VALLEY

luminated with flood lights until late into the night. Even in the summer, the ascent by cable car offers a spectacular view of the city and Vancouver Island. All this, together with occasional theater performances and a restaurant with panoramic views, conspires to make Grouse Mountain one of the city's top attractions.

Farther to the east is the **Lynn Canyon Bridge** in **Lynn Canyon Park**. Although it is only half as long as the Capilano Suspension Bridge, it hovers some 260 feet (80 m) above the canyon. There are interesting nature trails, films and exhibitions around the **Ecology Centre**.

Just over 8 miles (13 km) northeast of Vancouver lies **Mount Seymour Provincial Park**. Encompassing an area of nearly 1.5 square miles (3.5 sq. km), the park is a popular ski and hiking area centering around its 5,000-foot (1,453 m) peak. Several of the shorter hiking trails begin from the parking lot of the **Visitor Centre** at 3,270 feet (1,000 m), such as the **Loop Trail** around Goldie Lake.

In **West Vancouver**, you can take beautiful hikes through the rain forest in **Lighthouse Park**. There are more than 8 miles (13 km) of trails maintained in this area, and the view over to UBC is fantastic. In addition, there are inviting places on the rocks for sunbathing or picnicking.

Cypress Bowl Road winds its way up to **Cypress Provincial Park**, where, at altitudes of 2,600 - 4,500 feet (800 - 1,400 m), you have fabulous views all the way to Vancouver Island and even to the snow-capped American peak Mount Baker, 10,740 feet (3,285 m) high. Also in this park are the popular ski areas **Cypress Bowl** and **Hollytown**.

EXCURSION THROUGH WHISTLER & FRASER VALLEY

If your travel time is limited and you've decided to concentrate on Vancouver and perhaps Vancouver Island,

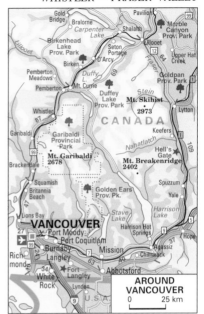

AROUND
VANCOUVER
0   25 km

you can still get a taste of British Columbia's diverse countryside on the following suggested tour, lasting three to four days. Only in summer can you drive the whole route in its entirety, as some of the roads are closed from late autumn to spring.

Starting point is **Horseshoe Bay**, the B.C. Ferries landing in the northwest part of the city. From here, Highway 99 winds along the fjord-like coast of Howe Sound. Expensive villas, carefully set in idyllic locations, nestle against the cliff walls.

Passing **Britannia Beach**, where you can tour an abandoned copper mine, the excursion continues on to **Squamish**. This town's economy centers on the timber industry. Once a year, however, the place goes wild: the first week of August sees the annual **Squamish Days**, when Canadian lumberjacks show what "real men" are made of. Crowds roar to cheer on contestants in wood-chopping and sawing competitions, while the beer flows like water.

Driving along the boundary of **Garibaldi Provincial Park**, which measures 780 square miles (2,000 sq. km) in size and has a wealth of hiking trails to offer, you come to **Whistler**, the most famous ski resort in B.C. (see p. 218) with its chalet-style lodges. Whistler offers anything but an experience of solitude in the mountain wilderness. While skiing is the sport of choice in the winter and the bars and restaurants bop year-round, in the summer you can hike, rent mountain bikes, go whitewater rafting, horseback riding, or golfing, or even enjoy summer skiing on the Black Comb Glacier. A few miles from town, hiking trails lead through the spectacular scenery of the **Coast Mountains**.

Pemberton, further on, lies in a valley that's devoted to raising livestock. Further on, **Duffy Lake Road** climbs from **Mount Curie** along Cayoosh Creek up to

Above: A cable car crosses safely above the rapids rushing between the perilously steep banks of the Fraser River at Hell's Gate.

a pass over the mountains. It's only 43 miles (70 km) from Pemberton to **Lillooet**, but in terms of climate, the two are worlds apart: for Fraser Valley, where Lillooet is located, is already one of the dry valleys characteristic of Interior B.C. The town achieved a certain prosperity in 1858, because gold diggers set out from here on their long journey through the Cariboo Mountains to Barkerville. The **Lillooet Museum** commemorates those wild days of the past.

Lytton, today known as the starting point of rafting tours along the Fraser River, began as an outpost of the Hudson's Bay Company named after the British colonial minister and writer Sir Edward Bulwer-Lytton, whose most famous book was *The Last Days of Pompeii*. The Fraser River claimed the lives of so many people attempting to canoe down it that in 1862 a road was carved out of the steep rock of the river valley. The road follows the river through this narrow valley and leads to **Hell's Gate**, the narrowest part of this powerful torrent. If you're not afraid of heights, the funicular ride over the rapids is exhilarating.

When it reaches **Yale**, the river shakes free of the untamed mountains and continues on toward the Pacific as a wide, placid current. Yale, incidentally, was where gold was first discovered in 1858, triggering a flood of fortune hunters who fought their way farther and farther up the river and deeper into B.C. Continuing on through **Hope**, where the film *Rambo* was shot in 1981, and **Harrison Hot Springs**, you come back into the Greater Vancouver area.

The edifice now known as **Fort Langley Historic Site** was once one of the most important forts of the Hudson's Bay Company. Established in 1827, it started to turn huge profits in 1858, when the gold diggers stocked up there on tools, coats and food. Now open to the public, it is a "living" fort where costumed guides recreate the glory days of the past.

VANCOUVER
Area Code 604

Accommodation

For hotel reservations in B.C., call 1-800-663-6000. *LUXURY:* **Waterfront Centre Hotel**, 900 Canada Place, tel. 691-1991, new, luxurious, centrally located, with tastefully furnished, large rooms, and good restaurants. **Hotel Vancouver**, 900 West Georgia St., tel. 684-3131. Opened in 1887, it serves as a local point of orientation and a piece of the city's history. **The Georgian Court**, 773 Beatty St., tel. 682-5555, intimate, well-run establishment with the exclusive restaurant "William Tell." *MODERATE:* **Holiday Inn**, 4405 Central Blvd. (Metrotown), tel. 438-1881. **Rosedale on Robson**, tel. 689-8033, new hotel on Robson St. **Park Royal**, tel. 926-5511, comfortable Tudor-style building 10 min from downtown. **Sandman Hotel**, 180 West Georgia, tel. 681-2211, efficient, beloved of groups, in proximity to Yaletown, Chinatown, Gastown. **Pacific Palisades**, 1277 Robson St., tel. 688-0461, renovated, great location. There are a number of moderate but slightly run-down **motels** on **Kingsway Ave**. *BUDGET:* **Sylvia Hotel**, 1154 Gilford St., tel. 681-9321, great site on the beach in the West End; a bit run-down, but still charming. **Youth Hostel of Downtown Backpackers**, 347 West Pender St., tel. 688-0112, clean and roomy. **City Centre Motor Inn**, 2111 Main St., tel. 876-7166, near the station, Sky Train terminal, and Science World; good value for money. **Hostelling International Vancouver**, 1515 Discovery St., tel. 224-3208, in a nice spot on Jericho Beach, Canada's largest hostel with public rooms where there's always something going on. **UBC** can arrange for rooms during the summer holidays, tel. 822-1010. The **Simon Fraser University** rents out rooms on its campus in Burnaby, tel. 291-4503. **YMCA**, 733 Beatty St., tel. 895-5830, a new building with one to four beds to a room, free health club.
B&B: **Vancouver B&B Registry** can arrange rooms, tel. 276-8616. **Shaughnessy Village**, 1125 W 12th Ave., tel. 736-5511, large place with little rooms decorated like ships' cabins, health club, restaurant, 24-hour service. **Manor Guest House**, 345 W 13th Ave., tel. 876-8494, turn-of-the-century villa. **Ocean Breeze**, 462 East 1st St., North Vancouver, tel. 988-0546.
CAMPING: **Capilano RV PARK**, tel. 987-4722, closest to the center of town, right by Lions Gate Bridge, clean, with pool; take buses 251, 252, 258 from Park Royal in the city center. **Burnaby Cariboo RV Park**, 8765 Cariboo Pl., tel. 420-1722, bus/skytrain to downtown Vancouver; attractive spot with whirlpool, pool, grill, fitness room; also suitable for cooler seasons.

Restaurants and Bars

The publication *City Food* is a valuable guide; it can be picked up in many restaurants and bookstores free of charge, and appears ten times a year for Vancouver, Greater Vancouver, Whistler and Victoria.
GASTOWN: Sitar, 8 Powell St., tel. 687-0049, very good Indian food at reasonable prices. **Blarney Stone**, 216 Carrall St., Irish pub with "pub grub" and live music, always hopping. **Hard Rock Café**, 688 W Hastings. **The Old Spaghetti Factory**, 53 Water St., tel. 684-1288.
DOWNTOWN, ROBSON AND WEST END: **Chartwell**, Four Seasons Hotel, 791 West Georgia St., tel. 689-9933, delicacies served in a lush "jungle" setting. **Imperial Chinese Seafood**, 3555 Burrard St, tel. 688-8191, good. **Joe Fortes**, 777 Thurlow Street, tel. 669-1940, *the* seafood restaurant in town: lovely decor, great atmosphere. **Cactus Club Café**, 1136 Robson, tel. 687-3278, excellent Tex-Mex, with large portions.
GRANVILLE ISLAND: Arts Club Theatre, bar and lounge, with Okanagan Springs beer on tap.
YALETOWN: Bar None, 1222 Hamilton Street, trendy late-night establishment. **"Y" Yaletown Breweries**, corner Helmcken/Hamilton Streets, chic restaurant with terrace.
VANCOUVER EAST: The Cannery, 2205 Commissioner St, tel. 254-9606, great seafood, excellent wines, harbor views.
KITSILANO: Caper's, im Plimley Block, steaks, salads, pasta.
LITTLE ITALY: Santos Tapas Restaurant, 1191 Commercial Dr, tel. 253-0444, tapas, live Latin American music.
NORTH VANCOUVER: Beach House, on Dundarave Pier, tel. 922-1414, good West Coast cuisine and seafood.

Museums

B.C. Golf Museum and Library, 2545 Blanca St., tel. 222-4653. **B.C. Museum of Mining**, Hwy 99 toward Britannia Beach, Howe Sound, tel. 688-8735, history and stories of local mining, very well displayed. **B.C. Sports Hall of Fame and Museum**, 777 Pacific Boulevard South, in the BC Place Stadium, tel. 687-5520, hand-on museum about the history of sports and famous athletes, Wed-Sun 10 am-5 pm. **B.C. Sugar Museum**, 123 Roger St., tel. 253-1131, Mon-Fri 9 am-4 pm. **Bloedel Conservatory**, 33 Ave./corner Cambie St., tel. 257-8570, open 10 am-5 pm in winter, until 9 pm in summer. **Canada Place**, Imax Theatre, tel. 682-4629 Canada Pl., tel. 682-2384, 9 am-5 pm. **Canadian Craft Museum**, 639 Hornby St., tel. 687-8266, artisan work, both modern and historic, with shop. **Capilano Suspension Bridge**, 3735 Capilano Rd., tel. 985-7474, May-Sept. 8:30 am-dusk, other times 9 am-5 pm. **Forest Alliance of B.C.**, 1055 Dunsmuir St., tel. 1-800-567-TREE, videos and exhibits about forestry. **Fort Langley National Historic Site**, 23433 Mavis Ave., Fort Langley, tel. 888-4424, 10 am-4:30 pm. **UBC Geology Museum**, Geological Science Centre, tel. 822-2449, fossils and minerals. **Granville Island Sport Fishing Museum**, 1502 Duranlean St., tel. 683-1939, 10 am-5:30 pm. **Gulf of Georgia Cannery National Historic Site**, tel. 664-9009 and **Steveston Heritage Fishing Village**, a historic fishing town; both located at the mouth of the Fraser River, S of Richmond, with antique shops, restaurants, fish market. **Harbour Centre**, 555 West Hastings St., tel. 689-0421, open 8:30 am-10:30 pm in summer, 9 am-9 pm in winter. **Lynn Canyon Ecology Centre**, 3663 Park Rd., tel. 981-3103, 9 am-dusk. **MacMillan Planetarium**, Vanier Park, tel. 738-7827, Tue-Sun in summer. **Maritime Museum**, 1905 Odgen Ave, tel. 257-8300, 10 am-5 pm, closed Mon in winter. **UBC Museum of Anthropology**, 6393 NW Marine Dr., tel. 822-3825 or 822-5087, 11 am-5 pm, Tue until 9 pm, admission free. **Roedde House Museum**, 1415 Barclay St., tel. 684-7040, call for opening times. **Science World**, with OMNI-MAX cinema, 1455 Quebec St., tel. 268-6363, 10 am-6 pm, Oct-May 'til 5 pm. **Sri Lankan Gem Museum**, 150-925 West Georgia St., tel. 662-7764, precious stones and a great café. **BBC Botanical Garden**, 6804 SW Marine Dr., tel. 822-9666, open daily 10 am-6 pm. **Vancouver Aquarium**, Stanley Park, tel. 682-1118, July-early Sept 9 am-8 pm, other times 10 am-5:30 pm. **Vancouver Art Gallery**, 750 Hornby St., tel. 662-4719, call for opening times. **Vancouver Museum**, 1100 Chestnut St., tel. 736-4431, Tue-Sun 10 am-5 pm, open daily in summer. **Vancouver Police Museum**, 240 East Cordova St., tel. 665-3346, all about fighting crime. **Vancouver Stock Exchange Visitors Centre**, 609 Granville St., tel. 643-6590, information about brokers and stock market history; reserve in advance.

Shopping

Murata Art and **Evergreen**, 390 Powell St., Japanese porcelain, kimonos, etc.

Punjabi Area (Main Street between 49th/51st Avenue), Indian foods, silk, jewelry.

Park Royal (any blue bus to N or W Vancouver stops at Park Royal), shopping center with various retail outlets, three department stores, an electronics shop, and low-priced sporting goods store.

Westminster Quay Public Market, New Westminster Skytrain Station, shops and a "gourmet court" on the Fraser River.

Metrotown, 4700/4800 Kingsway, huge malls with Skytrain station, 400 stores, cinema, restaurant, hotel (Holiday Inn; see "Hotels").

Tips for Kids

Bonkers, 1185 West Georgia St., tel. 669-9230, play area for children and adults. **Zoo** in Stanley Park. **Vancouver Childrens Festival**, in Vanier Park, tel. 280-4444. **Kids Only Market**, Granville Island, tel. 689-8447.

Cultural Events

Arts Hotline: For information about cultural events, call 684-ARTS. **Jazz Hotline**, tel. 682-20706. **Arts Club Theatre**, 1585 Johnston St., Granville Island, tel. 687-5315, modern theater. **C.B.C Festival of Music**, Queen Elizabeth Theatre, Hamilton St., in Sept. **Orpheum Theatre**: corner Smithe/Seymour Sts., tel. 665-3050, register in advance for guided tours through the home base of the Vancouver Symphony. **Cinema**: Half-price admission on Tuesdays to all Cineplex Odeon theaters, tel. 434-2463. **Pubs**: Many pubs offer live music; Thursday is concert day, when there's usually a $10 charge at the door. **A Touch of Hollywood**: Vancouver is often used as a filming site. Call 660-3569 for information. **Centre Culturel Francophone de Vancouver**, 1551 W. 7th Ave, tel. 736-9806, French-language cultural events. **Author's Readings** in the Railway Club, 579 Dunsmuir St., tel. 681-1625, 3rd Mon of every month; for more info on the literary scene, call 681-6330. **Ford Centre**, 777 Homer St., tel. 280-2222, musicals. **Simon Fraser University Teck Gallery**, 515 W Hastings, art, performances, readings; call 291-5075. **Theatre Under the Stars**, in the summer in Stanley Park, tel. 687-0174, open-air theater. **Yuk Yuk's Comedy Club**, 750 Pacific Blvd., tel. 687-5233, Thu, Fri, Sat comedy & cabaret.

Markets

Pacific National Exhibition Annual Fair, Exhibition Park, usually mid-Aug.-Sept. **Granville Island Public Market**, see p. 61. **Flea market**, on the grounds under the Skytrain tracks, Terminal Avenue at Thoronton, Sat and Sun 9 am-5 pm. **Londsdale Quay Market**, attractive shops and restaurants at the Seabus Terminal in North Vancouver.

Transportation

AIRPORT: The international airport is in Richmond, 20-30 minutes from downtown by car. The *Airporter* is a shuttle bus that runs to and from the airport (Level II) from about 5:30 am, stopping at the most important downtown hotels. Buses run every 15 to 30 minutes; a return ticket is $15, tel. 946-8866. A taxi will cost you around $20-25.

TRAIN: The **train station** is at 1150 Station St. **VIA Rail** is the official name of the Canadian railway. **Amtrak** operates trains to the U.S.A. The trip from Vancouver to Seattle or Seattle to Vancouver takes less than four hours; tel. 1-800-872-7245. From the B.C. Rail Station (1311 W First St., North

Vancouver), the B.C. Rail Cariboo Prospector offers sightseeing trips through Whistler and Lilloet to Prince George. The **Royal Hudson Steam Train**, tel. 687-9558, a historic steam train, chugs along the spectacular coastline to Squamish (a trip of about 2 hours); the return journey is then by ship, aboard the **MV Britannia** – one of the best tours in the Vancouver area. Tel. 984-5246 and 1-800-663-8238.

BOAT: **Cruise Ships** depart from Canada Place. **Ferries** travel approximately every hour from Horseshoe Bay (West Vancouver) to Nanaimo (Vancouver Island) and from Tsawwassen to Victoria (Vancouver Island) as well as to the Gulf Islands, which belong to Canada, and the San Juan Islands, which belong to the U.S.A. (B.C. Ferries tel. 669-1211, 7 am-10 pm; 24-hour recorded information line, 277-0277.) **SS Beaver Cruises** (from Coal Harbour, tel. 682-7284) run excursions aboard a replica of the first steamship in British Columbia. You can charter yachts of all descriptions from **Westin Bayshore Yacht Charters**, tel. 691-6936.

BUS: The bus station is located at 150 Dunsmuir Street. A new addition is the **Gold Leaf Dome Coach**, a luxury double-decker excursion bus that runs between Vancouver, Banff and Calgary: 74 passengers, service on board, stop at Kamloops for dinner, tel. 984-3131.

MUNICIPAL TRANSPORTATION: Vancouver has a city **bus** system, **trolleys**, the elevated **Skytrain** (Waterfront Centre, 20 stations in the suburbs, Burnaby, New Westminster, Surrey) and the **Seabus** from Canada Place to Londsdale Quay/North Vancouver, tel. 261-5100. The small mini-ferry to Granville Island, called **Aquabus**, runs in summer from 7 am-10 pm between the island, the Aquatic Centre, the Maritime Museum in Vanier Park and Stamps Landing. You can pick up bus and trolley timetables in the Tourism Vancouver office. West Georgia Street is a main axis for buses running either to North and West Vancouver or to the east.

If you want to get around Vancouver by public transportation – and it's a good option – make sure to pick up a copy of the brochures *Greater Vancouver Visitors Guide, Vancouver on Transit* and the *Transit Guide*: these contain maps, prices, fare zones, and tips on savings (such as a $6.00 day pass, good for all three zones).

CABLE CAR: **Skyride**, **Grouse Mountain**, 6400 Nancy Green Way, 9 am-10 pm, tel. 984-0661 for restaurant reservations and information about *Theatre in the Sky*.

CARRIAGE RIDES depart from the parking lot by the zoo in Stanley Park, 10:30 am-4 pm, about every half hour. Tel. 681-5115.

GUIDED CITY TOURS: Walkabout Historic Vancouver Tours depart from NE corner of Howe/Geor-

gia Sts., tel. 808-1650. Sightseeing bus tours in Vancouver, Victoria: **Pacific Coach Lines**, tel. 662-7575, or **Blue Mountain Tours**, tel. 298-1133.

Sports

Hastings Park Race Course, McGill St., horse racing, for information and times, call 254-1631. **General Motors Place**, Homer St., new home of the Vancouver Canucks and the Vancouver Grizzlies, also used for concerts. In this new, architecturally adventurous stadium, which seats 20,000, you have a good view even from the very last row. **Pacific Coliseum**, Renfrew St., roller hockey with the Vancouver VooDoos. **Baseball**: the **Vancouver Canadians** (minor league) play in Queen Elizabeth Park, at 33 Ave./Quebec St. On weekends, you can often observe **beach volleyball** competitions on local beaches. *SWIMMING:* **Kitsilano Outdoor Pool**, 450-foot (137 m) salt-water pool filled with beautiful people. **Vancouver Aquatic Centre**, 1050 Beach Ave., 165-foot (50 m) indoor pool, saunas, and more. *KAYAK RENTAL, COURSES:* **Ecomarine Ocean Kayak Centre**, 1668 Duranleau, tel. 689-7575. *TOURS, BIRDWATCHING:* **Outback Adventure Co.**, 206 1110 Hamilton St., tel. 688-7206. *BICYCLE AND ROLLERBLADE RENTAL:* **Bayshore Bicycle & Rollerblade Rentals**, 745 Denman St., tel. 688-2453 or 1601 W Georgia St, tel. 689-5071. *DIVING:* **International Diving Centre**, 2034 West 11th Ave., tel. 736-2541. **Divers World**, 1817 W 4th St, tel. 732-1344. *WINDSURFING SCHOOL AND RENTAL:* **Windsure**, Jericho Beach, 1300 Discovery St., tel. 224-0615. *SAILING:* **Sea Wing Sailing School**, 1818 Maritime, on Granville Island, tel. 669-0840, rental or charter of boats with captain.

Emergencies

Emergency: tel. 911. **Emergency Medical Service**: tel. 736-6400. The **College of Family Physicians** employs multi-lingual doctors; after 5 pm, the number is 682-2344. **Vancouver Grand Hospital**, 855 W Twelfth Ave., tel. 875-4111.

Tourist Information

Tourism Vancouver, Waterfront Centre, 200 Burrard St., tel. 683-2000. Walking Tours through Gastown led by guides in historical costume, free of charge, tel. 683-5650. **Vancouver Coast & Mountains Tourism Region**, 204-1755 W Broadway, tel. 739-9011. **Tourism Richmond Info. Center**, Highway 99, a bit N of the Massey Tunnel, tel. 271-8280. **The Georgia Straight**, which appears every Thu, has comprehensive listings of events, activities and tips, available free of charge in many stores, tel. 681-2000. **Internet**: **Euphony** is an on-line events listing, available free of charge at http://euphony.com. **Visitor's Choice** is a guide through the city, available free of charge.

VANCOUVER ISLAND

VICTORIA
FROM VICTORIA TO PACIFIC
RIM NATIONAL PARK
ALONG THE COAST
TO PORT HARDY

Vancouver Island, 280 miles (450 km) long with 500,000 inhabitants, is an island of contrasts. Even today, its wild and rainy west coast is almost inaccessible; while the east coast, with its popular beaches, is well-developed and densely populated. The island's attraction stems from a well-balanced combination of boutiques and high tea in Victoria, beach bars and first-class restaurants on the east coast on the one hand, and inland wildlife parks and secluded hideaways, such as Cape Scott Provincial Park on the island's northern tip, on the other. For the most part, the island is well developed; there's a range of outfitters for all sorts of water sports, while experienced outdoor enthusiasts can embark on one of the last true adventures: hiking the West Coast Trail.

As early as 1778, James Cook landed on the western coast of the island – but he assumed it was the mainland. Not until 1792 was the mistake corrected, when Captain George Vancouver discovered that this presumed "mainland" was actually the largest Pacific island off the North American coast. He promptly named Vancouver Island after himself.

Preceding pages: A boat festival in Victoria harbor. Left: An outdoor adventure for the truly daring: the West Coast Trail.

In 1843, the Hudson's Bay Company established Fort Victoria on the southern tip of the island, which was an extremely clever strategic move. At that time, the U.S.A. and Great Britain were negotiating about the border and had already set their sights on the 49th parallel. However, since the Hudson's Bay Company had already established their station farther south, the whole island area was annexed to Britain in 1849 – the only "runover" along the entire border from Manitoba to the west coast.

The legendary gold rush began in 1858: 27,000 miners poured into the city within a single summer. Temporary, makeshift quarters were hastily erected cheek by jowl with dignified English houses, marking what was probably the most exciting era in the history of Victoria. English society ladies with their parasols were forced to tolerate the provocative whistles of gold miners as they walked by. When British Columbia became a member of the Canadian Confederation in 1871, Victoria, the most important city in the West, was chosen as capital.

VICTORIA

Today, about 290,000 people live in Greater Victoria. Although the city can't really be considered small from the

73

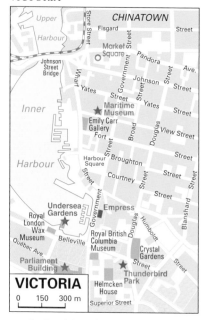

making the islanders in ways more British than the British themselves. Here, you'll find teatime and double-decker busses; the Union Jack waving everywhere; London tailors conjuring up jackets from fine tweed; and the requisite array of souvenirs emblazoned with images of the royal family.

A Walk Through Victoria

Picturesque and small of scale, the older section of town is ideal for exploring on foot. Best place to start is the **Inner Harbour**, where the larger ferries from Seattle and Port Angeles dock. Here, you can embark on a harbor tour through the inner-city waterway called **The Gorge** and to Juan de Fuca Strait with a view of the Olympia Mountains.

Crowning the harbor promenade is one of Victoria's landmarks: the luxurious **Empress Hotel** with its ivy-covered towers. Francis M. Rattenbury designed the Empress in 1905 as one of the plush railroad hotels. Every afternoon at 5 o'clock, traditional high tea, complete with delicate scones and cucumber sandwiches, is served in the hotel lobby. Although most of the guests are tourists, a few government officials and die-hard royalists also indulge themselves here.

standpoint either of size or population, its compact downtown area gives most visitors the impression of a small town – all the more so as Victoria has very few high buildings, apart from a few hotels. This provincial capital lies on the east coast, near the southern end of the island. Surrounded by the sea on three sides, Victoria boasts a mild, frost-free climate year-round, thanks to the warm Japanese current of Kuro Shio. This makes it an ideal place to live; in fact, partly as a result of the balmy climate, the city is often jokingly referred to as the "retirement capital," since more retirees live here than anywhere else in Canada.

Victoria truly does honor to the 19th-century English monarch for whom it was named. Queen Victoria would be pleased to find that British style has continued to flourish since the colonial era,

From the Empress, red double-decker busses, as befit a proper "British" metropolis, depart on city tours. Behind the Empress is the Crystal Garden, a glass structure which was architecturally revolutionary when it was built in 1925, and once hosted many a glittering ball. Today the Crystal, which is modeled after London's Crystal Palace, houses a small tropical garden with birds and monkeys, a café and souvenir shops. Excellent high teas with sandwiches and English butter cookies are also served in the Crystal Garden. If you don't want to continue on foot, you can always rent one of the bicycle rickshaws that stand in front of the Empress Hotel waiting for customers.

Right: While Asian immigrants embrace capitalism and seek their fortunes, young Victorians find Asian philosophies and martial arts "cool."

On the southern tip of the Inner Harbour, right next to the tourist information office, is the **Parliament Building**, a palace-like Gothic Revival edifice, built in 1897, which is another of the city's landmarks. The architect Rattenbury completed Parliament just in time for Queen Victoria's Diamond Jubilee; a statue of the Queen stands majestically in front of the building, while a gold-plated statue of Captain Vancouver looks down in solitary splendor from the top of the main dome. Surrounding Parliament is an attractive park with well-tended flower beds and lawns.

Opposite Parliament, the **Royal British Columbia Museum** presents excellent historical and cultural exhibits. The first floor is devoted to the history of the province and natural history; what really stands out here, literally, is the life-size mammoth. The second floor has Indian woodcarvings, mostly masks, as well as canoes and textiles; the colorful totem poles are particularly impressive. In addition, the museum presents everything

you might want to know about Vancouver Island: information about its native inhabitants, gold-mining towns, gold mines and even rain forests. An entire street of Victorian storefronts from the pioneer days has been reconstructed here. The Royal is among the best museums in the country; it style of presentation virtually "beams" the visitor back into the exciting world of the past.

There are more works of Indian art housed in **Thunderbird Park**, directly behind the museum: a range of modern totem poles (mostly replicas) and an Indian longhouse, which, however, seems a bit out of place in these surroundings. The planked Kwakiutl construction, the **Mungo Martin House**, is named after a well-known Indian painter and wood carver. In the summer months, West Coast Indians offer live presentations of the culture of their ancestors: in front of the longhouse, around the smoke of a bonfire, they perform enthralling mask dances to the steady exhilarating beat of tribal drums – another demonstration of

the unfortunate fact that traditional native culture tends for the most part to endure only in the form of a packaged tourist attraction. At the edge of the park, you can also visit **Helmcken House**, once owned by the first doctor in the rugged pioneer village. Looking at his mid-19th century instruments, you might have second thoughts about romanticizing "the good old days."

Not far from the Parliament buildings are two more tourist attractions. One is the **Pacific Undersea Gardens**, where, through glass panes, you can observe aquatic life or watch a scuba diver performing a show with his co-star, a gigantic octopus. The other is the **Royal London Wax Museum**, modeled on Madame Tussaud's in London, which groups its wax figures into 50 subjects, from fantasy monsters for the kids to British royalty for their parents.

Above: Tribal dances – not just for tourists.
Right: Perfection in landscape gardening –
Butchart Gardens.

After so much culture, you can move on to other pursuits – such as shopping. The historic old town center north of the Parliament Buildings and the area around Wharf Street are ideal venues. Following **Government Street**, the main shopping mile with a range of boutiques, and then **Johnson Street**, you come to **Market Square**. Here, in an old, renovated warehouse, there are forty small shops and restaurants around a historic courtyard. This is a great place to rummage for Indian art or such souvenirs as linen or English tea in pretty painted tins. You can buy delightful Indian jewelry, wood carvings and prints at **Hills Indian Crafts** on **Harbour Square**.

Just two blocks past Market Square, on Fisgard Street, is Victoria's tiny **Chinatown**, which despite its diminutive size remains North America's second-oldest Chinese community, after San Francisco's Chinatown, and was once infamous for its opium dens and brothels. At the end of Chinatown, fishmongers cry their wares, a vast range of fish and

seafood, at the picturesque **Harbour Public Market**.

Fans of kitsch should look in at **The Spirit of Christmas** store, located on Government Street, which offers designer Christmas trees and glittering Christmas ornaments, and is open year-round. If you manage to tear yourself away from the artificial snow, don't miss the **Emily Carr Gallery** on Wharf Street. In addition to original paintings depicting Indian themes or the scenery of western Canada, which you can get to know more closely on a guided tour, there's a film about the career of Ms. Carr (1871-1945), British Columbia's most famous artist.

Around Victoria

Beach-lovers of all ages should head for the west coast of Victoria towards Port Renfrew, where they'll find white sand and a beautiful coastline. In the little town of **Sooke** you can visit the **Sooke Region Museum**, where Nootka and Salish Indian textiles and wood carvings are on display. The museum also provides information about the program of events at the **Leechtown Gold Rush Site**, located on a spot where gold was discovered in 1864. The **East Sooke Park** is great for picnics, while on **Sombrio Beach** you can take beautiful walks along the Juan de Fuca Strait. A noteworthy sight outside **Port Renfrew** is the **Botanical Beach**, a veritable natural aquarium with saltwater ponds created by the low tide in the salt flats. If you're out for a walk, keep in mind that the strong winds and the changing tides can both be extremely dangerous.

Another excursion leads to the north of Victoria and continues out to the **Saanich Peninsula**, passing through affluent suburbs along the way. Starting at the Inner Harbour, take the **scenic marine drive** by following Dallas Road and then Beach Road along the coastline for a few miles, until you get to **Mount Douglas Park**. From there, take Cordova Bay Road north to Highway 17 and then turn on

77

Benvenuto Avenue to **Butchart Gardens**, the most famous public park in western Canada (about 15 miles/22 km north of Victoria). While Europeans tend to admire the rugged primeval nature of western Canada, Butchart Gardens captivates Canadians and Americans with its landscaping and planned gardens, which do attain a state of perfection here. Laid out in its 50 acres (20 ha) are a variety of thematic gardens: a lovely rose garden, an Italian garden, a Japanese garden, a sunken garden. The park is illuminated at night, and there are fireworks every Saturday; in the summer, it also hosts theater productions and concerts.

FROM VICTORIA TO PACIFIC RIM NATIONAL PARK

Heading north from Victoria on the four-lane **Trans-Canada Highway**, you can always count on hitting plenty of traffic. After about a half-hour's drive, the pass over **Mallahat Summit**, at a height of 1,100 feet (350 m) above sea level, commands a gorgeous view of the **Strait of Georgia** and the legion smaller islands scattered across it between Vancouver Island and the mainland. On a clear day you can even see the snow-capped summit of **Mount Baker** in the state of Washington.

Whippletree Junction, shortly before Duncan, is a little mall specializing in antiques and souvenirs; it's a complex of old wooden houses that were salvaged from a fire in Duncan's Chinatown. **Duncan** itself is a small town about 30 miles (50 km) from Victoria. Since 1986, the town has adorned itself with the epithet "City of Totems," and has made every attempt to live up to its name. Its inhabitants market Indian culture very professionally; it's also worth looking in at the **Cowichan Native Village**. A mile or so (2 km) north of town, a visit to the **B.C. Forest Museum** is a must: on its 100 acres (40 ha), it gives an effective presen-

tation of the history of Vancouver Island's logging industry, including an original lumberjack camp, an old narrow-gauge steam engine used to transport logs to the coast, and the various varieties of tree native to the area. Riding on the mini-steam train to the various exhibits gives you the sense of traveling back into the early days of settlement. Don't miss the exhibit of tree-felling techniques, which displays a full range of tools from the earliest axes to aggressive modern chainsaws.

If you should happen to spot the sign for **The Glass Castle** on the highway, make a quick detour to check out this highly unusual house constructed of 180,000 bottles.

After the sawmill in the former logging town of **Chemainus** was shut down in the 1980s, the inhabitants began looking for a new source of income, and came up with a new image for the town: art. The townspeople invited Canadian artists to paint their walls with scenes from the first days of settlement in the area; and

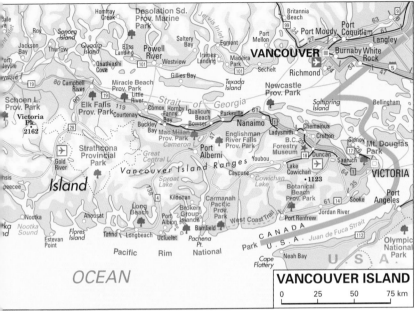

indeed, this decoration is a charming addition to this small community. The souvenir shops switched their focus to arts and crafts, and you can find a multitude of little gifts, from pottery to Indian masks. A rewarding excursion in the area is to cross over from Crofton (shortly before Chemainus) to **Saltspring Island**, to fish, climb on its rugged cliffs, or swim its turquoise waters. There are beautiful beaches at **Walker Hook**, **Cranberry Inlet**, **Vesuvius** and **Beddies Beach**.

Ladysmith, around 15 miles (26 km) north of Duncan, is an absolutely delightful town. The local museum is housed in the **Black Nugget**, a hotel built in 1881, and there is yet more to discover about Canadian trees and steam engines in the **Ladysmith Arboretum**.

Nanaimo

Just outside the city limits of Nanaimo is beguiling **Petroglyph Provincial Park**, where you can see Indian rock

carvings 10,000 years old. **Nanaimo** is the island's most important port, and therefore not particularly attractive, although the **Waterfront**, a promenade along the shore with parks, the yacht harbor and a modern harbor complex is quite nice, as are a few streets in the city center. From the ferry terminal in the north of the city, you can catch a boat over to the mainland town of Horseshoe Bay.

A much smaller ferry in the form of a miniature paddlewheel steamer crosses over to **Newcastle Provincial Park** on **Newcastle Island** in a matter of 10 minutes. Camping on the island is permitted, but don't expect quiet and solitude; it's often occupied by hordes of children on school field trips. However, you can walk around the island in two hours, and once you get away from the ferry landing, you do feel that you have the coves to yourself.

The old **Hudson's Bay Fort**, the city's trademark, now serves as a museum devoted to the history of the pioneer days. More details of the city's history

are exhibited in the **Nanaimo Centennial Museum** on Cameron Street; and old mining buildings are still standing near Piper Park. If you visit the city in mid-July, you can witness a most unusual competition, the **Bathtub Race**: daring men in motorized bathtubs race from here to the finish line in Vancouver, nearly 35 miles (56 km) away.

Englishman River Falls Provincial Park, southwest of the vacation spot of **Parksville** (5 miles/8 km along Route 8P), is a nice place for picnics and leisurely walks. A trail leads to the falls on the Englishman River, where you can have a great time swimming if you're not overly sensitive about cold water. From Parksville, Highway 4 leads to Port Alberni and on to the island's west coast. A few miles along this road, you arrive at the nature reserve **Cathedral Grove**,

Above: An enchanted land of ferns and mosses in Cathedral Grove. Right: Spraytossed and primeval – the island's west coast.

with towering trees, enchanting paths and dense ferns in one of the few original forests remaining on Vancouver Island. Douglas firs and giant West Coast cedars, as much as 800 years old and 245 feet (75 m) high, are particularly arresting; and there are educational nature paths for visitors on both sides of the highway. Detailed information boards illustrate the complex structure of the rain forest's unique ecological system. If you don't have time to go all the way to the west coast and won't have another chance to experience the mossy, humid atmosphere of the coastal rain forests, this reserve presents you with easy access to a very striking example of this kind of biotope. Cathedral Grove is only a part of vast **MacMillan Provincial Park**, which also boasts beautiful Cameron Lake.

Port Alberni

Technically speaking, the rather unappealing town of **Port Alberni** is actually on the west coast, since a deep fjord cuts

inland here, 30 miles (50 km) from the ocean proper. Oppressive and damp, although not particularly warm, the climate here is not suitable for people with circulatory disorders. The city boasts a deep-sea harbor, and one-fifth of all salmon caught off the coast of B.C. is brought to land here, making the harborside **market**, with its fresh fish and its hustle and bustle, well worth a visit. Nearby, the **Alberni Valley Museum** (Wallace Street) is devoted to local folk art and fishing. The newly renovated harbor area is the most attractive part of the city: it offers cafés, snack bars, sporting goods and fishing tackle stores, and a **Forest Centre** which is prepared to answer all sorts of questions.

For the most part, Port Alberni is a logging community; woodcutting has been going on in the forests around the town for more than 100 years, and there's a sawmill and a paper factory on the edge of town. Deforested slopes, in some places already clad in the green of reforestation, line the highway for miles on end, and heavily laden logging trucks roar ceaselessly by.

From here, you can opt for a particularly scenic route to the west coast: by boat. The little mail boat *Lady Rose* runs daily through the Alberni Canal to the coasts and fjords of the **Broken Group Islands** on the west coast, stopping either at **Bamfield** or **Ucluelet**. Here, you can find a touch of paradise: surrounded by turquoise water and sporting fine white sandy beaches, the little islands lie off the coast like diamonds in a necklace.

The west part of Vancouver Island is the windward side, but its admirers nevertheless find it one of the most beautiful places on Earth. Even in the summer, the region is often shrouded in fog, and mighty Pacific storms from the west pound the coastline. Anyone who comes with the sole objective of basking in the sun will be disappointed, but those who delight in beach walks and the beauties of raw, untamed nature have come to the right place. The weather conditions are ideal for the support of a lush rain forest,

which comprises a part of the **Pacific Rim National Park**. This narrow park extends along the coast in three sections: the southern part of the park contains the West Coast Trail; north of this, in Barkley Sound, are the Broken Group Islands, a paradise for anglers, kayakers and whale watchers; and finally, at the northernmost end, comes Long Beach, which is easily accessible by car.

West Coast Trail

Not until 1906 did the Canadian government decide to build a trail on the inaccessible coast as a route for the rescue of stranded seafarers. Experienced hikers should plan five days, or even better, a week to complete the trail, which is nearly 50 miles (77 km) long; and there's a quota for how many hikers can be on it at any given time. A small road (in poor

Above: Bald eagle. Right: Living "treasure" on Long Beach: starfish and green sea anemones.

condition) takes you the 55 miles (90 km) from Port Alberni to Bamfield, the northern end of the trail; if you're on foot, you should probably take the ferry. About 3 miles (5 km) outside of Bamfield, bear left to **Pachena Bay**; if you're hiking from north to south, the trail begins at the Information Centre here and ends at **Port Renfrew**. This walk is not suitable for inexperienced hikers, and overestimating your own abilities can be extremely dangerous to your health. This is no day hike or even a conventional hiking tour: rather, it requires strong nerves, excellent condition and a tolerance for frustration with a heavy backpack with a tent and the bare minimum of clothing weighing down your shoulders. After a day or two, sleeping on a camping mattress can become a torture, while everything in your pack is slightly damp, and never really dries out thoroughly. And you're always faced with new adventures: the swaying suspension bridge over **Logan Gorge**, for example, which calls for a certain amount of courage to cross; or the small cableway crossing the **Klanawa River**, which involves your sitting in a shaky little crate and pulling yourself along the river with a rope. Morasses and fallen trees can turn the route into an obstacle course, as can swiftly flowing rivers, such as **Walbran Creek**, where you secure yourself to a cable and wade through, backpack and all.

Hikers are rewarded for their efforts with spectacular views and magnificent natural beauties. The route leads past isolated coves with endless beaches of white sand and through impenetrable, impossibly green rain forests. At the **Tsusiat Waterfalls**, the spraying water cascades almost 60 feet (18 m) over a steep cliff to crash down onto the sandy beach below. Gray whales romp off the coast in May and June, migrating from Alaska to California; in May, too, pale pink faun lilies shoot up out of the sand. Even in the backwoods, in the island's interior, the

trail leads through unspoiled nature. Hidden away here is a dense, completely intact rain forest, the 12-mile (20 km) **Carmanah Valley**. Canada's tallest tree can be found there, a Sitka spruce towering 310 feet (95 m) high. However, the logging industry, with the government's permission, would like to clear part of the valley, leaving only the protected trees standing. Nature lovers and environmentalists are battling for the preservation of this unique verdant wilderness.

Ucluelet and Tofino

Highway 4 leads from Port Alberni past attractive Sproat Lake and on the 60 long miles (98 km) to the small fishing village of **Ucluelet** (an Indian word for "safe port"). Located here is the northern section of the Pacific Rim National Park: **Long Beach**, with its driftwood-covered sands. The **Wickaninnish Visitor Centre** perches high up on a cliff overlooking the Pacific: an excellently designed facility, it presents, among other

things, the sea creatures that live beneath the roar of the surf below: gray whales, sea lions and otters. It's worth your while to take part in a guided interpretive program, which lets you experience marine fauna "live" in the little coves behind the visitor center. At low tide along the 12-mile (20 km) beach, with a little luck, you can spot sea lions and seals on the rocks, violet starfish, and little crabs. Picnicking is permitted on **Florencia Beach**, **Wickaninnish Beach** and **Combers Beach**. 300-foot (96 m) **Radar Hill** is a delightful lookout point – the view extends across the mountains of the Island Range and the long sand beaches.

Inland, you can see impressive flora and fauna along **Bog Trail**: the roots of ancient fir trees cling tightly to the swampy ground, while carnivorous sundew plants catch unwary insects. The nature path **Rain Forest Trail** leads through the dense woods; its boardwalk means that you can keep your feet dry even as you explore the humid, primeval forest.

At the other end of Long Beach, 15 miles (25 km) away, is **Tofino**, which successfully combines modern comforts with the beauties of its natural surroundings. Seaplanes take off from the harbor of this quaint fishing village for **Ahousat**, **Hesquiat** or **Nootka**. In the summer, you can take boats out to sight gray whales, who rest here and search for food in the coves on their annual migration to Hawaii or Mexico. There are also boat excursions to the bubbling natural pools of **Hot Springs Cove**, northwest of Tofino, or the rain forests of **Meares Island**.

ALONG THE EAST COAST TO PORT HARDY

From Parksville to Campbell River

Past the quiet beach town of **Parksville**, a narrow road zigzags up inland,

Above: Tofino: a sailor's paradise between Vancouver and the Sunshine Coast. Right: Lucky fisherman on the Campbell River.

only to descend again to **Qualicum Beach**, a particularly tidy little town that's almost too perfectly set up for tourists with its array of waterfront motels, fancy restaurants, boutiques and ideal swimming conditions from its beach of fine, soft sand. The seaside resorts of **Bowser** or **Fanny Bay** are quieter and also boast beautiful beaches. From **Buckley Bay**, you can and should take a 15-minute ferry ride over to **Hornby** and **Denman Islands**; the latter is a little islet with lovely old churches and farmhouses.

Courtenay and **Comox** are typical retirement communities. Comox, set on a small peninsula, is a textbook example of an exclusive leisure community: its array of parks, golf courts, and neat and tidy houses seem to indicate that life on Vancouver Island must have been one of the inspirations behind the invention of the term "quality leisure time."

In summer, anyone interested in ethnology should look in at the **Courtenay & District Museum**, where Indian artifacts from pioneer days are on display.

From **Little River**, a ferry runs over to **Westview**, on the mainland. This is a good point of access to B.C.'s **"Sunshine Coast,"** where you can meander along the gorgeous inlets and fjords of the coastline and make your way back to Northwest Vancouver with the help of a number of little ferries. This is a good option if you don't feel like exploring the relatively undeveloped, heavily-logged northern part of Vancouver Island.

If you opt to stay on the island, however, and continue northward, you'll come to the attractive **Miracle Beach Provincial Park**, a nice place for beach walks, picnics, barbecues and camping. **Campbell River** is located at the halfway point of the east coast. Converging here are two bodies of water where fish naturally abound: Johnston Strait from the north and Georgia Strait from the south. As a result, this little town is a Mecca for fishermen. Campbell River proudly calls itself "Canada's Salmon Capital," and with good reason: sport fishermen catch fine specimens here, some weighing in at more than 65 pounds (30 kg). If you're interested, there's a plentiful supply of charter boats for hire.

Campbell River is also an ideal base for excursions to the islands off the coast. Every hour, a ferry makes the 15-minute trip over to **Quadra Island**, one of the Discovery Islands; at its south end stands the **Cape Mudge Lighthouse**, which is worth a visit. Nearby, there are Indian cliff drawings of fish and other sea creatures. The Kwakiutl Indian village of **Quathiaski Cove** is also worth a trip; the museum here displays masks, totem poles and cult items from the potlatch festival. When white settlers arrived, the Church denounced these works of art as "heathen" and confiscated them; not until more liberal Indian policies were introduced was it possible to recover these valuable ceremonial artifacts. The beach near **Rebecca Spit** is a beautiful place for a swim.

Strathcona Provincial Park

Located off the beaten tourist track, this provincial park is sought out mainly by locals who make their way from Campbell River into the untouched interior of the island. A good base for campers, not far from Campbell River, is **Elk Mill Falls**, with its spacious campgrounds on the nearby Quinsam River. **Strathcona Provincial Park** is the oldest and largest natural park in British Columbia: unspoiled nature as far as the eye can see, with inviting lakes for swimming and very few people. Here are virgin mountain forests, a popular hiking area with numerous trails and superlatives everywhere: the island's highest waterfall, the **Della Falls** (1,400 feet/440 m), and highest mountain, the **Golden Hinde**, with an elevation of almost 7,200 feet (2,200 m).

West of the park, the secluded little town of **Gold River** and the harbor of the same name truly deserve the designation "the end of the world." But even here,

Canadian shipping is alive and well: the former minesweeper *Uchuk III* is still in operation as a passenger ship, running to **Nootka Sound** and the historic location where Captain Cook first landed in 1778: **Friendly Cove**.

From Campbell River to Port Hardy

The extensive forests of this 335-mile (540 km) island off of Canada's west coast make Vancouver Island one of Canada's most important logging regions. Around 1.3 million cubic yards (1 million cubic meters) of driftwood pile up on its coasts every year. In the dense rain forests of the west coast, giant trees up to 1,000 years old thrust into the sky. The logging industry initially developed as a result of local demand, used for construc-

Above: Conflict between ecology and economy: the logging industry. Right: Whale watchers aren't always successful on the open sea – but at Vancouver's aquarium you're guaranteed an eyeful.

tion of the railroad and the mines. Even today, a large portion of the lumber is used for local construction; however, lumber has also become one of Canada's leading exports.

Up here in the sparsely populated northern part of the island, the logging industry doesn't even attempt to hide its tracks; in some other areas of Canada, loggers leave a few rows of trees standing to conceal the empty clearings of felled trees behind them. Greenpeace deserves thanks for exposing such practices and helping to force through political solutions. Today, thoughtless, mercenary deforestation has given way to a forest management which requires that for every tree that is felled, two new saplings be planted. *Forestry B.C.* grows more than 75 million saplings in its nurseries. Nonetheless, even Douglas fir saplings, which take 80 years to grow into full-size trees, can't wholly make up for the valuable resources that this industry wiped out in the past. And reports of scandals appear in the press time and

again – such as the Greenpeace's accusations concerning deforestation around Clayoquot Sound. Greenpeace is skilled at creating a maximum of media attention to help insure that its message will be heard. However, as it did in the much-publicized commotion involving Brent Spar, Greenpeace had to partially revise its statements against the forestry giant MacMillian Bloedel. The truth lies somewhere between the forest company's euphemisms and Greenpeace polemic. If you want to form your own opinion, request information from Greenpeace, take part in a Forestry Tour, and study the brochure "What Greenpeace does not tell Europeans" at the Forest Centre at the harbor in Port Alberni.

From Campbell River, Highway 19 continues on to **Port McNeill**, 124 miles (200 km) farther north. Ferries run from here to idyllic **Sointula** on **Malcolm Island**. Finnish coal miners founded this little village as their "Utopia" in 1901. Here you can marvel at the petroglyphs at Mitchel Bay or see exhibits about the early settlers in the Finnish Culture Museum. The Finnish heritage is unmistakable: even today, some inhabitants have blond hair and blue eyes, and the tidy houses and yards have a peculiarly Nordic flair.

Ferries also run from Port McNeill to Alert Bay, an Indian reservation, a trip of about 45 minutes. Take the time here to see the **U'Mista Cultural Centre**, housed in a Kwakiutl longhouse and displaying Indian works of art. Adjacent to it is an Indian cemetery with totem poles displaying grotesque faces. This island, in fact, boasts the tallest totem pole in the world, measuring nearly 240 feet (73 m) high.

Telegraph Cove, 11 miles (18 km) east of Port McNeill, styled the "Whaling Capital" of Canada, is the last of what used to be dozens of towns built on pilings along the east coast, expanded out when the coves proved too small to accommodate all the settlers. Telegraph Cove's tiny harbor, tucked into a bay, is a Mecca for whale watchers, who stream in

from all over the world for a chance to see the famous orcas or "killer whales."

Whale Watching

Every morning, Skipper Marty weighs anchor with a colorful and diverse group of visitors on board. Destination is **Johnston Strait**, which from May to October is home to a pod of orcas. Aside from the Juan de Fuca Strait off Vancouver's southern coast, this is the only region in the world where these creatures can be found so close to the coast. As the boat passes a chain of small islands, the air of suspense mounts among the excited Americans, Japanese and Germans who have arisen so early on this foggy morning. The aluminum boat quietly glides through the waves to the edge of the **Robson Bight Ecological Reserve**. The whales swim here to rub their bellies on the pebble beaches; human researchers

Above: For hard-core fans of the Inside Passage, there's no such thing as bad weather.

have yet to understand the reason for this unusual behavior. Orcas are a protected species and not to be disturbed; high-speed patrol boats thus ensure that no unauthorized vessels enter the reserve.

By radio, the skipper is informed that orcas had been sighted just beyond the next cove. Suddenly, the first fin surfaces, and a big cloud of spray rises into the air. Marty turns off the engine, and the boat glides on. Suddenly, everyone can see the fins: 5, 6 ,7 of them. Black, shiny bodies pass by the boat. Sometimes you may be lucky enough to see the shining black animals breaching, or leaping above the water: a spectacular sight. Marty tells his guests about the lifestyle of the animals: the orcas, also called killer whales, represent the largest group of toothed whales and belong to the dolphin family. Males can grow to be more than 30 feet (10 m) in length, weigh 11 tons and live to become 50 years old; the smaller females even live to be 80 or 90. The females lead the schools, which usually consist of 5 to 10 whales. The term "killer whale" is a bit misleading: yes, orcas do live off of other sea dwellers such as sea lions and bottle-nosed dolphins, among others, but they do not harm humans. Approximately 350 killer whales live in the waters around Vancouver Island.

Port Hardy and the North

Highway 19 ends after about 310 miles (500 km) in **Port Hardy**, almost at the northern end of the island. The city was named in honor of Sir Thomas Masterman Hardy, a Vice Admiral in the British Royal Navy. According to legend, it was he who, in the battle of Trafalger, held the dying Admiral Nelson in his arms. This small town is the connecting harbor to the mainland. In the summer, large ferries, such as *Queen of the North* and *Queen of Prince Rupert*, cast off from the **Bear Cove** terminal for their cruises through the **Inside Passage**. A visitor here can stroll up and down Market Street, have a picnic in the park, and see impressive Indian art in the **Port Hardy Museum** (Market Street). A large raven here illustrates the creation myth of the Kwakiutl Indians, which tells of a raven god that created the world and all its people.

If you want, you can continue on to the most northwesterly point of the island, Cape Scott Park. From Port Hardy, a narrow (and relatively poor) road leads to the hidden little town of **Holberg**, at the end of narrow **Holberg Inlet**, a small fjord that extends into the interior of the island. Here, you can unwind in the cozy *Scarlet Ibis Pub*, and forget that other tourists ever existed. At the island's northern tip, 40 miles (65 km) from Port Hardy, is its last nature reserve, **Cape Scott Provincial Park**. Even novice hikers can manage the 45-minute tour on **San Josef's Trail** through dense, moss-covered rain forest to the beautiful sandy beaches of **San Josef's Bay**.

VANCOUVER ISLAND
Area Code 604
Accommodation
Hotel reservations for B.C: 1-800-663-6000.

VICTORIA: *LUXURY:* **Sooke Harbour House**, 1528 Whiffenspit Rd., tel. 642-3421, 30 minutes from downtown, one of the best hotels in Canada with very good food and lovely views. **Empress Hotel**, 721 Government St., tel. 384-8111, traditional and elegant. *MODERATE:* **James Bay Inn**, 270 Government St., tel. 384-7151, historic hotel, excellent location downtown. *BUDGET:* **Motels** on exit roads such as Gorge Rd. and on Highway 1A. During summer vacation, you can rent rooms in the **University**, tel. 721-8396.
B&B: **AA Accommodation West B&B Reservation**, tel. 479-1986. **Victoria Vacationer B&B Reservation Service**, tel. 382-9469.

PORT RENFREW: *MODERATE:* **Arbutus Beach Lodge**, 5 Questso Dr., tel. 647-5458, nice beach location.

DUNCAN: *B&B:* **Fairburn Farm Country Manor**, 3310 Jackson Rd., tel. 746-4637, English country house with sheep farm, romantic and relaxing, open from April to October.

LAKE COWICHAN: *BUDGET:* **Pallie's Cottages**, 77 Nelson Rd. E, tel. 749-3524, bungalows on the river, quiet, nice setting.

NANAIMO: *MODERATE:* **Tally-Ho Hotel**, Terminal Ave., tel. 753-2241, ocean view, outdoor pool. *CAMPING:* **Living Forest Oceanside Campground**, tel. 755-1755, lovely campground, large, great location, 2 mi/3 km S of city center.

QUALICUM: *MODERATE:* **The Qualicum College Inn**, 427 College Rd, tel. 752-9262, historic boys' school-turned-inn, offers honeymoon packages and sports holidays.

HORNBY ISLAND: *MODERATE:* **Seabreeze Lodge**, Fowler Rd., tel. 335-2321, pretty little house with open fireplace.

COMOX: *MODERATE:* **Kye Bay Guest Lodge & Cottages**, 590 Winslow Rd., tel. 339-6112, quiet, on the water, with view over George Strait, library; a good place for a longer stay.

MIRACLE BEACH: *MODERATE:* **Miracle Beach Resort**, 1680 Miracle Beach Dr., tel. 337-5171, small bungalows on the beach. *CAMPING:* **Provincial Park**, tel. 954-4600, beautiful location surrounded by trees, right on the beach.

SOINTULA: *BUDGET:* **Malcolm Island Inn**, tel. 973-6366, romantic seclusion on the beach.

PORT HARDY: *MODERATE to BUDGET:* **Pioneer Inn**, Byng Rd., tel. 949-7271, quiet location in a park, with two good restaurants.

TOFINO: *MODERATE to LUXURY:* **Pacific Sands Beach Resort**, tel. 725-3322, dream loca-

tion right on an isolated beach, 4.5 mi/7 km S of Tofino, with verandas. *CAMPING:* **Crystal Cove Beach Resort**, tel. 725-4213, camping and bungalows, 2 mi/3 km S of Tofino; the bungalows are *MODERATE.*
BAMFIELD: *BUDGET:* **Woods End Landing**, tel. 728-3383, little wooden houses in the wilderness, space limited so call ahead; canoes and other amenities available.
ALERT BAY: *BUDGET:* **Pacific Hostelry**, tel. 974-2026, 26 rooms.

Restaurants

VICTORIA: **Chez Pierre**, Yates St., tel. 388-7711, the oldest French restaurant in town, expensive, features fine salmon and duck. **Pagliacci's**. 1011 Broad St., tel. 386-1662, good Italian food. **Sams Deli**, corner of Government/Wharf Sts., good sandwiches and snacks. **Green Cuisine**, vegetarian restaurant on Market Square. **High Tea** in the Empress Hotel: for reservations, call 384-8111. In the Botanic Gardens: **The Crystal Garden**, 713 Douglas Street, tel. 381-1213. **Canadian Steakhouse**, in Nootka Court, 645 Humboldt Street, huge steaks. **NANAIMO**: **Gina's**, 47 Skinner St., tel. 753-5411, excellent Mexican food. **COMOX**: **Lorne Pub**, pub and terrace in a venerable English country house. **PARKSVILLE/QUALICUM BEACH**: Typical pub food at the Tudor-style **George Inn**, 532 Memorial Ave.; very British. **Maclure House Inn**, 1015 East Island Hwy., tel. 248-3470, wonderful ocean views and good food. **PORT ALBERNI**: **Swale Rock Café**, on the way to the harbor; good salads and pasta. **UCLUELET**: On the beach by the visitors' center you can get good salads and sandwiches at **Wickaninnish**. Wonderful bay view. **PORT HARDY**: **Port Hardy Inn**, Grenville St., tel. 949-8525.

Museums

VICTORIA: **Maritime Museum**, 28 Bastion Sq., tel. 385-4222, Mon-Fri 10 am-4 pm, Sun noon-4 pm. **Royal British Columbia Museum**, 675 Belleville St., tel. 387-3701 (natural & local history, Indian culture) with **Thunderbird Park**, open daily 9:30 am-7 pm in summer, 10 am-5:30 pm in winter. Also in Thunderbird Park is **Helmcken House**, 10 Elliot St., tel. 361-0021, daily tours in summer, in winter Thu-Mon 10 am-5 pm. **Parliament Buildings**, 501 Belleville St., on the Inner Harbour, reserve in advance for guided tours, tel. 387-3046. **Pacific Undersea Gardens**, 490 Belleville St., tel. 382-5717, open daily. **Royal London Wax Museum**, 470 Belleville St., downtown on the Inner Harbour, open daily, tel. 388-4461.
DUNCAN: **B.C. Forestry Museum**, on Hwy 1, 1mi/2 km N of Duncan, tel. 715-1113, open daily May-Sept. 9:30 am-6 pm. **Cowichan Native Vil-**

lage, 200 Cowichan Way, tel. 746-8119, open in summer 9 am-6 pm, other times 9:30 am-5 pm. **COURTENAY**: **Courtenay & District Museum**, 360 Cliffe Ave., tel. 334-3611 May-Aug daily, other times Tue-Sun 10 am-4 pm. **NANAIMO**: **Nanaimo District Museum**, tel. 753-1821. **QUADRA ISLAND**: **Kwakiutl Museum**, open in July and August. **SOOKE**: **Sooke Regional Museum & Travel Info Centre**, tel. 642-6351. **ALERT BAY**: **U'Mista Cultural Centre**, Front St., tel. 974-5213, May-September. **PORT ALBERNI**: **Valley Museum**, 4255 Wallace St., tel. 723-2181, Tue-Sat 10 am-5 pm, Thu 10 am-9 pm; brochure available for a historic walking tour of town. **UCLUELET**: **Wickaninnish Centre**, tel. 726-7333, May-Sept, opening hours according to individual interpretative program.

Events

VICTORIA: **Victorian Days**, with a **Parade** on May 21 to mark Queen Victoria's birthday, and the **Swiftsure Regatta**. **NANAIMO**: Mid-July sees the great **bathtub race** from Nanaimo to Vancouver across the Strait of Georgia. **CHEMAINUS**: Festival of **wall painting** in July: artists paint new walls. **PARKSVILLE**: In mid-July is the **International Sandcastle Competition**; call 954-3999 for info. **CAMPBELL RIVER**: **Salmon Festival** in July and **salmon fishing contest** in August. **PORT HARDY**: **Filomi Day**, fishing festival in Aug with woodcutting, fishing contests, lots of beer.

Tips & Trips

FLIGHTS: There's air service to Vancouver from every major city in Canada. You can fly from Vancouver over Seattle and the Gulf Islands on an **Air B.C.** seaplane (tel. 640/753-1255) or from Vancouver in a **Helijet Airway** helicopter (tel. 1-800-665-4354) or on **Air Canada** (tel. 640/753-1255).
FERRIES: From Vancouver to Victoria, **B.C. Ferries** from Tsawwassen to Swartz Bay, 2 hrs. 7 am-9 pm, 1.5 hours. Service from Horseshoe Bay (Vancouver) to Nanaimo. **B.C. Ferries**, 7 am-9 pm, 2.5 hours; tel. 386-3431. **Black Ball Ferry** from Port Angeles (Washington) to Victoria, tel. 386-2202. **B.C. Steamship Company**, Seattle to Victoria, May-Sept, tel. 386-1124. **Washington State Ferries**, from Anacortes (Wash., U.S.A.) to Sidney, 20 mi/30 km N of Victoria on the Saanich Peninsula, tel. 381-1551 (Victoria) or 206/464-6400 (Seattle).
SMALLER FERRIES: From Port Alberni, the *M.V. Lady Rose* runs to **Bamfield** (start of the West Coast Trail) three times a week (Tue, Thu, Sat; for pedestrians only); there are also half-day boat trips through the Broken Island Group to **Ucluelet** (Mon, Wed, Fri, as well as Sun in July, Aug). **Little River to Powell River**, daily 7:30 & 11:15 am, 3:15 & 7:15 pm.

HARBOUR TOURS: From May to October, departure in the Inner Harbour from the pier opposite the Empress Hotel. Info: 381-1511.

BUS: **Pacific Coach Lines** buses depart approximately every hour from Vancouver for destinations in Vancouver and Victoria. Tel. 385-4411 (Victoria) or 604/662-8074 (Vancouver). *Bus service on Vancouver Island:* **Laidlaw**, tel. 388-5248, 6 buses a day from Victoria to Nanaimo, among others.

SIGHTSEEING IN VICTORIA: City tours in horse-drawn carriages (from the Parliament Buildings) or bicycle rickshaws (from the Empress Hotel). **Tally-Ho Sightseeing**, tel. 479-1113, tours depart opposite the Royal London Wax Museum. **Grey Line Tours**, several times a day in summer, tours depart from the Empress Hotel, tel. 388-5248. **Walk-A-Bout Victoria**, guided city tours, tel. 382-2127, June-early Sept from the Tourist Information Centre, 812 Wharf Street.

FORESTRY: **Timber Tours** (tel. 1-800-661-7177) gives free tours concentrating on woodlands and forestry, such as a 3-day "wood tour" around Lake Cowichan, with a visit to the Kaatza Museum. Tours leave from Timber West Forest, Information Centre Downtown Lake Cowichan. On Vancouver Island there are 5 Timber West bases: Courtenay, Lake Cowichan, Mt. Newton Seed Orchard/Saanichton, Campbell River and Port McNeill.

SALMON FISHING: **Campbell River: Dunn's Premier Outfitter**, 632 Erickson Rd., tel. 923-2236. **Bamfield: Bamfield Fishing Charters**, tel. 728-3286, with or without a guide.

WHALE WATCHING: In Johnston Strait, in front of Telegraph Cove by Robson Bight Ecological Reserve, you can see narwhals in their natural habitat; between June and early October, you can book a 4- to 5-hour boat tour with **Stubbs Island Whale Watching**, tel. 928-3185. **Seasmoke Tours**, Alert Bay, tel. 974-5225, run 3-5 motorboat tours a day (about 4 hrs., c. $60). Sailboat or motorboat tours from Alert Bay/Cormorant Island and Alder Bay Campsite. Gray whale tours, March-May from Tofino (**Jamie's Whaling Station**, 606 Campbell St., tel. 725-3919, also runs tours to Hot Springs Cove) and Victoria (**Marine Adventure Centre**, Inner Harbour, 950 Wharf St., tel. 995-2211, also arranges kayak, motorboat, bike tours, moped rental). Boat tours on the *Lady Rose* from Ucluelet and Port Alberni to the Broken Group Islands.

HIKING: **West Coast Trail**: only for experienced hikers: an adventurous 4-7 day hike through Pacific Rim National Park, from Bamfield to Port Renfrew, tel. 663-6000 (reservations required). Book tip: *The West Coast Trail and Nitinat Lakes*, Sierra Club of Western Canada, Douglas & McIntyre, 1992. Buses run from Victoria and Port Alberni to the respective ends of the trail. **San Josef Trail**: easy 45-minute walk in Cape Scott Provincial Park to San Josef Bay. **Cape Scott Trail**, for experienced hikers only: wilderness hikes of 4-7 days exploring forests and rocky beaches in the N of the island. Consult the Information Centre in Port Hardy.

WINE: On Vancouver Island there are vineyards and cider producers; see the brochure *Vineyards and Cideries of the Cowichan Valley*.

NANAIMO: Three heritage walks lead through the old city; brochures available at the Visitors' Centre. **ZEBALLOS: Gold-digging** at Zeballos Bay. From Hwy 19, detour W; behind Woss, just before Lake Nimpkish, a little road leads off to Zeballos. **CAMPBELL RIVER**: Sea-bird watching, 13 mi/20 km E of Campbell River in the **Mitlenatch Island Bird Sanctuary**, reached by boat; North Island Charter: tel. 287-3137.

DENMAN and HORNBY ISLAND: Hourly ferry service to the **Gulf Islands** from Buckley Bay (50 mi/80 km N of Nanaimo). The ferry dock is a short walk from **Denman**, where there's a small museum and gallery. Various cultural events are held on **Hornby Island**.

HOT SPRINGS COVE: Day trips from Tofino by boat (through **Seaside Adventurer**, tel. 725-2292) or plane. Boat charter: **Canadian Princess**, Ucluelet, tel. 726-7771, Tofino: **Noahs Ark Boat Rentals**, tel. 726-4229.

National Park

The **Pacific Rim National Park** is on the west coast, some 4 hours from Victoria. Sea lions, seal colonies, beaches, parks (Long Beach Park) and nature trails (Rain Forest Trail, Bog Trail). 48 mi/77 km of wilderness hiking on the West Coast Trail (see "Hiking"), March-Oct, tel. 729-4212 & 726-7721. **Butchart Gardens**, 14 mi/21 km N of Benvenuto Ave., near Bentwood Bay, tel. 652-4422.

Tourist Information

Tourism Association of Vancouver Island, Suite 302-45, Bastion Sq., Victoria, tel. 382-3551. **VICTORIA**: **Travel Infocentre**, 812 Wharf St., on the harbor, tel. 953-2033. **NANAIMO**: **Travel Infocentre**, 2290 Bowen Rd., tel. 756-0106. **PARKSVILLE**: **Travel Infocentre**, Island Hwy., Parksville, tel. 248-3613. **CAMPBELL RIVER**: **Travel Infocentre**, 1235 Island Hwy., tel. 286-1616. **PORT HARDY**: **Travel Infocentre**, 7250 Main St., tel. 949-7622. **PORT McNEILL**: **Travel Infocentre**, 7250 Main St., tel. 956-3131. **PACIFIC RIM NATIONAL PARK**: Superintendent, P.O. Box 280, Ucluelet, B.C. V0R 3A0, tel. 726-7721. **Pacific Rim Visitor Service**, on the Ucluelet-Tofino road, tel. 726-4212 (March-Oct). **Tofino-Long-Beach Travel Infocentre** 351 Campbell St., Tofino, tel. 725-3414.

THE CANADIAN ROCKIES

SOUTHERN ALBERTA
CALGARY / BANFF N. P.
KOOTENAY N. P. / YOHO N. P.
JASPER NATIONAL PARK
CENTRAL BRITISH COLUMBIA
QUEEN CHARLOTTE ISLANDS

SOUTHERN ALBERTA

In comparison with empty Saskatchewan, Southern Alberta seems to be much more densely populated. The pleasant landscape is divided up between farms, small towns and industrial plants. According to legend, **Medicine Hat** was the site of a battle between the Cree and Blackfoot Indians, "where the Cree medicine man lost his hat" – this proved a bad omen, as the Cree lost the battle. The city is known for its porcelain industry. Visit the **Clay Products Interpretive Center** for an illustration of the various stages of creating porcelain. Children can even try their hands at ceramics. Also here is the **Medicine Hat Museum & Art Gallery**, which in addition to a range of temporary exhibitions houses a permanent one on the history of settlement in the region. If you want a more in-depth view of the city center, take the self-guided *Downtown Historical Walking Tour* (maps available from the Visitor Information Center). And from Medicine Hat, you can take interesting excursions to Dinosaur Provincial Park and Cypress Hills Provincial Park (see pp. 180-182).

Preceding pages: Calgary, city of millions, has a Western streak a mile wide. Left: The spectacular setting of Moraine Lake.

The area around **Lethbridge**, the region's agricultural center, has also seen the mining of high-quality coal since 1870; together with oil and natural gas, this coal is one of the province's riches. In Lethbridge itself, take time to visit the peaceful **Nikka Yuko Japanese Garden** (corner of 7th Ave. and Mayor Magrath Drive), a Japanese garden with a pagoda and a room for tea ceremonies which was created as a gesture of Canadian-Japanese friendship. The garden is located in **Henderson Park**, a leafy oasis in this otherwise industrial town (where there are picnic tables, sports grounds, boat rental, a golf course, and a rose garden).

If you want to find out more about Lethbridge you can enquire at the Visitor Information Center at the west end of 1st Avenue, right next to the attractive **Brewery Gardens** with its impressive rockery. Southeast of Lethbridge, past the town of Milk River, you come to **Writing-on-Stone Provincial Park**, which derives its name from its large collection of Indian petroglyphs and pictographs. It is also known on account of its many *hoodoos*, bizarre columns of sandstone.

Indian Battle Park, on the Oldman River, is named after the last bloody battle between native peoples in North America: in 1870, the Cree fought here

95

against the Blackfoot Indians. The former whiskey trading post of **Fort Whoop-Up** is one of the stations of the North West Mounted Police, who were assigned here – as they were in Cypress Hills or Fort Macleod – to keep the peace as sly traders tricked the Indians with watered-down whiskey in exchange for their valuable furs. Visitors to the fort today can see a museum and an impressive audio-visual show or enjoy a bumpy ride in a covered wagon.

As you drive westwards along the **Crowsnest Highway**, you'll see the snowcapped peaks of the Rockies and eventually come to the small town of **Fort Macleod**, which looks more like the set for a Western than a real-life community. After passing through a defensive ring of recently-built motels, you come to a Main Street lined with facades from the pioneer age; a passage leads

from this street to the fort. Built in 1874 as the new headquarters of the North West Mounted Police, it was named after its first commander. Fort Macleod was the first Mounties post in the West and is therefore of special historical importance for Canada. The **Fort Museum** paints a heroic picture of these men, but also tells of their hard lives full of deprivation. One whole gallery is even devoted to the lives of the first women in the west. The *Red Serge Wives* did not have an easy time in the rough men's world, and many historical accounts are all too quick to forget them.

Showcased displays illustrate how buffalos were hunted; while another wall is covered with an impressive collection of photographs. Around 1880, Henry Pollard photographed trappers and Native Indians, hand-colored the pictures, and ultimately produced striking contemporary documents. Reconstructed living quarters give even more insight into lives divided between the wilderness and the civilization they'd left behind: buffalo

Above: Go West – everyone wants to go to the Rockies. Right: The white man managed virtually to exterminate the buffalo.

96

horns hang next to old English porcelain plates. The individual buildings, lovingly fitted out, include a smithy, church, canteen and medical center. Being ill during the pioneer age must have been a real punishment in itself, judging by such objects as the "sputum bowl," the spine-chilling dentist's chair or the "pneumonia jacket."

In July and August, the traditional Mountie "Musical Rides" are held four times a day, although the riders are actually students in reproductions of the actual uniforms. Real Mounties only wear their red coats on rare and special occasions.

Not far from Fort Macleod, Highway 785 leads to an unusual place which was declared a UN World Heritage Site in 1981, and is today marked by an astonishing museum. **Head-Smashed-In Buffalo Jump**, its name striking in itself, outlines Native Indian hunting practices in a manner which is intelligent, emotional and unconventional. Inside the museum, there's a floor plan of the tour which begins on the building's top story

(take elevator 1 to the 3rd floor, then follow the bison's prints to elevator 2 to reach the platform). Up here, above the windswept rocks, the Indians ran bison herds over the lip of the cliff so that they crashed to their deaths below (hence the graphic name): a method that took advantage of the bison's naturally poor eyesight and its strong instinct to follow the leader of the herd. Popularly known as "buffalo," a term which isn't quite accurate from a zoological standpoint, these gigantic creatures can reach a height of just over 5.5 feet (1.7 m), weigh up to 2,200 pounds (1,000 kg), and attain speeds of more than 30 miles (50 km) per hour.

The museum's exhibits illustrate the many uses to which the Indians put the bison. Before the white settlers arrived, there were around 60 million bison roaming the plains of North America. Their subsequent extinction was a tragedy in more ways than one: as these animals died out, the traditional Indian way of life was also extinguished forever.

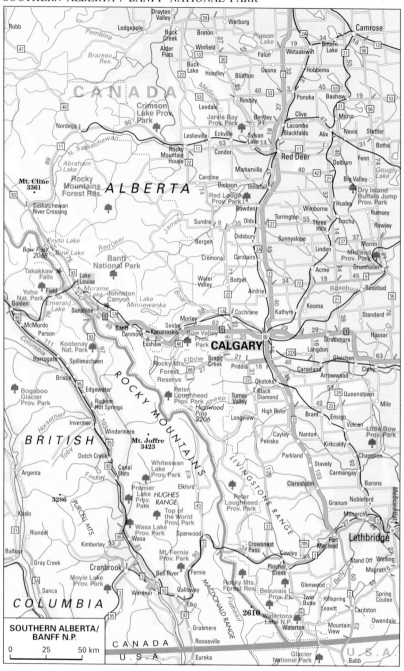

SOUTHERN ALBERTA/
BANFF N.P.

0   25   50 km

Waterton Lakes National Park

While many visitors to Canada tend to head from here straight for Calgary, there is an unspoiled scenic treasure to the south which is every bit as attractive as the better-known Rocky Mountain national parks. Highway 6 leads through the Hutterite settlement of **Pincher Creek** to **Parkgate North** of **Waterton Lakes National Park**. The park abuts onto Glacier National Park in Montana (U.S.A.), and the two parks are also known collectively as **Waterton-Glacier International Peace Park**. If you're driving in on Highway 6, Bison Paddock Road leads off on the right, and from the parking lot it is only a few hundred yards to **Bison Paddock Viewpoint**. Here, you have a first taste of the park's unique combination of prairie landscape and mountains, hilly grassland and small lakes. And rising up abruptly behind the panorama is the dramatic backdrop of the Bellevue Hills, which are themselves overshadowed by the towering Rockies.

The park's main valley is U-shaped, a typical form created by glacial erosion when a glacier moved in and rounded out the originally V-shaped walls. Reaching a depth of 513 feet (157 m), **Upper Waterton Lake** is the deepest glacial lake in the Rockies, and extends an impressive 6.8 miles (11.1 km). **Waterton** itself is a small, attractive town catering to tourists with various hotels, such as the *Prince of Wales*, campgrounds and tour operators. You have the best view out over the town and Upper Waterton Lake from the observation point of **Bear's Hump**, by the Park Information Center, roughly half a mile (1 km) north of town. Since the path takes in some 650 feet (200 m) of vertical ascent in about half a mile (about 1 km), it's not an easy climb. On the other hand, the view is more than

Above: Colorful natural spectacle in Red Rock Canyon.

adequate compensation, and, thanks to the strong gusts of wind for which the area is notorious, there is little danger of getting too warm.

Less tiring, but just as interesting, is a round-trip walk of less than 2 miles (3 km) around the town. Starting from the **Heritage Center**, you continue along the lake shore and, at **Cameron Creek**, make your way up to **Cameron Falls**. Geologists believe that the rock below the falls is the oldest in the Rockies, some 1.5 billion years old, thrust up through the forces of compression from the earth's interior to its surface. About a third of a mile (500 m) south of these falls is the start of the path to **Lower Bertha Falls**. A brochure available from the **Park Information Center** describes eight highlights along the way. In an unusual gesture of commemoration, the falls are named after a lady who circulated counterfeit money.

Red Rock Canyon is arguably the park's major highlight. Made of argillite, a sedimentary rock with a high iron con-

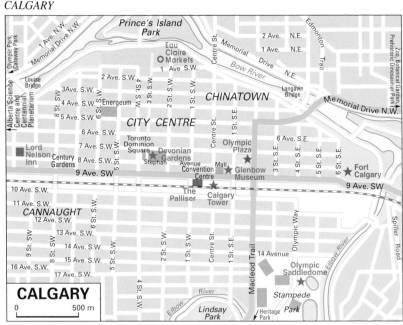

CALGARY

0   500 m

tent, it gets its characteristic red hue from the oxidation that occurs when the stone comes in contact with air. The green and white segments are also composed of argillite, but argillite threaded with an iron derivative that does not oxidize. Even 8,000 years ago, the canyon was already a magical place for the native peoples. In the intervening years, however, and especially in the last decades of intense tourist activity, millions of feet and sweaty hands have taken their toll. Anyone with any sort of feeling for nature is therefore advised to keep damage to a minimum by staying on the trails and bridges.

From Pincher Creek, **Crowsnest Highway** heads over the pass of the same name and through several communities which are jointly known as *Municipality of Crowsnest Pass*. It was here, in 1903, that a landslide led to a mining accident which virtually wiped out the mining

Right: Trademark of the cowboy city of Calgary is its Saddle Dome.

town of Frank. The **Frank Slide Interpretive Center** features displays on the cause and effects of the slide, as well as the tremendous difficulties of building the railroad. Visitors can also walk along interpretive trails near the site of the disaster. In Frank itself, the **Crowsnest Museum** deals with the history of the pass from 1899-1950, while the **Crowsnest Pass Ecomuseum** tells of the uniqueness of this once-isolated region, with information on local archaeology, geography and the landslide as well as on mine revolts, people who took justice into their own hands, and train robbers.

If you're making for Calgary from the south, you have a choice between several routes. The quickest option is Highway 2 via **Claresholm**, where horse lovers might like to stop off to see the **Appaloosa Museum**.

If time is not an issue, Highway 22 offers the more scenic route through the **foothills**. It also allows people who aren't in the mood for a big city to bypass Calgary altogether and continue on Highway

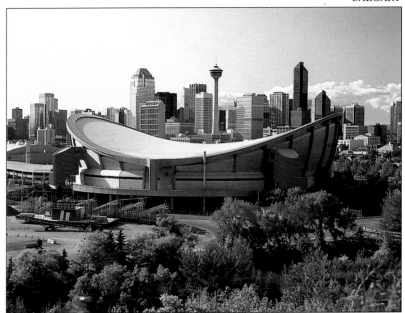

541 through Kananaskis County. The 199-square-mile (508 sq. km) **Peter Loughheed Provincial Park** is home to large numbers of grizzlies, black bears, elks, beavers, wolves and pumas. Park rangers can suggest a few routes for possible walks.

Note that Highway 22 is only open from roughly mid-June to October; in this period, however, the journey over the 7,213-foot (2,206 m) **Highwood Pass** is one of the highlights of the Rockies. Incidentally, this is the highest pass in Canada which is negotiable by car. After this, it can be quite a shock to the system to emerge, at **Serbe**, onto the main "race track" through the Rockies, that is to say, Trans-Canada Highway 1.

CALGARY

In Calgary, Western Canada's largest city in area, there's no trace of the relaxed driving so typical of other parts of Canada; rather, traffic jams and congestion are the order of the day.

Established in 1875 at the confluence of the **Bow** and **Elbow Rivers**, Fort Calgary was originally a military post built in the middle of Blackfoot Indian territory to deal with whiskey smugglers, before the coming of the railroad in 1883. Until 1914, the town was able to survive exclusively from processing the meat that resulted from its lush pasturage and flourishing cattle-breeding. Then oil was discovered in Turner Valley, 31 miles (50 km) south, and 1923 saw the construction of the first refinery in Alberta. This historical success story is often derided by inhabitants of the province's capital, Edmonton, who claim their city was a thriving trading post much earlier on, and not a rough, uncivilized military post like Calgary.

There is a long-standing rivalry between the two cities. Calgary is a center for white-collar workers in the headquarters of Canada's oil companies (80% of all Canadian mineral oil and natural gas business is conducted here), while Edmonton is more a center for production.

Edmonton, unabashed, counters by belittling Calgary as a cowtown. There is some truth in this, given that Calgary's initial development came about thanks to Anglo-Saxon cattle breeders – it's no accident that the city's first-ever millionaire happened to be the owner of a slaughterhouse. Edmonton, on the other hand, owes its rise to grain farmers.

In Calgary, people take the designation "cowtown" as a compliment, and its use is encouraged rather than otherwise. Although it's a modern, optimistic and forward-looking city in a continual process of change, the cowboy image and love of horses remain essential elements of everyday life. Pride of the city is the **Spruce Meadows Equestrian Center** (at the junction of Highway 2 and 22X West), a renowed thoroughbred breeder which also hosts top-flight equestrian

Above: Half of Canada makes the annual pilgrimage to the Calgary Stampede. Right: 20 seconds on a bucking bronco can feel like an eternity.

events. The city's main shopping boulevard, **Stephens Avenue Mall**, is lined with varieties of cowboy boot running the gamut from plain brown to patterned and embroidered creations made of the skins of rare creatures.

Since hosting the Winter Olympics in February, 1988, the city has gained a major landmark in the **Olympic Saddledome**, the winter sports arena shaped like a cowboy's saddle. Any visitor coming in from the south should stop off in **Stampede Park** to see the Saddledome and take a few snapshots of the best view of Calgary's skyline.

For ten days in mid-July, the city hosts the largest **rodeo** in North America. Both genuine and wanna-be cowboys mingle during this spectacle, which combines the flavor of the Wild West and that of a county fair; industrial and agricultural shows are also held at the same time. Apart from traditional rodeo disciplines such as bronc-riding with and without a saddle, or throwing bulls with one's bare hands, another highlight of the **Calgary**

Stampede are the daily races between covered wagons, drawn by four horses and accompanied by enthusiastic whoops and cheers from the crowd. Rounding out the picture are evening performances by acrobats or comedians; a Las Vegas-style revue; and exhibits of prize animals or the wheeling and dealing of slippery horse dealers. Even the range of food captures something of the spirit of Calgary: Alberta steaks next to Asian snacks, tradition and internationalism side by side.

Calgary's downtown is a pleasant place, with patches of green and the signature **skywalks**. The latter are glass tubes for pedestrians running between the skyscrapers some 16 feet (5 m) above the ground, which add a distinctive touch to the cityscape. They also provide a way for pedestrians to get around untroubled by Calgary's notorious weather, which is prone to rapid, extreme changes. In winter, the warm chinook winds can cause the temperature to rise as much as 75°F (25°C) within an hour – a fact that

became known to the world during the Olympic Games.

Best place to start a pedestrian tour of downtown is **Olympic Plaza**, which commemorates the winners of the 1988 Winter Olympics. Diagonally opposite is the excellent **Glenbow Museum** (corner of 9th Ave. and 1st St.), a good introduction to the history of Western Canada with information on explorers, fur traders, railway men, missionaries and Mounties. The museum also has in-depth information on the native peoples of the West Coast, particularly the Inuit; as well as collections of minerals and weapons, archives and a library.

Passing through the **Convention Center** you come to 9th Avenue, site of another famous landmark: **Calgary Tower**. The view from this 625-foot (191 m) tower with its revolving restaurant, observation deck and cocktail bar is spectacular enough, taking in the prairies and the Rockies, to be well worth the five-dollar price of admission. The Olympic flame at the very top of the tower is lit for

103

special political, sporting, or cultural occasions; it is not, however, the same flame in which Calgary residents irreverently toasted marshmallows in 1988, much to the horror of IOC functionaries.

Crossing Center Street brings you back to Stephen's Avenue Mall. Here, on the third floor of the **Toronto Dominion Square** complex, neither rain, snow nor wind can spoil anyone's pleasure in the **Devonshire Gardens**; these indoor gardens, laid out over about 2.5 acres (1 ha), are a veritable oasis with more than 20,000 tropical and native plants, as well as waterfalls, rest zones, and restaurants.

One block further north is yet another biotope, albeit of an artistic nature: the **Lunchbox Theater** (5th Avenue SW, Bow Valley Square) plays theater, cabaret and musicals at lunchtime, an interesting way of putting one's lunch break to good use – and free of charge! Heading west along 5th Avenue SW, you come to the **Energeum**, a highly interesting exhibition outlining the exploitation of oil, coal and natural gas, and providing information on geology. Visitors are even allowed to dip a hand into crude oil – protected, of course, by a glove. Following 7th St. SW to the south will bring you, after two blocks, to the **Alberta Sports Hall of Fame**, honoring the sporting achievements of Canadian athletes.

To get to the **Alberta Science Center and Centennial Planetarium**, you can either take the **LRT (Light Rail Transit)** that runs along 7th Avenue SW or walk. This entertaining museum features hands-on exhibits on astronomy, space shuttle missions and meteorites; and telescopes are available for star-gazers. A walk along Bow River leads to **Prince's Island Park**, an island which is an ideal venue for relaxing or having a picnic after traipsing around the city. At the end

Right: Mount Rundle, 9,643 feet/2,949 m high, rises up behind the Vermillion Lakes.

of Barcley Mall in the **Eau Claire Market** complex (stores, market, restaurants) there is an **IMAX Theater**. The area between River Front Ave. and 3rd Ave. SW is Calgary's small **Chinatown**.

Outside the city proper, four other attractions deserve a mention.

To the southwest, on Glenmore Reservoir, is **Heritage Park Historical Village**, where more than 100 restored buildings convey the flavor of life in a small prairie town around 1900. Capping the illusion that the past has come to life are the vintage steam train and paddle-wheel steamer that bear visitors on land and on lake.

To the southeast is **Fort Calgary**, the site of Calgary's original settlement, today a 40-acre (16 ha) park. Little remains of the fort, apart from Calgary's two oldest houses, but the Information Center describes the work of the North West Mounted Police and gives a picture of the lives of the first settlers.

The settlement's location at the confluence of the Bow and Elbow rivers is very picturesque, and a short stroll brings you over to **George's Island**, where you can visit the **Calgary Zoo, Botanical Garden and Prehistoric Dinosaur Park**. The name says it all: in addition to 1,400 animals, including a large gorilla population, there are magnificent greenhouses with tropical plants and life-sized replicas of dinosaurs.

Olympic Park lies some 15 minutes northwest of town. One look at the exposed ski jumps here, which stand 228 and 294 feet (70 and 90 m) high, and you can easily understand that during the 1988 Winter Olympics the winds often swept through to "blow out" the proceedings. Even without the chinook, this is a breezy place. Visitors can take guided tours, get their thrills on the rollercoaster-like bobsled simulator, and tour the **Olympic Hall of Fame**. Canadians' pride in "their" Olympics is palpable: exhibits of every conceivable kind crowd

the three floors. Next door, the huge amusement park of **Calaway Park** is evidence of the links between the Canadian and the American way of life; the faceless suburbs that you pass through on the way to the mountains, with their anonymous rings of fast-food outlets, gas stations and motels, are equally reminiscent of Canada's neighbor to the south. But some 60 miles (100 km) on, you put this all behind you, engulfed in the awesome, desolate landscape of the Rocky Mountains.

BANFF NATIONAL PARK

The Trans-Canada Highway 1 bound for Banff sees heavy traffic; campers are much in evidence in high season, and *Brewster Gray Line* buses with their destinations marked in Japanese characters thunder westwards so as to reach Banff as quickly as possible. **Bow Valley Provincial Park** benefits from its location slightly away from the main route to Banff National Park – and its concentration of shy animals and rare plants, notably high for such a small area, also profits from quiet isolation.

Turn off about 50 miles (80 km) west of Calgary towards Highway 1a to reach the **Visitor Centre**, from where you can set off on foot on the **Montane Trail**, 1.4 miles (2.2 km) long. Along the trail various features of the glacial scenery formed during the Ice Age are explained, including some textbook examples of "osers." These ridges of debris were formed by fast-flowing meltwater streams that ran parallel to the glacier. Further along Highway 1a, 10 miles (16 km) west of the junction with 1x, a steep ascent leads up to **Grotto Canyon**, where you stand on the valley floor surrounded by steep cliff walls rising threateningly, vertically into the sky. Occasionally, you may spot a free climber hanging on the rocky walls, but usually it is quiet, evoking the special atmosphere that inspired aboriginal Canadians to execute rock paintings here some 1,000 years ago. The exact location of the

paintings is no longer advertised for fear that too many visitors could cause too much damage. Should you chance on a picture, please resist the temptation to touch it and look with your eyes only!

Banff National Park, 2,590 square miles (6,641 sq. km) in area, is linked to Jasper National Park, which borders it to the north, via the famous panoramic road "Icefields Parkway." Shortly past the park gate you reach the town of **Banff**, acknowledged international hub of the Canadian Rockies, with its best-known feature, the 9,643-foot (2,949 m) high **Mount Rundle**. In 1883, railway workers discovered hot springs here and were worldly enough to demand an admission fee from anyone who wanted to visit them. This did not go down well with the railway association, which proceeded to create a nature park around the springs that was later enlarged to take in

Above: Big city traffic in the heart of the Rockies – Banff Avenue. Right: A different kind of winter sport at Banff Hot Springs.

the area around Lake Louise. A vacation center grew up by the springs; today this historic site has been reconstructed as the **Cave and Basin Centennial Centre** in original, 1914-vintage style (with thermal pool and visitor center).

Purists complain that Banff is like a fairground and therefore should not be part of a national park. True, in the high season it gets very crowded, and even out of season the town could hardly be called quiet. Nevertheless, it is possible to find less-frequented places within reasonable walking or biking distance; furthermore, even long-distance walkers enamored of solitude tend to enjoy a taste of civilization now and again.

Even within city limits, Banff has so much amazing scenery that it makes sense to rent a mountain bike for a day to see it. Starting at the castle-like Banff Springs Hotel (built in 1888), you can continue via the golf course to small **Bow Falls**, from where there is a wonderful view into the **Bow River** valley. If, immediately past the bridge, you turn right

toward Banff Avenue, Tunnel Mountain Drive will bring you to the **Hoodoo Trail** (walk from Surprise Corner Viewpoint). Alternately, you can also continue along Tunnel Mountain Drive and make for the viewpoint close to the campsite, where you can also see the hoodoos and even climb a bit around these tall, eroded pillars of sandstone.

Banff Avenue will take you through the center of town to the **Park Museum**, a Victorian building with a rustic interior which informs visitors about the park's flora and fauna. Another museum, the **Whyte Museum** (Bear Street), is concerned with the history of the Rockies, not so much from a geological standpoint as an entertaining one, presenting events from the point of view of the pioneers, mountain climbers and first tourists. Following Bow Avenue and Gopher Street, you come to a parking lot which marks the start of the **Fenland Trail**. Armed with an explanatory brochure (available at the start of the trail; walk in a clockwise direction), walkers can discover 10

interesting features of the distinctive flora and fauna of this moist biotope.

Beyond the bridge spanning the Bow River (to the right as you face the Banff Springs Hotel), there are several attractive trails leading through the **Bow River Valley** (there are also several riding stables, some catering to novices). Mountain Road leads up to the **Upper Hot Springs**, where you can soak in an outdoor thermal pool or unwind in one of the steam baths, their air perfumed with aromatic oils, wrapped in a warmed towel – especially to be recommended if you've just climbed **Sulfur Mountain** (around two hours). If you don't like to hike, you can take a funicular to the top of this 7,459-foot (2,281 m) elevation, where three observation decks and a restaurant command stunning panoramic views. **Vista Trail** leads to nearby Samson Peak.

Banff is a firm favorite with Japanese travelers, in particular for its traditional, fairytale **Banff Springs Hotel** (see "Hotels," p. 238), which became famous all over the country after it was featured in a Japanese soap opera.

Since organized tours tend to stick to well-trodden paths, they seldom venture as far as the two pretty picnic lakes **Two Jack Lake** (with canoe rental) and the locals' favorite, **Johnson Lake**. In 1941 the water in **Lake Minnewanka** (Devil's Lake), some 7 miles (11 km) east of Banff, was dammed: it rose by 72 feet (22 m), and grew 5 miles (8 km) in length, making it the largest lake in the park. In the process, the village of Minnewanka Landing sank beneath the surface, and for divers it can be a memorable experience to swim through the underwater ruins.

Like so many other lakes in the Rockies, this one makes you question how it could come to be such a vivid blue. Once again, glaciers are the cause: when glacial meltwater flows into a lake, it carries tiny particles which either settle on the bottom or float in the water. These tiny particles reflect green and blue from the light spectrum. When an entire glacier melts, it introduces a very high number of particles into the lake, and the water appears to be a particularly deep blue or turquoise.

To get to Lake Louise, you have a choice between the newer, better Highway 1 or the older 1a; the latter briefly touches spectacular **Johnston Canyon**. A surfaced path leads the half a mile (1.1 km) to the **Lower Falls**, and continues a further 1.7 miles (2.7 km) to the canyon's **Upper Falls**. There are actually 7 waterfalls in the canyon, but the Upper Falls are, at 98 feet (30 m), the highest. The waterfalls result from the meeting of two kinds of stone, dolomite and limestone: the water rushes over the edge of the harder dolomite and wears away the soft limestone below, hollowing it into ever deeper basins. At some point the eroded

basin undercuts the dolomite projecting above it; the dolomite lip then breaks off, and the waterfall moves another notch upstream.

Anyone traveling along Highway 1 should make a detour to **Sunshine Village**. This ski resort marks the close of its season, at the end of May, with a "fun run" which ends with the costumed skiers trying to jump over a pool; most of them fall in, much to the delight of the onlookers. From the parking lot in Sunshine, the mountain trail to **Rock Isle Lake** is some 5 miles (8 km) long. The snow often doesn't melt here until the beginning of July; from mid-July to the end of the month, the meadows are transformed into a sea of flowers. At the end of the trail, you climb up to the **Rock Isle Viewing Point**, which lies beyond the Continental Divide – the demarcation line between the river systems which flow into the Pacific and those which flow into the North Atlantic. The view out over the lake with the meadows in the foreground and the enormous gray mountains forming a backdrop is one of the most attractive sights in the Rockies. If you choose, you can continue to hike on to Standing Ridge, another lookout point, or to **Rock**, **Grizzly** and **Larix Lakes**.

Lake Louise

Shining, turquoise **Lake Louise** (5,660 feet/1,731 m) is the best-known and the most beautiful lake in the Rockies. Overshadowing this grandly located moraine lake is 11,311-foot (3,459 m) Mount Victoria, whose glacier reaches almost as far as the shore.

The village of Lake Louise is no more than a crossing in the road with gas stations, supermarkets and a sporting goods store. Look in at the **Old Railway Station**, which has been converted into a delightful restaurant, and is a pleasant place to stop off for a cup of coffee during the day. It's furnished with elements of the

Right: Picture postcard view – Lake Louise and its famous hotel.

original ticket hall, vintage railway seating, and an array of nostalgic photos.

When people refer to Lake Louise, they are usually talking not about the village but **Château Lake Louise**, a luxury hotel. During the high season its parking lot is generally choc-a-bloc with day visitors keen to catch a glimpse of the luxury. Note that neither eating cake on the terrace nor lunching in the deli is an overly expensive undertaking; and even the restaurants catering to the evening trade are generally affordable. Top of the list, at least for the Japanese, is the *Walliser Stube*, where cheese is melted into a creamy fondue that seems highly unusual to Asian eyes. Most guests are also perfectly satisfied with the Swiss coats-of-arms that add another "authentic" touch to the interior decor, and probably won't notice that the animal on Bern's coat-of-arms is actually the Berlin bear.

The château makes a good starting point for walks, but it's futile to look for solitude here; the days of Walter Wilcox, the man who surveyed this deserted region for the railroad, are long gone. One popular walk leads along the shore of the lake, which is usually frozen over from November to June. Indeed Lake Louise is the most "wintry" community on the classic route through the Rockies and an ideal skiing area: two and a half months of summer, and snow the rest of the year. Even in August, the lake doesn't "warm up" above a brisk 39°F (4°C). On the far shore opposite the hotel there are boats waiting to transport walkers back, but if you are feeling energetic you might like to continue to the **Plain of the Six Glaciers** (4.5 miles/7 km each way from the parking lot; accessible only in the height of summer; wear warm clothing). A tea house perches at a height of 6,981 feet (2,135 m); almost a mile (1.5 km) further on, walkers reach a spectacular outlook point. Visible from here are all six of the eponymous glaciers: **Lower Victoria, Upper Victoria, Aberdeen, Lefroy, Upper Lefroy** and **Popes**.

One of the best-known walks in the Rockies leads to **Lake Agnes**, named for

the wife of Canada's first prime minister. For the first mile and a half you go through thick forest, but then there are some fantastic views out over Lake Louise before the path makes a 180-degree turn and goes on past circular **Mirror Lake** to Lake Agnes, lying at 6,664 feet (2,038 m) like the floor of an ancient amphitheater carved out of the rock. The original **Tea House** here was the first of its kind in the Rockies, built in 1901, but the present-day building is a reconstruction dating from 1981 (usually open mid-June to late September).

Another of the Rockies' most-photographed subjects can also be reached from Lake Louise: Moraine Lake Road leads up to **Moraine Lake**, which long graced the Canadian 20-dollar bill. From the parking lot, you walk over a little bridge to reach the lookout point: in the foreground is the deep blue lake; in the

Above: Which way to the Matterhorn? A taste of Switzerland in the Rockies. Right: Mountain goats.

background, the **Wenkchemna Peaks** (a name derived from the Stoney Indian word for "ten," referring to the number of peaks on view). From here, a path roughly 2 miles (3 km) long leads to the **Consolation Lakes**, surrounded by awe-inspiring, treeless scenery. Upper Consolation Lake can only be reached by scrambling over gravel scree and rocks.

KOOTENAY AND YOHO NATIONAL PARKS

The main highway continues straight on to the north; the tourist buses from Banff and Lake Louise make for Columbia Icefield, and most of the campers drive towards Jasper. Considerably less crowded, yet no less attractive, is the loop through **Yoho** and **Kootenay National Parks**, which are actually part of British Columbia. This trip is all the more spectacular if you travel through Kootenay to Radium Hot Springs and then via Golden back to Lake Louise.

Just a few miles after the turn-off to Highway 93, you get a first breathtaking view out across **Twin Lake** and **Vista Lake**. A little further on, a signpost indicates that you've reached the border of the province and the Continental Divide.

From **Kootenay Parkway**, it's a lovely walk to the **Stanley Glacier**; at the end of the hike you have magnificent views into side valleys and the main valley, which owes its trough shape to glacial erosion. The first 1.5 miles (2.4 km) take in 719 feet (220 m) of vertical ascent, while the remaining mile or so (1.8 km) is less steep. The route also leads through the site of the devastating bushfire of 1968, which destroyed 6,575 acres (2,630 ha) of forest. Interestingly, the sections that were destroyed by the fire now house twice as many types of plants as were known before. But the burned area is also exposed to erosion, and avalanches cause considerable damage.

After this, the road descends rapidly. Another 4.5 miles (7 km) along, make sure to stop off to see the three small orange and ocher-colored ponds known as the **Paint Pots**. A nature trail leads the half a mile (1 km) from the parking lot. After the suspension bridge you come to the **Ocher Beds**, clay deposits filled with water containing iron. Before the advent of white settlers, the Kootenays made use of this phenomenon, forming a kind of cake of the clay, baking it and then pulverizing it, adding animal fat, and employing the resulting mixture to paint designs on clothes, teepees and faces. Around 1900, white businessmen began to collect the pigment systematically, but the undertaking failed in the long run, partly because of the difficulties transporting the ocher the long way to Calgary; and the abandoned machinery they used is still rusting on the site today. At the end of the trail are the aptly-named Paint Pots – three mineral springs colored by the clay deposits. The holes are conical in form, since the build-up of iron deposits

keeps raising the edges higher and higher. The deeper the water is, the more pressure it produces to work against the pressure of the spring water rising from below; the spring water accordingly seeks another exit, and creates isolated holes around the larger ponds.

The vegetation here is adapted to the drier, warmer climate of the **Columbia Valley**. Anyone traveling in Canada between mid-May and mid-June will find Lake Louise still frozen and covered with snow, and then emerge into the spring at the thermal source of **Radium Hot Springs**.

From **Golden**, you can continue eastwards to **Yoho National Park**. "Yoho" is a Cree word denoting awe or miracle, and the first natural wonder visitors encounter here are the **Wapta Falls**, reached after a walks of about a mile and a half (2.4 km) through the woods. The falls are fed by **Kicking Horse River**; this river shares its name with the pass leading to Lake Louise. This name originated with the Palliser expedition, a part

of which, led by the Scottish doctor and geologist James Hector, reached the area above Wapta Falls in 1858. On the trail, Hector and a packhorse took a tumble, and the horse kicked him in the chest, causing him to lose consciousness. His companions took him for dead, and indeed had already begun to dig his grave, when Hector blinked and opened his eyes. Although in considerable pain, he rode on with his fellows the next day; and the river has been known as Kicking Horse ever since.

Field, an old railway settlement, is important for tourists in that it's the site of the park information center, where there are also desks of the tourist offices of both B.C. and Alberta. Here, you can learn more about one of the park's highlights, **Lake O'Hara**, which is only available to a restricted number of visitors at a time, and only by shuttle bus

Above: Bow Lake in early summer. Right: Prairie dogs are popular models above Peyto Lake.

(reserve well in advance for campsites and seats on the bus). In this way, the park protects a delicate ecosystem as well as preserving a memorable landscape for the benefit of true nature-lovers. A small number of camping spots are, however, available at shorter notice: inquire in the center the day before you wish to visit. East of Field, there are more than 530 million old fossils in the **Burgess Shale Fossil Beds**. This site, which was first discovered in 1909, can only be visited on a guided tour.

Field is also the starting point for trips to **Emerald Lake**, 6 miles (10 km) away. This deep blue mountain lake shines against the imposing glaciers and peaks (up to 10,000 feet/3,000 m high) of the President Range. A pleasant three-mile (5 km) walk leads around the lake; on the shore opposite the parking lot, between mid-June and mid-July, you can spot yellow lady's slippers in bloom. This (protected!) type of orchid grows in shady areas, but also in gravelly soil close to ground water.

After around the middle of June the **Yoho Valley Road** is open, leading to the exquisite **Yoho Valley** and imposing **Takakkaw Falls**. Falling 1,256 feet (384 m), these grandiose falls are the third-highest in all of Canada. Appropriately, the word *takakkaw* means "it is wonderful" in the Cree language.

At the beginning of the road is Kicking Horse Campground, from where you can take a very interesting, brief stroll into the history of railway construction, following the so-called **Walk in the Past**, whose six highlights are described in a brochure at the start of the trail. The walk leads past old coal depots – deserted since the advent of diesel locomotives in 1956 – along the original course of the tracks, to a locomotive dating from 1885. Normally, locomotives could only cope with a gradient of 2.2%, but "Big Hill" required them to ascend a 4.8% gradient over a distance of some 9 miles (14 km), pulling 14 cars and 700 tons of freight. This tremendous feat took more than an hour, and delays were inevitable, since

trains literally stopped in their tracks on the way up and often derailed on the way down. Avalanches and mudslides compounded the difficulties, and the CPR railway company suffered the loss of many lives and six-figure sums of money. Not until 1909 did the situation improve with the construction of two tunnel systems known as the **Spiral Tunnels**. This revolutionary and brilliant feat of engineering cost 1.5 million dollars, employed 1,000 workers and used 700 tons of dynamite to blast out the route.

On account of their shape, the tunnels are popularly referred to as "the pretzel." Atop **Spiral Tunnel Viewpoint**, there's a model that best illustrates the technical workings of these tunnels; there, too, with a bit of luck, you can take in the sight of a locomotive at the front of a seemingly endless freight train emerging from the upper tunnel while its last cars are still disappearing into the lower tunnel. One model for this construction was the train tunnel of the Gotthardbahn in Switzerland.

From Lake Louise to Jasper on the Icefields Parkway

Icefields Parkway is the nickname for Highway 93, which traverses Banff and Jasper National Parks. First point of interest on this 143-mile (230 km) drive is **Bow Lake**. Tourist buses deposit large groups of people close to the Num-Ti-Jah lodge, souvenir shop and restaurant – generally, however, only for a brief photo and shopping stop before continuing on their journey. This means that most miss the walk along the lake to its alluvial deposits: the glacial meltwater carries sediments which pile up further and further into the lake. The walk continues along the canyon to the foot of **Bow Glacier**, which seems to hang threateningly over the onlooker. A second stop is the Bow Summit look-out point, also called **Bow Pass** (6,726 feet/2,068 m). There's an

Above: Winter tires required – special buses on the Columbia Icefield. Right: Athabasca Glacier, highlight of the Icefields Parkway.

other spectacular view over **Peyto Lake** from another observation point which can only be reached on foot. When you walk from the parking lot to the summit, you'll note immediately that, while the forestation is normal around the parking lot, only isolated groups of trees cling to the heights of the summit. Indeed, due to the 327-foot (100 m) difference in altitude the wind is twice as strong, explaining why tree growth is stunted and most trees grow horizontally rather than vertically.

The parkway heads on through the Mistaya and the Saskatchewan valleys before winding its way up to the 6,654-foot (2,035 m) **Sunwapta Pass** and Columbia Icefield. White "mountain goats" clamber over the rocks – not goats at all, in fact, they are more closely related to Asian mountain antelopes, and are easy to distinguish from bighorn sheep with their twisted horns and a brown coat. The white "goats" are more timid than the sheep, who are known to cheekily beg for food through the open windows of visi-

tors' cars. Please resist, however, the temptation to feed them.

Athabasca Glacier, which is part of the Columbia Icefield, owes much of its renown to the fact that it's so easy to get to. It makes sense to start by visiting the **Icefield Park Center**, which provides interesting information on glacial activity; from here, special buses run directly out to the glaciers for so-called *iceseeing*. Alternatively, you can walk to the ice over gravel and moraine and climb up part of the glacier's tongue (make sure to bring hiking boots and a thick jacket!). A sobering accent are the boards posted with dates documenting the gradual but steady retreat of the glacier – almost a mile (1.6 km) since 1870 – a process which is accelerating due to the combined effects of erosion and global warming.

The entire **Columbia Icefield**, the main attraction of the Parkway, covers an area of 127 square miles (325 sq. km), making it the largest in the Rockies. The ice averages a thickness of 1,200 feet (365 m); in places, it's up to 2,950 feet (900 m) thick.

The route north of the Columbia Icefield is less spectacular and gradually descends on its way to Jasper. Some 37 miles (60 km) before Jasper, you can detour off to the impressive **Sunwapta Falls**. At the junction of Highway 93 and 93a, the **Athabasca Falls**, also worth stopping off for, plunge into a narrow gorge. Several bridges and paths lead to observation points which command a view of this attractive sight.

JASPER NATIONAL PARK

Founded as early as 1907, the famous **Jasper National Park** covers 4,242 square miles (10,878 sq. km), making it the largest park in the Canadian Rockies. At the Columbia Icefield, it borders on Banff National Park, although no actual gate or entrance marks the boundary.

Lying at an altitude of 3,460 feet (1,058 m), the town of **Jasper** is also surrounded by high mountains, but the val-

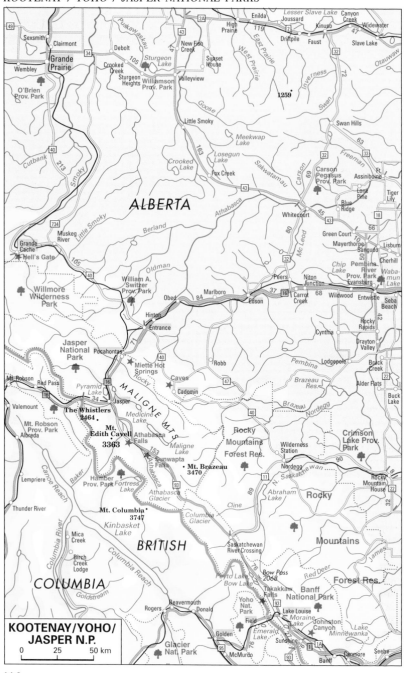

**KOOTENAY/YOHO/
JASPER N.P.**

0   25   50 km

ley is wide enough that they don't appear as threatening as do those at Lake Louise. This former railroad town is pleasant enough, but nothing to take your breath away. Its main street is lined with stores, restaurants and souvenir shops. Another striking feature are the town's many churches, including the Lutheran church, faced with cedar shingles, and the Catholic church of St. Mary's, built in the style of a castle.

If Canada aficionados light up at the sound of the name Jasper, it's because of the stunning landscapes that lie all around the little town, including both memorable mountains and beautiful lakes. As far as mountains go, the 8,057-foot (2,464 m) local mountain **The Whistlers** (named for the shrill call of its resident marmots), is a popular destination year-round. The Jasper Tramway covers the 3,270 feet (1,000 m) of vertical ascent in just 7 minutes, and a path just under a mile (1.4 km) long leads from the tram station to the summit. It's rare – except in Banff – to have such easy access to such a spectacular view, so it is hardly surprising that some 150,000 people a year make the most of the opportunity – tramping heavy-footed through the delicate wilderness. Nature-lovers are asked to keep to the paths so as to keep ecological damage to a minimum.

Jasper is surrounded by a large number of lakes, each unique in its own way, starting with **Pyramid Lake**, which serves as an open-air swimming pool for Jasper's residents. **Lake Edith** and **Lake Annette** on the way to Jasper Park Lodge are also pleasant for swimming. Lake Edith has a sand beach; at Lake Annette, you can walk or cycle around the lake through woods, past weekend cabins each with its own little private stretch of lake shore. If you want a more in-depth experience of the Canadian way of life, rent a room at traditional **Jasper Park Lodge** on picturesque **Beauvert Lake**.

The unique combination of mountains and lakes, fauna and flora is especially charming in July on the sub-alpine meadows below **Mount Edith Cavell**. This 10,997-foot (3,363 m) mountain was known among the Cree as "white spirit" on account of the strange light that was visible above its snow-covered peak on moonlit nights. It received its present name in memory of the courageous British nurse Edith Cavell, who was executed for helping Allied prisoners to escape during World War I. Edith Cavell Road, roughly 9 miles (14.5 km) from Highway 93a, leads to a parking lot (the road is unsuitable for large campers) which is the starting point for two walks. From the first, the aptly-named **Path of the Glacier**, you can see Angel Glacier high above, clinging to the edge of the cliffs of Mount Edith Cavell, while the second, **Cavell Meadows**, leads you through meadows covered with heather.

Yet such walks are only a first taste of greater things to come. **Maligne Road** (pronounced ma-LEEN) leads to one of the greatest natural spectacles in the Rockies. In the course of the last Ice Age, the Wisconsin Period, powerful valley glaciers carved the main valleys into deep U-shaped troughs; however, the smaller glaciers in the little valleys on either side of the main troughs only cut into the earth as far as the upper surface of the larger glaciers. After the large glaciers melted, these higher-lying side valleys suddenly ended in nothing and seemed to hang over the larger valley floors. The Maligne Valley is such a "hanging" valley. The river once plunged as a waterfall down to the main Athabasca valley below, but over thousands of years it gradually cut a steep gorge through the limestone, resulting in the **Maligne Canyon**, one of the most grandiose canyons in Canada. There are several entrances to the canyon. If you park at the Sixth Bridge parking lot, you can hike up the canyon for 2.3 miles (3.7

km); from Fifth Bridge parking, it's just 1.7 miles (2.7 km), while from the main parking lot by First Bridge "the loop" is only about half a mile (1 km). The further back you start, however, the more rewarding the walk. By the second bridge, the canyon reaches its deepest point at 180 feet (55 m).

Above, by the tea house, you can admire the so-called **potholes**: over the years, eddying water, mixed with sand, bores a hole in the earth. If a largish stone is trapped in the hole, it becomes even larger. Years later, when the current changes direction, the holes are left behind, filled with standing water or moist earth. As such they make ideal natural "pots" for ferns and shrubs.

After so many scenic highlights, the **tea house** offers a pleasant ambience in which to relax. The food is good, and the crowds disembarking from the tourist

Above: On Pyramid Lake. Right: The bashful moose is seldom willing to pose this photogenically.

buses only stay for a quick coffee and a browse through the souvenir shop before leaving you in peace once more.

Some 10.5 miles (17 km) further on you reach **Medicine Lake**, which fills steadily up until July and then drains away in the fall, a phenomenon that prompted the natives to talk of *big medicine*, or magic. The lake drains into the Maligne system of underground limestone caves; its water surfaces again by the fourth bridge of the canyon, or ends up in some of the lakes around Jasper Park Lodge. Before the road was built, enterprising captains tried to set up small ferry services to transport tourists across the water. However, the strong currents often caused the boats to capsize, prompting the frustrated boat people to try filling in the holes on the lake floor with newspapers and mattresses.

Finally, you come to the high point of the journey. Canada has a wealth of picturesque lakes, but none of them can compare with **Maligne Lake**, some 13.6 miles (22 km) long, up to 1.2 miles (2

km) wide, tucked at an altitude of 5,471 feet (1,673 m) into the Maligne valley and an incredible, intense blue. Its most photogenic and most familiar face, with Spirit Island in the foreground, is visible on a boat trip to the lake's south shore.

Henry Macleod, an inspector for the Canadian Pacific Railroad, was unimpressed by the lake's beauty. But then, he had been traipsing for many long miles on foot when he chanced upon it in 1875; hence he dubbed it "lake of the inflamed feet," and wrote it off as "an unpleasant corner of the earth." The Stoney Indians, by contrast, had long appreciated the lake. When Mary Schaffer, a white explorer, began to develop an interest in the area, an Indian chieftain named Sampson Beaver sketched out a fairly rough map for her. In 1908, Schaffer's expedition succeeded in finding the lake; she then built a boat and charted its waters in three days. **Schaffer's Lookout** (roughly half a mile/1 km along the lake), named after this courageous woman, is in fact the best vantage point from which to view the

lake in all its beauty. From this little bay a path leads off the left and through woods and clearings back to the parking lot. The chances of seeing moose around Maligne Lake are pretty good. These timid creatures, which stand almost 6.5 feet (2 m) high at the shoulder, often venture out in the early morning and evening.

In Jasper, the main tourist path bears off to the west, and even if you're actually heading for the Pacific coast it is worth making a detour to the eastern borders of Jasper Park. The mountains recede and the mighty **Athabasca River** winds its way through one of the most beautiful valleys in the Rockies – a particularly attractive sight at twilight.

Pocahontas, on Meitte Hot Springs Road, was founded in 1908 when Frank Villeneuve discovered coal. Anticipating the construction of a second railroad line through the Rockies and the increased demand for coal this would create, he gave the area the promising name of "Pocahontas" after a highly successful mine

119

in Virginia. The mining community quickly swelled to 2,000 inhabitants, but their joy was short-lived. Granted, the railway did come, but the tracks were later taken up again because of the great need for steel in World War I, leaving Pocahontas without a rail link. Mismanagement, a spate of mining accidents and a strike in 1919 combined to put an end to the town's hopes of riches. In 1921 the mine was closed down for good. Today, visitors can explore the few remains of the mine on an interpretive trail, or embark on a somewhat longer walk up to the lovely campground.

Miette Hot Springs are the warmest mineral waters in the Canadian Rockies, emerging at a temperature of 129°F (54°C) and cooling to 102°F (39°C). It is a wonderful sensation to soak in warm water with the Rockies in the background; furthermore, the baths, with their outdoor pools, are wonderfully old-fashioned and never overcrowded.

From Jasper to Edmonton

The first larger community after Jasper is **Hinton**, a town with an industrial air whose economy is largely based on forestry. The **Alberta Forest Service Museum** gives visitors an insight into this field, and **Weldwood Sawmill** offers guided tours. Hinton can hardly be called attractive, but the area around it is beautiful. Adventure-seeking wilderness fans should take the road to **Grande Cache** and on to Grande Prairie: you drive through expanses of forest reaching as far as the eye can see, dotted with rivers but with hardly a trace of human settlement. Some 3.7 miles (6 km) north of the attractive town of Grande Cache, **Smoky River**, which is ideal for canoeing and kayaking, forms the spectacular canyon of **Hell's Gate**. In Grande Cache there are a number of operators who know the almost inaccessible **Willmore Wilderness Park** like the backs of their hands:

beautiful Rocky Mountain landscapes without the overcommercialization of so many comparable sites. If you find so much solitude unnerving, **William A. Switzer Provincial Park** contains an "adventure lodge" which offers "wilderness complete with instructions."

Highway 40 southbound also leads through a sparsely-populated region: Coal Branch. In this area are ghost towns such as **Mercoal**; the caves near **Cadomin**; and glorious views of the watershed between the Saskatchewan and Athabasca rivers known as the **Cardinal Divide**. And the people you encounter are truly happy to welcome any visitors who happen to pass through.

Building the **Yellowhead Highway** meant cutting a path through seemingly endless forests. Here and there a dirt road leads back into the forest; apart from these, there isn't much in the way of sights until you reach Edson.

Edson is a typical small Canadian town. The **Galloway Station Museum**, overlooking a small park, displays various artifacts connected with the region's history. Also worth visiting is the **Red Brick Arts Centre and Museum** in the old schoolhouse (1913). The old classrooms have been restored and filled with pictures and other objects relating to the days of the pioneers. Here, you can really start to appreciate the feats of the early frontiersmen. In 1910, the railroad brought in the first settlers, who continued on northwards in covered wagons. Anyone traveling to **Fox Creek** and on to **Grande Prairie** can get an idea of how strenuous this journey must have been. Even if you don't make the entire journey, do try to detour over to the **Rosevear Ferry** (on the McLeod River), one of only two river ferries in Alberta still in operation.

Wabamun Lake, where you can swim, boat or golf at the pretty resort of **Seba Beach**, is already within the catchment area of Greater Edmonton.

CALGARY
Area Code 403
Accommodation
LUXURY: **The Palliser**, 133 9th Ave. SW, tel. 262-1234, one of the loveliest hotels in western Canada; excellent service. *MODERATE:* **Crossroads**, 2120 16th Ave. NE, tel. 291-4666. Fitness room, whirlpool, sauna, casino. **Lord Nelson Inn**, 1020 8th Ave. SW, tel. 269-8262, pleasant place in central downtown location. *BUDGET:* **Holiday Inn Airport**, 1250 McKinnon Dr. NE (Trans-Canada Hwy 1 & 19th St NE), tel. 230-1999, pool, sauna. **University**, rooms to rent during the summer holidays, tel. 220-3202.

Restaurants
The Red Carpet, tel. 255-1173, elegant and expensive. **The Ranchmans Inn**, a Calgary institution with huge steaks, spare ribs, Western atmosphere. **Dean House**, 806 9th Ave., historic house in a pleasant riverside setting, also serves tea. **Franzl's Gasthaus**, 2417 4th St. SW, tel. 228-6882, German and Austrian cooking, homemade *strudel*, beer garden. **Schwartzies Bagels**, downtown, 100 Penny Lane, 7616 Ellbow Dr., all kinds of bagels.

Museums
Glenbow Museum, 130 9th Ave. SE, tel. 268-4100, Tue-Sun 10 am-6 pm. **Calgary Tower**, 101 9th Ave. SW, tel. 266-7171, Mon-Sun 8 am-11 pm, until midnight in summer. **Science Centre**, 701 11th St. SW, tel. 221-3700, daily July-Labour Day, other times Wed-Sun. **Energeum**, 640 5th Ave. SW, tel. 297-4293, June-August Sun-Fri 10:30 am-4:30 pm, other times Mon-Fri 10:30 am-4:30 pm. **Calgary Zoo, Botanical Garden & Prehistoric Park**, 1300 Zoo Road NE, tel. 232-9300. **Fort Calgary Historic Park**, 750 9th Ave. SE, tel. 290-1875, May to Thanksgiving Day 9 am-5 pm. **Heritage Park**, **Historical Village**, 14 St. SW/Heritage Dr., tel. 259-1900, Mid-May to early Sept daily, then until mid-Oct by appointment. **Canada Olympic Park**, Highway 1 West, tel. 247-5452, 10 am-5 pm.

Shopping
Laemmle Western Wear, 115 8th Ave. SW, cowboy gear, boots, the works.

Festivals / Rodeo / Events
Calgary Folk Festival, late July, free noon performances in the Stephens Avenue Mall, Century Park Garden and Olympic Plaza. Evening performances by local and international artists in various venues, such as the Kensington Deli Café and King Edward Hotel. For information, call 225-5256.
International Native Arts Festival, in **Calgary**, mid-August, features a range of traditional dances, music, artisan work and crafts of Native Americans as well as other native populations from all over the world.

The **Calgary Stampede** is held in the second week of July and lasts 10 days (always starting with a big parade on a Friday). Most of the events of this popular cowboy festival are held in Stampede Park, but there's plenty going on in other parts of the city, as well. Information & tickets: **Calgary Exhibition & Stampede**, Box 1060, Station M. Calgary T2P 2K8, tel. 261-0101 or 1-800-661-1260. **Calaway Park**, amusement park, 6 mi/10 km W on Hwy 1, Springbank exit, tel. 240-3824; July-Aug daily; weekends in May, June, Sept. and Oct. **Calgary Tower**, 9th Ave., tel. 266-7171, open daily, 625 ft/191 m high, restaurant, souvenir shop.
Spruce Meadows, 3 mi/5 km SW of Calgary, a famous center for horse-breeding and training, riding lessons and tournaments. The grounds are open to visitors every day. At the beginning of Sept, it hosts the only international jumping tournament in North America, **The Masters**. Tel. 254-3200.

Transportation / Tips & Trips
The **Greyhound bus station** is at 850 6th St. NW, tel. 265-9111. **Red Arrow Express** is a luxury bus that runs between Calgary and Edmonton; its terminal is at the Westward Inn, 119 12th Ave. SW, tel. 265-8033. A lovely **train trip** is the two-day excursion from Calgary to Vancouver with the private railway line **Rocky Mountaineer Railtours**, tel. 604/606-7245. Calgary's **LRT Train System** links the city's northwest, northeast and southern districts with the center. It's a good idea to leave your car at one of these suburban stations and take the train in to downtown. For the whole downtown area between City Hall and the corner of 7th Ave. SW and 10th St. SW, you can ride the LRT free of charge.

Tourist Information
Calgary Convention and Visitors Bureau, Tower Centre, 237 9th Ave. SE, tel. 263-8510.
Writing-on-Stone Provincial Park, 26 mi/42 km from Milk River, tel. 647-2364.

THE ROCKIES
Area Code 403, unless otherwise specified
Accommodation
MEDICINE HAT: *MODERATE:* **Medicine Hat Lodge**, 1051 Ross Glen Dr., tel. 529-2222, well-tended, with casino, English pub, pool with water slides. *BUDGET:* **Medicine Hat Inn**, 530 4th St. SE, tel. 526-1313
LETHBRIDGE: *MODERATE:* **Lethbridge Lodge**, 320 Scenic Dr., tel. 328-1123, with pool. **Best Western Heidelberg Inn**, 1303 Mayor Magrath Dr., tel. 328-8846.
FORT MACLEOD: *BUDGET:* **Kosy Motel**, Box 625, tel. 553-3115, clean, pleasant motel with comfortable rooms.
PINCHER CREEK: *BUDGET:* **Heritage Inn**, Box 399, tel. 627-5000, well-run establishment.

WATERTON: *MODERATE:* **Prince of Wales Inn**, tel. 859-2231, in Waterton Lakes National Park, a noble building resembling a castle. **Kilmorey Lodge**, Box 100, Evergreen Ave, tel. 859-2334, cozy lodge in a dream location right on Waterton Lake with a very good restaurant. *BUDGET:* **Storey Brook Farm**, tel. 627-2841, in a spectacular setting, pretty rooms, sauna, lavish farmer's breakfast.

KANANASKIS COUNTRY: *LUXURY:* **The Lodge at Kananaskis**, K. Village, tel. 591-7711. *MODERATE:* **Rafter Six Ranch**, Seebe, tel. 673-3622, lodge, bungalows, camping, Indian museum, petting zoo. *CAMPING:* **Boulton Creek**, P. Lougheed Provincial Park, tel. 591-6344.

BANFF and Environs: *LUXURY:* **Banff Springs Hotel**, Box 960, tel. 762-2211, a fairy-tale hotel with every imaginable luxury. *MODERATE:* **Baker Creek Chalets**, between Lake Louise and Banff on the Bow Valley Parkway, tel. 522-2783, lovely, quiet, comfortable resort with luxurious amenities. **Johnston Canyon Resort**, Box 875, tel. 762-2971, lovely setting, very comfortable. **Hidden Ridge Chalets**, Tunnel Mt. Rd. in Banff, tel. 762-3544, studios and vacation apartments in a lovely setting. *BUDGET:* **Banff Voyager Inn**, 555 Banff Ave., tel. 762-3301, with pool, sauna.

KOOTENAY / YOHO: *LUXURY:* **Emerald Lake Lodge**, Box 10, near Field, tel. 250/343-6303, luxury accommodations nestled against a deep blue lake. *MODERATE:* **Kootenay Park Lodge**, tel. 762-9196. *CAMPING:* **Lake O'Hara**. Only accessible by shuttle bus after registration at the Visitor's Center in Field (Yoho National Park), in summer 8 am-8 pm, other times to 6 pm.

LAKE LOUISE: *LUXURY:* **Château Lake Louise**, tel. 522-3511, a fortress from outside, the lap of luxury within, in an absolutely gorgeous setting. **Post Hotel**, tel. 522-3989, luxury accommodations in high-rise style.

MODERATE: **Paradise Lodge & Bungalows**, Box 7, tel. 522-3595, log cabins near the château.

JASPER: *LUXURY:* **Jasper Park Lodge**, tel. 852-3301, luxury-class bungalows in extensive grounds, quiet; the nicest resort of the CP group. *MODERATE:* **Alpine Village**, from Hwy 93a, tel. 852-3285, attractively furnished bungalows, open fireplaces, gorgeous setting, large outdoor pool. **Sunwapta Falls Resort**, Box 97, tel. 852-4852, lovely bungalows in a wilderness setting, S of Jasper on Icefields Parkway. *BUDGET:* **Patricia Lake Bungalows**, Box 657, tel. 852-3560, wonderful lakeside location. Pocahontas Bungalows, Box 820, tel. 866-3732, rustic bungalows, pool, restaurant; just past the entrance to the park as you come from

Edmonton. *B&B:* Jasper's Visitor Information Center has a brochure listing 80-some private accommodations. *CAMPING:* In the national park are **Honeymoon Lake,** tel. 292-4444, in a very beautiful setting, with hiking trails around the like, S of Jasper on Icefields Parkway; **Whister Campground**, large, spacious; and **Pocahontas**, in a beautiful forest setting on the road to Miette.

HINTON and Environs: *MODERATE:* **Blue Lake Adventure Lodge**, Box 6150, tel. 865-4741 Lodge with a wide range of leisure opportunities. *BUDGET:* **Folding Mountain Resort**, Box 6085 Hinton, tel. 866-3737, wooden houses, shops, and camping.

EDSON: *BUDGET:* **Aspenhill Country Lodge**, Box 7439, tel. 723-6019, turn off on Schlick Road, 4 mi/7 km W of Edson; lodge in the wild.

SEBA BEACH: *CAMPING:* **Kokanee Park**, Box 264, Seba Beach, tel. 797-3058, well-tended campground with a driving range for golfers.

Restaurants

OKOTOKS: **The Ginger Tea Room**, 43 Riverside Dr., tel. 938-2907, lunch and tea served until 5 pm in a lovely Victorian house; on Friday, there's also a romantic dinner.

BANFF: **Magpie & Stump**, 203 Caribou St., tel. 762-4067, excellent, comfortable Mexican. **Grizzley House**, 207 Banff Ave, a Banff institution, a cozy room where you can choose between 40 kinds of fondue; reserve in advance: tel. 762-4055.

WATERTON: **Cobblestone Manor**, 173 7th Ave. W, Cardston, 25 mi/40 km E on Hwy 5, tel. 653-1519. Historic stone and wood building (1889) furnished with antiques, serving hearty American meals and homemade cakes.

LAKE LOUISE: **Lake Louise Station**, 200 Sentinel, tel. 522-2386; dine in a renovated train station. **Post Hotel**, *the* gourmet dining experience in western Canada, tel. 522-3989.

JASPER: **Mondis**, in the Whistler Inn, tel. 852-4070; fine Italian food. **Truffles & Trout** in the marketplace, corner of Patriza/Hazel Sts., high-class delicatessen with fancy sandwiches and cappuccino.

WILDWOOD: **Wildwood Hotel**, a mix of hotel, pub, laundromat and restaurant.

Museums

MEDICINE HAT: **Clay Products Interpretative Centre**, 703 Wood St. SE, tel. 529-1070, mid-May-late Oct., 10 am-6 pm. **Museum & Art Gallery**, 1302 Bomford Cresc. SW, tel. 527-6266.

LETHBRIDGE: **Nikka Yuko Japanese Garden**, Mayor Magrath Dr. in Henderson Park, tel. 328-3511, Victora Day-mid-June and Labour Day-late Sept. 9 am-5 pm, mid-June-Labour Day 9 am-8 pm, tel. 328-3511. **Fort Whoop Up**, Indian Battle Park, tel. 329-0444, Victoria Day-Labour Day Mon-

Sat 10 am-6 pm, Sun noon-5 pm, other times Tue-Fri 10 am-4 pm, Sun 1-2 pm.
FORT MACLEOD: **Fort Museum**, tel. 553-4703, May-June 9 am-5 pm, July-Labour Day 9 am-8:30 pm, Labour Day-mid-Oct 9 am-5 pm, other times 9:30 am-4 pm. **Head-Smashed-In Buffalo Jump**, Box 1977, tel. 553-2731, open Victoria Day-Labour Day 9 am-8 pm, other times 9 am-5 pm.
CROWSNEST: **Frank Slide Interpretive Centre**, Crowsnest Pass, tel. 562-7388. **Crowsnest Pass Ecomuseum**, Old Court House, 20 Ave, Blairmore, tel. 562-8831. **Crowsnest Museum**, downtown Coleman, tel. 563-5434.
CLARESHOLM: **Appaloosa Horse Club Canada Museum**, 3rd St. E, tel. 625-3326.
BANFF: **Park Museum**, 91 Banff Ave., tel. 762-1558, open June-Aug 10 am-6 pm, other times 1-5 pm. **Wythe Museum**, 111 Bear Street, tel. 762-2291, mid-May-mid-Oct. 10 am-6 pm; July, Aug also Tue-Sat until 9 pm; other times Tue-Sun 1-5 pm, Thu until 9 pm.
EDSON: **Galloway Station Museum**, 5425 3rd Ave., tel. 723-5696, June-Sept 10 am-4:30 pm. **Red Brick Arts Centre & Museum**, 4818 7th Ave., tel. 723-3582, May-Sept Mon-Fri 9 am-5 pm, Sat/Sun to 4 pm, other times Mon-Fri 9 am-4:30 pm.

Tips & Trips

MEDICINE HAT: A **self-guided tour** leads you past turn-of-the-century buildings; you can pick up the brochure at the Tourist Centre, corner of Trans Canada Highway and Southridge Dr., tel. 527-6422.
BANFF HOT SPRINGS: Open mid-May-mid-Sept 9 am-11 pm, other times 10 am-10 pm, tel. 762-1515. **MIETTE HOT SPRINGS:** Late June-late Aug 8:30 am-10:30 pm, mid-May to late June and Sept-mid-Oct 10:30 am-9 pm, tel. 866-3939.
BOAT TOURS / CANOE: **Cruises on Waterton Lake**, with stops for photos, tel. 859-2362. Boat trips on **Lake Minnewanka**, info line in Banff 762-3473; transportation can be arranged from Banff; fishing trips also possible. On the **Athabasca River** near Jasper you can book canoe trips in calm water with an accompanying interpretive program through the Jasper Adventure Centre, tel. 852-5595.
RAFTING: **Whitewater Voyages**, Box 1983, Golden, tel. 250/762-9117, whitewater rafting on the Kicking Horse River, tours of several days. **Alpine Rafting Company**, Box 1409 Golden, tel. 250/344-5016, half-day and all-day trips on the Kicking Horse River. **Hydra River Guides**, Box 2708 Banff, tel. 250/762-4554, tours on the Kicking Horse River. **Kootenay River Runners**, Box 81, Edgewater, tel. 250/762-5385, rafting on the Kootenay and White Rivers; pick-up service from Banff, Radium, Golden. **Whitewater Rafting**, Jasper; reserve at Avalanche Esso, 702 Connaught Dr., tel.

852-4386 or at Jasper Park Lodge, tel. 852-6052, various rafting trips around Jasper.
SNOWCOACH: **Columbia Icefield Snowmobile Tours**, P.O.Box 1140, Banff, tel. 762-6735.
CABLE CAR: **Sulphur Mountain Gondola**, Banff, tel. 762-2523, mid-May-late August 8:30 am-8 pm; September-October 9 8:30 am-6 pm; October 10 to late November, 9 am-4 pm. **Lake Louise Summer Sightseeing Lift** to Whitehorn Lodge, in the ski area, only June-late Sept 9 am-9 pm, tel. 522-3555. Jasper Tramway, Box 418 Jasper, tel. 852-3093, early April-late Oct.
HELICOPTER TOURS: **Alpine Helicopters**, 91 Bow Valley Trail, Canmore, tel. 678-4802.
RIDING: **Warner Guiding and Outfitting**, Box 2280, Banff, tel. 762-4551, 1- to 2-hour rides around Banff for beginners; day trips; rides to outdoor camps. **Tonquin Valley Pack Trips**, Box 23, Brule, tel. 865 4417, wonderful excursions of 4 days and longer. **Skyline Trail Rides**, 3- to 4-day riding tours; also provides pack mules for hikers. **Sunrider Stables**, 1- to 2-hr rides around Lake Annette. Both through Jasper Park Lodge, tel. 852-4215.
MOUNTAIN BIKING: **Adventures Unlimited**, 209 Bear St., Banff, tel. 762-4554, organized tours in the Rockies and bike rental. **Free Wheel Cycle**, 618 Patricia St., Jasper, tel. 852-3898, also provides a brochure with tours of up to 19 mi/30 km around Jasper. *HIKING:* Local tourist offices can recommend trails. For more casual routes, pick up the guide *Easy Walks and Hikes in the Canadian Rockies* by Graeme Pole.

Parks

Banff National Park, Visitor Centre, 224 Banff Ave., tel. 762-8421 or 762-1550. **Lake Louise Visitor Centre**, tel. 522-3833. **Jasper National Park, Visitor Information Center**, Jasper, tel. 852-3858. **Peter Lougheed Provincial Park**, tel. 591-6344, closed in April. **Waterton Lakes National Park**, tel. 859-2224. **Yoho National Park** Visitor Centre, tel. 343-6783, Lake O'Hara reservations, call 343-6433, 8 am-4 pm.

Tourist Information

Chinook Country Tourist Association, 2805 Scenic Dr. MM, Lethbridge, Alberta, tel. 1-800-661-1222, information about the whole area between the American border (S), the B.C. border (W), Calgary (N) and Taber, Vauxhall (E). **Evergreen Country Tourism Council**, Box 6007, Edson, tel. 723-4711. **Lake Louise Visitor Centre**, Samson Mall, tel. 522-3833. **Medicine Hat Tourist Centre**, corner Trans Canada Hwy./Southridge Dr., tel. 527-6422. **Trail of the Great Bear**, brochure describing a route from Yellowstone National Park (Montana) to Jasper, available from tourist information offices of most of the surrounding towns.

CENTRAL BRITISH COLUMBIA

Mount Robson Provincial Park

If you're coming from Jasper and cross the 3,486-foot (1,066 m) high **Yellowhead Pass**, the first park you'll reach in British Columbia is **Mount Robson Provincial Park**. The **Fraser River** widens here to become long, thin **Moose Lake**, so named for the creatures who often graze along its swampy eastern shore. Some 50 miles (80 km) west of Jasper is the highest mountain in the Canadian Rockies, **Mount Robson**. Measuring 12,930 feet (3,954 m) in height, it appears even higher due to the fact that it rises up vertically almost 9,800 feet (3,000 m). Head first for the visitors' center, where you can pick up information and route suggestions for various walks. One such walk is the 13.6-mile (22 km) **Berg Lake Trail**, although access is restricted due to its popularity; walkers have to apply for a permit several days in advance. Also popular, yet much shorter – just over 3 miles (5 km) in length – is the walk to **Kinney Lake**. The vegetation here is reminiscent of the coastal rainforests, thanks to the high precipitation produced by the clouds that gather around Mount Robson's peak. Just under a mile (1.5 km) east of the visitors' center is the starting point for the trail to **Overlander Falls**, named for the gold-diggers who, in 1862, became the first to dare the overland route to the gold fields at Kamloops.

Wells Gray Provincial Park

Anyone bound south for Kamloops should take the time to visit **Wells Gray Provincial Park**, which bears traces of volcanic activity. The park is relatively easy to reach. At **Blue River**, an unpaved

Right: One of the most popular Canadian leisure pastimes: the barbecue.

road leads to a parking lot that's the starting point of a pleasant 1.5-mile (2.5 km) walk to blue-green **Murtle Lake**. You can also enter the park through **Clearwater**, where a Travel Infocentre stocks useful information for hikers – and for canoers, as Wells Gray is a paddler's paradise. But the park's attractions are open even to the less athletic, thanks to more than 20 trails of varying length. Outside Wells Gray, in **Spahats Creek Provincial Park**, **Spahats Falls** and their 399-foot (122 m) deep canyon make popular subjects for photos. Wells Gray Park itself boasts 59-foot (18 m) **Dawson Falls** and gigantic **Helmcken Falls** which plunge 448 feet (137 m) – twice as high as Niagara Falls.

Prince George

Heading northwest, the **Yellowhead Highway** continues 140 miles (226 km) through Fraser Valley before reaching **Prince George**. This transportation hub grew to prominence thanks to the forestry industry, but it is also known for **Fort George** and the park of the same name on the banks of the Fraser River. Classical music can be heard floating across the patio of the Civic Center, a reminder that Prince George has its own symphony orchestra. **Connaught Hill Park** is a popular meeting place for residents: the younger generation basks in the sun, lovers walk hand in hand, and office workers come here on their lunchbreak. A heritage walk provides a more in-depth introduction to the town.

Detour to Barkerville

From Prince George, you can make an interesting detour on the **Cariboo Highway** (Highway 97) southwards along the Fraser River to **Quesnel**. This small town, founded during the gold rush, is sometimes referred to as "Gold Pan City"; it contains an old Hudson's Bay

Trading Post, faithfully restored and back in operation. Another 56 miles (90 km) further east on Highway 26 is **Barkerville Provincial Historic Park**, one of the most interesting living museums in Canada. This typical gold rush settlement, framed by the Cariboo Mountains, sprang up virtually overnight after Billy Barker struck gold in Williams Creek in 1862. Until 1868, Barkersville was the largest town west of Chicago. One notably successful sector of the population were the Chinese merchants, something attested to by the large number of restored Chinese stores. After 1875, however, the former boom town sank back into oblivion.

Among the 125 historic buildings here today are a barber's shop, a printer's, a hotel, a saloon and the **Theater Royal**, which stages music-hall style productions. From late June to early September, the town really comes to life: people wearing period costumes stroll its sidewalks alongside streets busy with horse-drawn wagons and mail coaches.

Bowron Lake Provincial Park, further to the east, is considered a paradise for canoers; one popular route is a five- to ten-day, 72-mile (116 km) circular trip taking in 7 portages. For canoe rental and permits – only 50 people are allowed to start the route each day – enquire at the **visitors' center**.

Detour to Fort St. John

As you drive north on the **John Hart Highway** (Hwy 97), your first stop should be **Bear Lake**, which enjoys a wonderful location, has sandy beaches and a fantastic campground – so fantastic that even mosquitoes feel right at home. Smaller provincial parks with attractive lakes follow one after another along Highway 97; the landscape is reminiscent of Alaska. **McLeod Lake** is of great historic significance: it was the first settlement west of the main ridge of the Rockies and north of San Francisco. Simon Fraser set up a trading post here as early as 1805; today, however, this his-

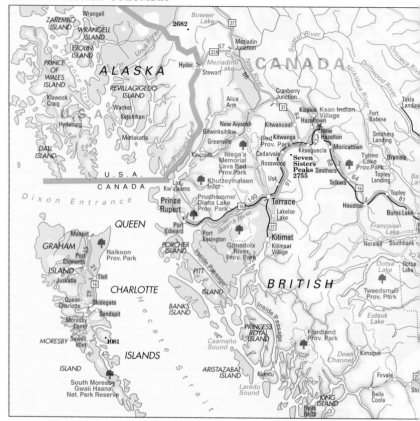

toric site is little more than a truck stop and hangout for Native Indians from the nearby reservation. Scaling the 3,051-foot (933 m) **Pine Pass**, the road leads on to **Chetwynd**, a town completely given over to the timber industry.

After a scenic stretch on Highway 29 you come to **Hudson's Hope**, a community which courts tourism in a pleasant manner. Local campgrounds are free, although voluntary donations are pretty much *de rigeur*; xeroxed handouts describe the area's sights; and local volunteers tend to the museum, the church, and guided tours of their town. There is contention among local history experts as to the derivation of the town's name. Some say it is meant ironically and refers to the

redoubtable efforts of the Hudson's Bay Company to set up a trading post here in the early 19th century. Others claim the name goes back to the old English sense of the word "hope," that is to say, a small valley. The local **museum** in the former general store of the Hudson's Bay Company houses a mixed collection ranging from prehistoric finds and trapping equipment through old waffle irons to a picture of Marga MacDoughall. This courageous woman handed out vitamin tablets to undernourished Indian children and taught Indian women how to knit in 1940 – at a time when contact with the native population was anything but fashionable. Romantic **St. Peter's Church** next door was built of logs at the

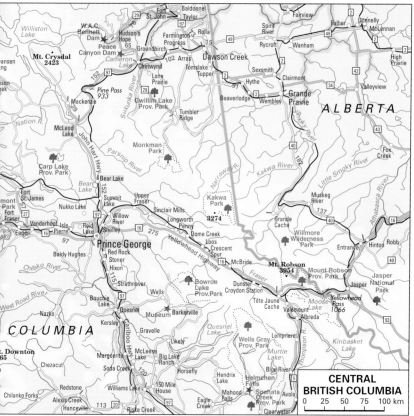

end of the 1930s. Hudson's Hope is picturesquely situated on the **Peace River**, a huge, meandering river with islands and rapids, which you can examine at closer range on a stroll along its banks in **Alwin Holland Park**. You can also take a lovely walk up to Cameron Lake (for maps and tips, ask at the tourist information center). But ther river also serves to generate electricity; the enormous structures of the **Peace Canyon Dam** (3 miles/5 km south of town) and the **W.A.C. Bennet Dam** (15 miles/24 km west of town) are open to the public. At the latter, you can examine an underground power station with gigantic turbines and generators and visit an exhibition about the dam.

The next stretch of Highway 29, continuing on to **Fort St. John**, is one of the most attractive in Western Canada, commanding breathtaking views out over the deep valley of the Peace River. (For a description of Fort St. John and the trip on the Alaska Highway, see p. 203.)

On the Yellowhead Highway to the Pacific

The wooden town of **Vanderhoof** has a small, attractive **Pioneer Museum** consisting of several buildings and a café serving traditional meals and home-baked goods. Vanderhoof is also the starting point for a detour up north to **Fort St. James**, attractively situated on

Stuart Lake, founded in 1806 by the explorer Simon Fraser. Here, the fur-trading heyday of the Hudson's Bay Company, around 1896, comes to life: dressed in period costume, the employees impart facts and tell anecdotes from the rough days of the frontier. Visitors can also taste salmon smoked in the original manner used by the native tribes.

Fort Fraser, to the west, has a pleasant small church, although this seems to be decidedly less frequented than the local bar. The latter is an ideal place to hear first-class fishermen's tales; you are, after all, about to enter "Lake Country." At the east end of **Fraser Lake**, the sand beaches of **Beaumont Provincial Park** lure visitors. The route then continues through ranch country to reach **Burns Lake**, a settlement consisting of little more than a main street lined with various stores. From Burns Lake, you can

Above: Carrying on old traditions in the Ksan woodcarving school Right: "Longhouse" in the Ksan Indian Village.

continue to **Tchesinkut Lake** and **François Lake**. François Lake boasts a ferry dock, departure point for a vessel that transports cars to the other side of the lake, to **Southbank**, several times a day. Overnight accommodations are available at **Uncha Lake** and **Takysie Lake** (lodge, cabins, camping facilities). Fishing, again, is *the* major activity in this region. For those more attracted by the idea of adventure than angling, the 5-day "Tweedsmuir Boat Trek" is one of the greatest outdoor experiences to be had in Western Canada. Starting at **Ootsa Lake**, the trek continues by boat through the almost inaccessible **Tweedsmuir Provincial Park**. Participants stay overnight in rustic cabins, portage the boats overland on rails, and are immersed in absolute solitude.

Further westwards on the Yellowhead Highway there is a turn-off in Topley to **Granisle** on **Babine Lake**. Since the copper mines here were closed, this small settlement has become a center for hobby fishermen.

Looking around the town of **Houston**, one can't help thinking that, lacking any real attractions for visitors, it creatively invented a few of its own. At the center of town visitors can admire the largest fishing rod in the world. What is more, the town boasts that the largest steelhead, a local and particularly contentious variety of trout, was caught here. Houston has also titled itself a "Forestry Awareness Community" and offers guided tours through "demonstration forests" and a sawmill.

Telkwa – in Cree the name means "where the rivers meet" – is a pretty, well-tended village whose buildings date back to 1908. Passing through here puts you in the proper frame of mind for **Smithers**, another neat-looking small town filled with chalet-style houses. Set at a right angle to the highway is the main street, a pleasant boulevard lined with stores and restaurants; and the town's set-

ting, against a backdrop of mountains, only heightens the agreeable overall impression. Smithers is a mecca for mountaineering and skiing enthusiasts in summer and winter alike; sports and mountaineering supply stores, mountaineering and skiing schools are all available. The Travel Infocentre is also happy to give advice on routes and has taken a few details about specific walking trails from an excellent published guide to hikes in the area (see "Guidepost").

Moricetown, a little ways along, offers a spectacular vista; from there, the route continues on to **Hazelton** (including South and New Hazelton). From the restaurant "Humming Bird" there are fantastic views of the **Seven Sisters Peaks**. The small town is so beautifully restored that it is like walking through a museum; its real attraction, however, is the **Ksan Indian Village**. In the 1950s the art of the Gitksan people, the first natives on the west coast, had almost completely disappeared. Granted, traditional celebrations were still held in private, but

hardly anyone still practiced the traditional fine arts and crafts. Then, in an attempt to preserve something of his people's culture, one member of the tribe set up a museum for works of art in 1959. The response from the tribe was overwhelming: nearly every family contributed valuable objects that had been created by their ancestors and handed down from generation to generation. The Ksan Village was created in 1970, and has been steadily enlarged ever since. Recreated here are the traditional longhouses of cedar planks, which were home to several families. Today, one of these houses accommodates a **woodcarving school**, in session from October to April; students complete their training in 4 years.

Another longhouse serves as a **museum**; even behind glass, the exhibits seem to exude some mystical power. One striking element here are the *bent boxes*, cedarwood boxes which were used for a variety of purposes: for storage, as coffins, for cooking, even as drums.

In the village park, **totem poles** tower up into the sky. The Gitksan hollowed out the wooden poles to make them lighter to transport, and carved various figures, faces and grimacing animals' faces in the red cedarwood. The poles were between 10 and 69 feet (3 and 21 m) high, depending on the importance of the clan chieftain in question. Somewhat comparable with the coat-of-arms in Europe, they could symbolize the clan, represent the relationship between man and animal, or serve as a kind of memorial to someone who had died. Prisoners were never tied to them, as the first Europeans assumed. Today, original totem poles are either in museums or rotting away somewhere in the inaccessible rain forests on the west coast. Only in a few cases is the original site accessible enough to permit visitors in to view them: in **Kispiox**, for instance, there are 15 poles with a variety of themes. A particularly attractive example is the famous totem pole *Hole in the Sky* in **Kitwancool**. It is the oldest totem still standing in its original location.

Kitwanga is the starting point for an interesting tour; the first stop might be **St. Paul's** missionary church, a log cabin structure dating back to 1893. **Kitwanga National Historic Site** marks the location of the country's only Indian fort, occupied by Tsimshian Indians who lived on an earthen hill within a palisade.

If you don't feel drawn to continue on to Alaska, turn off west at **Cranberry Junction**, some 22 miles (35 km) past Kitwancool Lake, and continue on an unpaved road (it's wise to check in Hazelton about its present condition and opening times) to **New Aiyansh**. Here, a visitors' center provides detailed brochures and maps on **Nisga'a Memorial Lava Bed Provincial Park**, an ecologically sensitive area that was created in the wake of a volcanic eruption some 300

years ago. The legend goes that boisterous native children caught a salmon and inserted small sticks of burning wood into its back. Shortly afterwards the earth started to quake, smoke and flames shot up over the land, and the mighty god Gwa Xts'agat sent lava streaming into the valley. Many of the Nisga'a Indians died, because the spirit of the mountain was angered by this wanton act. Fish was the native population's wealth; misuse of this treasure led to this disaster.

At Terrace, you come back to the Yellowhead Highway. **Terrace** may not be a very inviting place, but the **Heritage Park** here is well worth visiting: it features nine log cabins, dating from between 1910 and 1935, some of which serve as exhibition areas. Governing principle of the displays is evidently the notion that anything that anyone has found worth saving must be worth displaying. Terrace has a full range of stores and gas stations; it has to, since the next 82 miles (132 km) through the valley of the mighty, salmon-filled **Skeena River** (once an important route for Indians and settlers) is for the most part devoid of the trappings of civilization.

Anyone interested in getting better acquainted with the region should detour over to **Kitimat**, which lies on a Pacific fjord in the midst of the rain forest. Some 62 miles (100 km) southeast of here, 792,500 acres (317,000 ha) of boreal rainforest have been made into a protected area (campsites can be reserved). The forest lies in the tribal area of the Haislaa Indians, who refer to the region in their language as *husduwachsdu,* meaning "spring of cloudy-blue water." Kitimat itself is a center for various industrial plants, which are open to the public, including Eurocan Pulp & Paper, Methanax (petrochemicals) and Alcan (aluminium smelting).

Those making for Prince Rupert might like to stop off at **Prudhomme/Diana Lake Provincial Park**, which makes for

Right: Most important means of transportation in Prince Rupert: the seaplane.

a good picnic stop and also has two short yet attractive trails: the 1.2-mile (2 km) **Diana Creek Trail** and 1.5-mile (2.5 km) **MacDonald Trail**, the latter leading to a lookout which commands views of both lakes.

From Prince Rupert, it is worth making a detour to **Port Edward** to visit the old fish factory in the **North Pacific Cannery Village Museum**. This industrial memorial is an unpleasant reminder of conditions in factories at the turn of the century: people worked for a pittance in damp buildings, carefully segregated by ethnic groups: Europeans, native peoples and Chinese.

Prince Rupert

Rain is an all too common phenomenon in **Prince Rupert**: the lush vegetation of the coastal rain forest thrives on the rain clouds that hover over the mountains on the coast. The region around the **Khutzeymateen Inlet** is a typical rain forest area, as well as a protected area for

grizzlies (bear-watching tours leave from Prince Rupert). However, even within city limits you see enormous red cedars. If you're coming from Port Edward, there is a parking lot just before the industrial area. On the left side of the road a track leads to the **Tall Trees** and on to **Mount Oldfield**. On the right side you can walk to **Morse Basin** and, at **Butze Rapid Viewpoint**, observe a series of rapids that change direction with the tide. Go on past **Grassy Bay** to circle back to the parking lot.

Prince Rupert's residential areas are pleasantly located along the coast, but the downtown area is rather disappointing. If you follow the road to the old railway station you can visit the small **Kwinitsa Railway Museum** there, which recalls the heyday of rail transport and the busy harbor at the turn of the century. Railway tycoon Charles M. Hays did much to help the town. An iron stairway leads up to the center of town, where a **memorial park** documents how many locals died at sea: each brick in the sizable brick wall here bears the name of a single victim. The building with the tourist information office also houses the **Museum of Northern B.C.**, which sheds light on the 10,000-year history of settlement on the northwest coast with Indian arts and crafts, finds from the pioneer age, old photos and documents. Also here on Market Place is the **Court House**, a building dating back to 1921, set in a pleasant little park.

Continue three blocks west along 2nd Avenue and you come to an attractive ensemble composed of **City Hall**, the **Besner Building** (1928), and a totem pole and statue of Charles Hays. These last symbolize the most important influences on the city: the culture of the coastal Indians and trading.

The Inside Passage

The **Inside Passage**, the water route through the fjord-like landscape of the west coast, from **Prince Rupert** to Bear Cove near Port Hardy, is the highlight of any trip to Western Canada and understandably attracts large numbers of tourists: during the peak season, drivers should book at least two months in advance, although foot passengers and cyclists can travel at shorter notice. The **B.C. Ferries** are comfortable and a good range of quality food at reasonable prices is available both in the restaurant and cafeteria. Having said that, eating should not occupy too much of your time, as there is much to see on deck during this 20-hour journey. The ferry makes its way through a narrow, fjord-like channel past wooded islands; bald eagles circle overhead, and you can sometimes spot a gray whale. The ship doesn't stop anymore at Bella Bella, a lively community whose population is part native Indian. The 124-mile (200 km) stretch to Port Hardy is

Right: A cruise with impressive landscapes: the Inside Passage.

only a short section of the 12,400-mile (20,000 km) coastline.

As long as 10,000 years ago, hunter-gatherer peoples lived around these seemingly impenetrable fjords. However, it was not until George Vancouver charted the region and its economic potential came to light that the Europeans became aware of the area. Fur traders came and offered the Indians worthless goods in exchange for their valuable skins. A hundred years ago, it was gold-seekers who made use of this protected sea route on their journey to the gold fields of the Klondike. Next, a number of people out to make a fast buck recognized the enormous potential of the rich fishing grounds here and set up the first canning factories, such as the ones in Port Edward.

At the beginning of this century, groups of Scandinavian "utopists" arrived to found Christian communities in an attempt to flee industrial society. Most of those who tried their luck here failed on account of the poor soil, the inclement weather, and, above all, the isolated location. Even **Port Hardy** on Vancouver Island was still an inaccessible wilderness of rain forest as late as the 1920s.

QUEEN CHARLOTTE ISLANDS

Anyone who has the time should certainly travel to the **Queen Charlotte Islands**, whether by ferry (7-9 hours) or seaplane. More than 150 in number, these islands, sometimes nicknamed the Canadian Galapagos, are a paradise for a wide range of avifauna, misty rain forest oases with expanses of fantastic beach. On the other hand, the logging industry has left its mark in places. **Graham** and **Moresby** are the two largest islands in the group; ferries dock on Graham Island at the harbor in **Skidegate**. The Haida Indian longhouse on the beach is a popular subject for photos. The totem pole in front of it was fashioned by Haida artist

Bill Reid, and illustrates the history of the village in fascinating carvings.

The **Queen Charlotte Islands Museum** has excellent displays on the culture of the Haida Indians, as well as on the flora and fauna of the coastal rainforests.

There are roads along part of the east coast. You can take the Yellowhead Highway to **Tl'ell**, a farming community founded in 1904 by the legendary "Mexican Tom," who set up a ranch here in defiance of the harsh weather conditions. It lies at the edge of the 273-square-mile (700 sq. km) **Naikoon Provincial Park**. Naikoon means "long nose" in the Haida language, a fitting name for a park that seems, at its northern end, to poke out into the sea (Rose Spit). In the park you can wander through coastal rainforest from, for example, the Tl'ell River Bridge to the picturesque wreck of the *Pesuta*, a wooden ship that capsized here in 1928. In **Port Clements**, the **Port Clements Museum** sheds light on the difficulties of forestry and fishing on such

isolated islands. **Juskatla** is a painful reminder of how respect for other cultures and their religious beliefs can take a back seat to economic interests. Large-scale logging has cleared the area, and it's of little advantage that a Haida canoe that was discovered during the logging has been able to remain on the spot where it was found; for all that's to be seen around it is a forest of sad-looking stumps.

In the North lies the largest settlement on the islands, **Masset**. The Indian reservation of Old Masset, home to some 600 Haida Indians, has been restored as the **Haida Heritage Village**, where visitors can watch Haida artists at their woodcarving.

From Skidegate, you can take a boat south to neighboring **Moresby Island**. There, from **Sandspit**, a logging community, you can drive south to **Gray Bay** with its deserted sand beaches. Within **South Moresby/Gwaii Haanas National Park** is the Indian settlement of **Ninstints** on **Anthony Island**, which has been declared a UN World Heritage Site.

CENTRAL BRITISH COLUMBIA
Area Code 250 (Greater Vancouver: 604)
Accommodation
MOUNT ROBSON PROVINCIAL PARK:
MODERATE: **Mt. Robson Lodge**, Box 17, Valemont, tel. 566-44821, historic ranch with accommodation in log cabins.
WELLS GRAY PROVINCIAL PARK:
MODERATE: **Jasper Way Inn Motel**, 57 E Old North Thompson Hwy., Clearwater, tel. 674-3345. *BUDGET:* **Beaver Ranch Resort**, Box 518 Clearwater, tel. 587-6567, on Dunn Lake Rd., three magnificient log cabins on a private lake. **Dutch Lake Resort**, 361 Ridge Rd., Clearwater, tel. 674-3351, cabins and camping, site of Timberline Eco Adventures (see "Tips & Trips").
PRINCE GEORGE: *MODERATE:* **Coast Inn of the North**, tel. 563 0121, not exactly attractive, but well-run, with pools, sauna, and good food. *BUDGET:* **Roblyn Motel**, 3755 Hart Highway, tel. 962-7081, appealing little motel. *B&B:* The brochure *Explore Prince George* has detailed listings.
ALONG JOHN HART HIGHWAY: *CAMPING:* **BEAR LAKE: Crooked River Provincial Park**, tel. 565-6340, gorgeous spot on Bear Lake with sand beach. **Whiskers Bay**, Macleod Lake, tel. 565-9591, bungalows, campsites and restaurant, great location. **Pine Ridge Campground**, Mile 22 on Highway 29, tel. 262-3229, ideal location in the spectacular Peace River Valley.
HUDSON'S HOPE: *BUDGET:* **Sportsman's Inn**, 10501 Charter Ave., tel. 783-5523, very good value for money.
CAMPING: **Gething Park**, tel. 783-9901, well-kept campground which the community makes available free of charge, with showers.
BURNS LAKE / LAKELAND: *CAMPING AND LODGES:* **Beaver Point Resort**, on Tchesinkut Lake, tel. 695-6519, camping and wooden bungalows, small shop. **Moosehorn Lodge**, on Uncha Lake, tel. 694-3730, camping, lodge, riding, fishing, and gorgeous wilderness setting. **Takysie Lake Resort and Motel** on Takysie Lake, tel. 694-3367, lovely wooden bungalows and campsite in the middle of nowhere.
SMITHERS: *MODERATE:* **Hudson Bay Lodge**, 3251 East Highway 16, tel. 847-4581, well-tended, good food. **Stork Nest Inn**, 1484 Main St, tel. 847-3831, neo-Alpine style, pleasant and quiet.
HAZELTON: *MODERATE:* **Sportsman Kispiox Lodge**, on the road to Kispiox, tel. 842-6455, log cabin complex in a lovely setting, popular with fishermen.
CAMPING: **Ksan Campground**, tel. 842-5940, by the Ksan Indian Village, attractive riverside location.

KITIMAT: *CAMPING and MOTEL:* **Kitimat Motel**, 656 Dadook Cresc., tel. 632-6677, camping and bungalows, quiet and green.
PRINCE RUPERT: *BUDGET:* **Parkside Resort Motel**, 101 11th Ave., tel. 624-9131, pleasant hotel a bit north of downtown. **Aleeda Motel**, 900 3rd Ave. W, tel. 627-1367, centrally located, some rooms with kitchenettes. *B&B:* **Eagle Bluff**, 201 Cow Bay Rd., tel. 627-4955, nice house right on the water.

Restaurants
PRINCE GEORGE: Bamboo House, 1208 6th Ave., good Chinese. **BX Neighbourhood Pub**, Carney St./5th Ave., turn-of-the-century style, inside and out. **The Keg**, 582 George St., representative specimen of this steaks-and-salad chain. **Rosel's**, 1624 7th Ave., cozy, very good restaurant in an old house of wood and stone.
HUDSON'S HOPE: J&J Restaurant, fast food, good tacos and salads. **Sportsman's Inn**, good cooking in the dining room.
MACLEOD: Macleod Lake Lodge, nice restaurant on the lake.
BURN'S LAKE: Mulrannys Pub, snacks and plenty of beer.
HAZELTON: Humming Bird Restaurant, wonderful food and a gorgeous setting in view of the Seven Sisters mountain chain; terrace.
TERRACE: The White Inn, in the Coast Inn of the West, homey family restaurant.
PRINCE RUPERT: Peglegs, 101 1th Ave., by the memorial park; great view over the bay; good food, terrace. **Smile's Seafood Cafe**, 113 Cow Bay Rd.; tasty seafood and great desserts.

Museums
HAZELTON: Ksan Indian Village, Box 326, Hazelton, tel. 842-5544.
PORT EDWARDS: Cannery Village Museum, tel. 628-3538, May-Sept 10 am-7 pm, other times 10 am-4 pm Wed-Sun only.
PRINCE RUPERT: Museum of Northern B.C., tel. 624-3207, June-Sept, Mon-Sat 9 am-8 pm, Sun to 5 pm, other times Mon-Sat 9 am-5 pm.

Shopping
PRINCE GEORGE: Capricorn Strings, 1769 Nicholson St., large selection of folk music instruments.

Tips & Trips
INSIDE PASSAGE: reserve through B.C. Ferries, 1112 Fort St., Victoria; for reservations call 386-3431, late May-late September. Runs every second day in both directions. Prices run around $540 one way for two adults and a camper.
PRINCE GEORGE: Hiking has a new flavor when your luggage is transported by pack llama. **Strider Adventures**, tel. 963-9542.

PRINCE RUPERT: Tours to the **Khutzeyma-teen Valley**: *By Plane*: **Harbour Air**, tel. 623-1341, daily at 2 pm. *By Boat*: **Ecotours by Sunchaser Charters**, tel. 624-5472; 4-, 6- or 10-day trips, with bear-watching; care is taken not to disturb the natural habitat. There's a tremendous range of offers for cruises, boat charter, and fishing trips; contact the tourist information office for details.

BARKERVILLE: An old gold-diggers' settlement has been transformed into a museum village, open year-round, events and tours June-mid-Sept, 8 am-8 pm, tel. 994-3332.

LOGGING INDUSTRY: **Pulpmill/Sawmill Tours:** A number of wood-processing plants give informative tours of their facilities and even pose some critical questions. **North by Northwest Tourism Association** offers more details (see "Tourist Information"). **Northwood Pulp & Timber**, Prince George, tel. 562-3700. **Babine-Augier Tour**, a 33 mi/54 km self-guided interpretive tour with 9 stops; pick up the brochure at Burns Lake Infocentre, tel. 692-3773. **Houston Forestry Tours**, contact the Houston Chamber of Commerce, tel. 845-7640. **Kitimat Industrial Tours**, reserve through Travel Info Centre, Box 214, tel. 632-6294. **Hinton Weldwood of Canada**, tel. 403/865-2251, brochure available at the Tourist Centre in Hinton. **Chetwynd, Forestry Capital of Canada**, a hiking trail through the woods, with possible visits to Canfor & Canadian Forest Industry, by arrangement: Infocenter, tel. 788-3345.

HUDSON'S HOPE: W.A.C. Bennet Dam, tel. 783-5211, one-hour tour, 9 am-6 pm in summer; in winter by arrangement. Self-guided tour of the **Peace Canyon Dam**, tel. 783-5211, 8 am-4 pm.

CANOE: **Kanata Wilderness Adventure Ltd.**, Kanata, Box 1766, Clearwater, tel. 674-2774, also offers other tours including dogsled trips, riding, rafting, hiking.

WELLS GRAY PROVINCIAL PARK: Timberline Eco Adventures, 361 Ridge Rd., Clearwater, tel. 674-3351. Canoes, hiking, fishing, dogsleds.

RIDING: **Fort Graham Lodge**, Box 238, Hudson's Hope, tel. 783-5248, real wilderness lodge on Williston Lake, with charming owners; rides from one hour to tours of several days.

HIKING: Local tourist offices can recommend hiking routes. For the region around Smithers (Burns Lake to Kitimat), you can pick up Elmar Blix's excellent guide *Trails to the Timberline* (Fjelltur Books), available at the bookstore **Mountain Eagle Books** in Smithers, among others.

Transportation
PRINCE RUPERT: Greyhound Terminal, 822 3rd Ave., tel. 624-5090.

Tourist Information
Bowron Lake Provincial Park, tel. 398-4414. **Clearwater Travel Info Centre**, 425 E Yellowhead Hwy., Box 1988, Clearwater, tel. 674-2646; information about **Wells Gray** and **Spahats Creek Provincial Parks**, with leaflets and brochures for hikers and canoers. **Tourism Prince George**, 1198 Victoria St., tel. 562-3700. **District of Hudson's Hope**, Box 330, tel. 783-9901.

North By Northwest Tourism Association, Box 1030, Smithers, tel. 847/5227, excellent cooperative effort of the communities between Mt. Robson Park and Prince Rupert/Queen Charlotte Island; ask for the *Vacation Planner*.

B.C. Yukon Circle Tour: a brochure outlining this round-trip excursion through northern B.C. and briefly into the Yukon is available from the North by Northwest office.

Smithers Chamber of Commerce, Box 2379, tel. 847-5072.

Nisga'a Memorial Lava Beds: for information, contact B.C. Parks, Skeena District, 3790 Alfred St., Smithers, tel. 847-732.

QUEEN CHARLOTTE ISLANDS
Accommodation
LUXURY: **Langara Fishing Lodge**, tel. 873-4228, exclusive lodge on the island of Langara, pick-up service from Vancouver, a dream for anglers.

BUDGET: **Moresby Island Guest House**, tel. 637-5300, lovely lodge on the ocean right on Shingle Bay by Sandspit. **Dorothy & Mike's Guest House**, 3125 2nd Ave., tel. 559-8439, two pretty little wooden houses in a garden.

CAMPING: **Misty Meadows Provincial Park**, reservations: 847-7320, in Smithers: a dream campground with 40 mi/64 km of beaches, in the north of Naikoon Provincial Park.

Tips & Trips
Ferries to Queen Charlotte: **BC Ferries**, 1112 Fort St., Victoria: for reservations, call 386-3431. Departures from Prince Rupert daily except Tue, late May-late Sept., about $190 one-way for two adults and a camper. There's also **seaplane** service several times a week.

Drivers on the **Queen Charlotte Islands** should note that there are restrictions to access on some logging roads between 7 am and 5 pm. Information: 637-5436 (Moresby), 557-4212 (Graham).

Because of the Indian settlement Ninstints, **Anthony Island**, in **Gwaii Haanas N. P.**, is on the U.N.'s list of world heritage sites; it's only accessible by boat or plane from Sandspit. Info and reservations for individual travelers: Parks Canada, tel. 559-8818; Gwaii Watchman, tel. 559-8225.

THE VALLEYS OF SOUTHERN BRITISH COLUMBIA

**COLUMBIA VALLEY
OKANAGAN VALLEY
SIMILKAMEEN AND
TULLAMEEN VALLEYS
NICOLA VALLEY**

British Columbia (or B.C.) is best known as the province with the high mountains of the Columbia range, snow and glaciers, and seemingly never-ending forests; and people tend to associate it with winter sports and mountaineering. Fewer people know that B.C. also offers lake swimming, sand beaches, and even vineyards. Southern B.C. is traversed by three long valleys which run from the American border northwards to between 95 and 125 miles (150-200 km) into the province's interior. And here, in what is known as "Interior B.C.," the protected zone between no fewer than four mountain ranges (from east to west: the Rockies, the Purcell Mountains, the Selkirk Mountains and the Monashee Mountains) boasts a veritably Mediterranean climate, especially in the orchard and vineyard region of the Okanagan Valley.

COLUMBIA VALLEY

From Radium Hot Springs to Fort Steele

The contrast is amazing: anyone heading south out of the Rockies and through

Preceding pages: The little town of Fort Steele – a living folk museum. Left: Fire hydrant à la Kimberly.

Kootenay National Park in the early summer will be astonished at the gradual transition from bare, wintry tree branches to increasingly lush greenery. **Radium Hot Springs**, then, presents full-fledged summer: it isn't only the springs that are hot; the weather usually is, as well. Tourists in shorts sit outdoors in sidewalk cafés and eat ice cream. Located at the junction of Highway 95 and 93, the town consists of dusty-looking motels and restaurants decorated in *faux*-German-Alpine style. Opposite the "Old Salzburg Restaurant" is a building that's a cross between a fairy-tale villa and a fortress, presided over by a local character named Rolf Herr, a wood-carver who sells his antic sculptures in his own souvenir shop. The **thermal bath** itself, located further up the valley, evokes the spirit of the somewhat run-down spas you find in the former East Bloc. It's not exactly a haunt of the international jet set; nonetheless, it's pleasant enough, and a soak in the outdoor pool is very relaxing.

The broad valley of the **Columbia River**, especially enchanting in spring and fall, not only offers excellent opportunities for water sports, but has also become a center for golfers: the "big five" courses here are high up on the lists of Canada's best golf courses, at least in terms of popularity (see "Golf," p. 226).

139

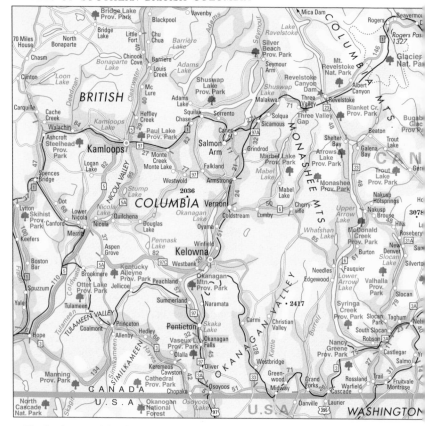

The landscape of the Columbia Valley south of Radium Hot Springs is equally beautiful: the Columbia River meanders along and broadens between Inverness and Canal Flats into **Lake Windermere** and **Columbia Lake**. In the background, the snow-covered Rockies form a stark contrast to the southern tip of the lake (**James Chabot Provincial Park**, with beach), where girls in bikinis stroll across the street, beach boys tote their surf-boards and it is not unusual to see someone sorting out his diving equipment in the middle of town.

Invermere is an attractive resort combining beach life, Western flair, touches of the pioneer era, and Alpine folk color. Those interested in the days of the pion-

eers should visit the **Windermere Valley Museum**, which depicts those days in exhibits spread through seven buildings. In the town center, in contrast, signs over shop doors have a slightly European accent: *Alpen Meats & Delicatessen*, or *European Sausage*.

Apart from the relaxed atmosphere of a bathing resort, **Windermere**'s attractions include the restored **General Store** and **Stolen Church**. The latter is a special feature of the town: when Celina Kimpton moved to Windermere from Donald, she missed her church so much that her husband Rufus took it apart, moved it, and rebuilt it in Windermere.

In the thermal baths of **Fairmont Hot Springs**, water temperatures range be-

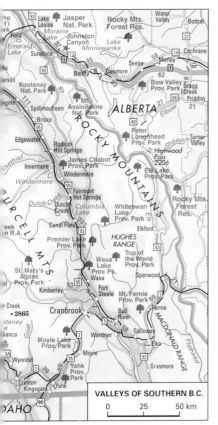

VALLEYS OF SOUTHERN B.C.

0   25   50 km

tween 84.5°F and 118°F (35°C and 48°C). On the way there, the landscape is not unlike vistas one encounters in Europe, notably in the Swiss Alps. The road crosses **Dutch Creek**, and at the roadside one can see fine examples of **hoodoos**, sandstone pillars of the type you can also see around Banff. Just after Canal Flats, a road turns off to **Whiteswan Lake Provincial Park** where the idyllic, natural **Lussier Hot Springs** bubble up out of the earth. Almost every Canadian who has visited the park has his own personal bear story to recount, and as more and more beer is consumed around the campfire, the bears become larger and more dangerous with each retelling. You can also hear stories about enormous fish and

bears in **Premier Lake Provincial Park** (turn off at Skookumchuck), another attractive park which also tends to be frequented mainly by Canadians.

Top of the World Provincial Park offers pure wilderness and nothing but. Even at the height of summer, when the ground is dry, the access road is at best an adventure; and it leads only to a parking lot from which the park itself is a two hours' walk away. But then one comes to **Fish Lake**, which is breathtakingly beautiful, and spectacular **Mount Morro** (9,522 feet/2,912 m) is near enough to touch.

Kimberly is one of the more questionable attractions in the Rockies. In 1972, when the local mine was forced to close down and the village was in danger of becoming a ghost town as its residents drifted away in search of jobs, some enterprising souls came up with the ingenious idea of creating a "Bavarian village." Grouped around the *Platzl* or main square are a blend of Bavarian souvenir shops, Swiss fondue joints, Black Forest restaurants and other outlets of a similar nature. The Canadian concept of the Alps seems over-generous at best: the *Schnitzelhaus* menu offers a Beethoven schnitzel – the composer's closest contact with the Alps having presumably been on journeys from his birthplace in Bonn to his later residence in Vienna – as well as a Louis Armstrong one. Kimberley is a good base for tours to the picturesque **Purcell Mountains**, and **St. Mary's Alpine Park** is ideal for hiking.

East of Kimberley is **Fort Steele**, a former outpost of the North West Mounted Police which has been superbly restored. The settlement came into being in 1864, when the gold rush spread to Kootenay Indian territory at Wildhorse Creek, but it didn't get its name until 1888, when it was christened in honor of commander Sam Steele, who succeeded through skilled diplomacy in preventing Indian uprisings. However, 1898 was the year

that the railroad bypassed the fort, opting instead for route through Cranbrook; and Fort Steele gradually became a ghost town. Not until 1961 did the concerted efforts of the provincial government result in the creation of **Fort Steele Provincial Historic Park**, an open-air museum with Victorian-style buildings and a costumed staff recreating the appropriate historic atmosphere. More than 60 buildings over this extensive area were restored: the smithy, the Windsor Hotel, the theater, the Prospector Print Shop and the churches. The bakery sells bread hot out of the wood-burning oven; the International Hotel serves Victorian dishes; and, walking on a wooden plank sidewalk past pioneer-age facades, you feel you've been transported back to the 19th century – although Dr. Watt's shingle promising *painless dentistry* doesn't inspire much confidence.

Above and left: A double adventure near Golden – river rafting and Abbott's Ridge Trail in Glacier National Park.

From Radium Hot Springs through Golden to Revelstoke

The drive from Radium Hot Springs northwards through Columbia Valley is so beautiful that it's hard to know where to look, or what to photograph: the river's winding course through the valley, the doughty mountains behind it, or the color accents provided by the red cars of passing freight trains.

Golden may not be a spectacular place in itself, but it's a good base for walkers, fishermen and whitewater rafters. The District Office stocks information on walks, such as the one to pretty **German Lake**. A boat tour on the Columbia River is also an interesting and relaxing activity. Anyone interested in the area's history should visit the **Golden and District Museum**, which has a range of information on everything from Swiss mountain guides to mining and other aspects of life in the pioneer age. The museum society also saved an old schoolhouse from Brisco and restored the old railway station –

on a rather modest scale, it's true, but appealing because of the human involvement and dedication that produced it.

From Golden, you can opt to drive west towards Revelstoke. Here, in the inaccessible wilderness of the Columbia Mountains, it becomes evident once again what tremendous effort must have been involved in continuing the construction of the railway and road. Not until 1881 did Major A. B. Rogers succeed in penetrating this far west into the **Selkirk Mountains** in his search for an appropriate route for the railway. Later, he was honored by bequeathing his name to **Rogers Pass**, a 4,339-foot (1,327 m) elevation atop which a visitors' center present exhibits about various natural disasters that have hit the area. In the 19th century, legion avalanches blocked the railway line time and again; today, the tracks run under the mountains through a 5-mile (8 km) tunnel. Here, in **Glacier National Park**, some 12% of the land is covered in ice; around 140 glaciers advance on the valley; and the weather is often just as unwelcoming as the glacier region itself.

In **Mount Revelstoke National Park**, the probability of rain or snow is even higher than in Glacier National Park. The pleasant town of **Revelstoke**, squeezed in between the Selkirk and Monashee mountains, is a typical railroad town. If the weather is good, it is worth taking a drive along **Summit Road** up to the top of 6,337-foot (1,938 m) **Mount Revelstoke**, from where you can hike, especially from the end of June to August, when the meadows are carpeted in masses of wildflowers.

Anyone fascinated by things technical should examine 572-foot-high (175 m) **Revelstoke Canyon Dam**, some 6 miles (10 km) further on, where the Columbia River is dammed to form **Revelstoke Lake**. A spectacular 87-mile (140 km) drive upstream leads to **Mica Dam**, at 791 feet (242 m) one of the highest dams in Western Canada (you can arrange for guided tours through the tourist information office in Revelstoke).

From Revelstoke to Kootenay Lake

The **Selkirks region** between the Purcell and Monashee mountains is a relatively isolated area. Rugged mountain scenery is interspersed with agricultural areas, which are particularly evident in the south between Nelson and Trail. Many of the farms in the **Kootenays** in the southeast are still worked by the Doukhobor, members of a religious community originally based in Russia which rejected military service and the oath of allegiance to the Czars. Persecuted at the end of the 19th century, they fled by the thousands to Canada, where they founded their own social system based on communal property. While the older generation tries to preserve its traditional values and language, the children are less interested in speaking Russian: they want to become Canadians like their friends.

Above: Alpine folklore draws tourists in interior B.C. Right: Orchards and vineyards line the slopes of the Okanagan Valley.

But the Kootenay region retains its own flavor in any case, lying somewhat off the main tourist routes and no longer of any significant economic interest: the boom period of silver mining is long since over.

Some of the former silver mining communities along the west bend of the Columbia River not only sank into oblivion, but quite literally sank altogether, swallowed by the rising waters resulting from the **Arrow Lake** dam project. Indeed, water plays a dominant role in this region; tourists delight in the romantic little ferries that stand in for absent bridges in many places along the river. You can cross, for example, from **Shelter Bay** to **Galena Bay**, from where one can continue on to **Nakusp**. Next to this is the town of **Nakusp Hot Springs**, where the two thermal baths remain at temperatures of 102°F and 111°F (39°C and 44°C) respectively. From Nakusp, you can reach the Okanagan Valley by taking the ferry across Arrow Lake from Fauquier to Needles and then continuing on Highway

6 through magnificent wild, deserted country.

Driving southeast from Nakusp on Highway 6 you come to **New Denver**, a sleepy place that would make an authentic setting for a movie about the pioneer age, although it is hard today to imagine the busy saloons or the shoot-outs that broke out among the miners. Even more imagination is required of the visitor to **Sandon**, which you reach by following a dirt road. All that is left of this once-bustling town are a few foundation walls and piles of rubble peeking out thrugh the greenery as nature reclaims the area. Yet in 1886, Sandon not only had some 5,000 inhabitants but also the luxury of electricity, while people in many other areas were happy if their petroleum lamps worked. To ensure that the town's history, at least, is not forgotten, there's a small **museum** with fascinating old photos.

Highway 6 heads south to **Slocan**, which provides the best access point for **Valhalla Provincial Park**. This 125,000-acre (50,000 ha) wilderness is ideal for backpackers who are up for walking to remote campgrounds set in the midst of unspoiled nature.

Nelson, on the banks of the Kootenay River, is an especially nice little town which has carried its Victorian charm over into the present, thanks to the loving restoration of more than 300 turn-of-the-century buildings. This is no open-air museum, however, but rather a vibrant little town which manages successfully to combine tradition and the modern.

Driving east from New Denver on 31A you come to **Kaslo**, where the *S.S. Moyie*, an old paddle-wheel steamer, now serves as a **museum** of local history. Another boat still operates on **Kootenay Lake**, some 22 miles (36 km) to the south: the ferry between Balfour and Kootenay Bay. Between Kaslo and the ferry dock is **Ainsworth Hot Springs**, once a cosmopolitan spa with thermal baths; the place has retained much of its charm, even if the venerable hotel has been replaced by a modern building.

OKANAGAN VALLEY

Many people who toy with the idea of emigrating to Canada dream of living either on Vancouver Island or in the Okanagan Valley. In terms of climate, the valley is blessed: winters are relatively mild, although there are a number of ski areas within a one-hour drive; spring begins dependably in April; and most of the rainfall is restricted to the month of June. After this, the area reminds one of nothing so much as Andalusia for three wonderful months: hot, dry sunny summers with temperatures higher than 86°F (30°C) mean that only sparse vegetation can grow on the mountain ridges, generally such plants of the arid vegetation zone as Ponderosa pine and sagebrush. In September and October, the foliage turns wonderful, brilliant colors which glow in the sun of the warm days of "Indian summer," while the grape harvest, Thanksgiving celebrations and other gourmet events are a last burst of exuberant life before the valley sinks into a short winter sleep. Axis of the landscape are the valley's clear, warm lakes: together, Osoyoos Lake, Skaha Lake and Okanagan Lake extend for 74 miles (120 km) through the valley, offering sand beaches and a full panoply of water sports.

Many years ago there lived in the valley a wise Indian who loved animals and was called *Old Kan-He-Kan*. One day the malicious *Kel-Oni-Won*, who was possessed by the devil, came and killed the old man. From that time on, the people in the valley called it "Okanagan" in the old man's memory, and asked the gods to avenge him. The gods accordingly let *Kel-Oni-Won* stew in his sins until he had turned into a horrible sea serpent called *Ogopogo*.

Originally, in the late 18th century, the land that is today a center for fruit-growers and vintners was devoted to cereal farming. At that time, the grain had to be transported out on packhorses, then transferred to canoe on its way to the markets outside the valley. When the railway arrived, local farmers were able to switch to fruit, since there was now a way to transport perishable produce quickly out of the valley, and, while grain could be cultivated in a number of areas, this region had a monopoly on the sunny, warm conditions necessary to grow fruit. The period between June and October sees the growth of cherries, apricots, pears, apples, plums and grapes; when the fruit is ripe for harvest, *U-Pick* signs indicate sites where the public can come in and gather their own bounty (for a price). Then there's the grape harvest: 11 of B.C.'s 14 wineries are located in the Okanagan Valley (see p. 228).

Keremeos, just before the main valley as you approach from the west, is noted for its fruit stands and especially for **Crisp Mill**, built in the year 1877. One of the last mills in Canada, this building is so well-preserved because its upper story has been put to a range of different purposes since its construction – it has served as everything from a chicken coop to an artist's studio – and the roof, therefore, has always been kept in good condition. After the mill ceased operations, nobody ventured into the lower story where the old machines were stored, kept away by rattlesnakes and stinging nettles. Today, the mill is a registered landmark because it is clear testimony to the course of technological progress. At first, the mill used huge millstones which crushed the grain. A first innovation were smaller millstones which only touched the grain briefly, separating the kernel from the husk. Next, machines with stationary millstones were developed; one from the year 1880 is of immeasurable value. The museum team was – and is, for the work is continuing – faced with the challenge of reconstructing the mill piece by piece,

Right: An endearing relic of technology and progress – Keremeos Crisp Mill.

a task that requires a good amount of detective work; sometimes it's by pure chance that someone figures out how one of the old pieces lying around fit into the puzzle. The mill is set in an attractive park where there are also exhibition grain fields and orchards. The **tea house**, with an outdoor terrace and a pleasant souvenir shop, offers old English charm and excellent baked goods.

Osoyoos, near the country's southern border, recalls the plains of Mexico, for cacti flourish here in the dry climate of the **ecological reserve** 5 miles (8 km) north of town. Such desert vegetation can also be found in some balmy spots further north in the valley. But the town itelf, attractively situated on a peninsula thrusting into the pleasantly warm waters of **Osoyoos Lake**, also has a hint of a Mexican or Spanish air.

In **Okanagan Falls**, a road turns off at the bridge to the **LeComte Estate**. The terrace of this excellent winery commands one of the best views in the whole valley (for wine tour information, see "Guidelines"). Fitting right in to this warm climate are the 130 different kinds of animals from around the world, including such exotic specimens as zebras, giraffes and rhinos, who dwell on the **Okanagan Game Farm**, 5 miles/8 km south of Penticton. Within this reserve, visitors can go on a 3-mile (5 km) safari by car.

Penticton, its name meaning "the place to stay forever" in the language of the Salish Indians, is the tourist center in the southern part of the valley. The city has more than 10 hours of sunshine a day during July and August and is picturesquely located between two lakes popular with swimmers, Okanagan Lake and Skaha Lake. The main promenade is at **Okanagan Lake**, where motels and restaurants line the sand beach and a paddle-steamer is anchored: the *S.S. Sicamous* was once the only means of crossing the lake. Today, it has gone into a much-deserved "retirement," but is still open to visitors. Art works, mainly by local artists, are on display at the **Art**

Gallery of the South Okanagan Valley. Many of the pictures have a vibrancy to them which is hardly surprising given the quality of life the region offers. For a comprehensive history of the region and its native peoples, visit the **Penticton Museum**.

There are northbound roads on both sides of Okanagan Lake. Traveling along the east shore brings you to **Okanagan Mountain Provincial Park**, which is very popular with mountain bikers and hikers.

The road along the west shore follows the rocky cliffs. Along this shore, the **provincial parks** are more the size of picnic sites – which is what they are intended to be. **Summerland** nestles amidst orchards between the cliffs; on Lakeshore Drive South, you can visit a trout farm and learn all about the life and death of the rainbow trout. Everything about **Peachland**, also surrounded by or-

Above: Kelowna – city of beach parties.
Right: Horse breeders on Shuswap Lake.

chards, is small, down to its tiny harbor and shopping arcade.

Kelowna

Kelowna is the next town of any size on Okanagan Lake, something drivers can infer from the daily rush hour on the pontoon bridge that leads from **Westbank** to the downtown area. Before crossing the bridge, you can take a left off the highway to the **Lakeview** neighborhood, where you can inspect **Butterfly World** and the adjoining **Parrot Island**. These consist of gardens and greenhouses filled with a wealth of tropical flora where colorful butterflies and parrots flit to and fro.

Insiders refer to **Kelowna** as "tiny town." These insiders are a pretty varied crew, running the gamut from rich yacht owners to back-to-nature hippies who reject consumer society and spend their summers here doing odd jobs when not engaged in what seems to be an endless beach party. Kelowna has a beautiful

City Park, built around **Veedam Park**, which was created in 1986 in recognition of Kelowna's Dutch sister city. At the waterfront are a playground for children and a sand beach. Near the intersection of Abbott and Bernard Streets is the landing of the paddle-wheel steamer **M.V. Fintrey Queen**, which offers round trips, with dinner, on Okanagan Lake. Pedestrians can continue their stroll along the shore, past the yacht harbor, over to the new complex of the **Lakefront Grand Hotel**, where the excellent restaurants are also open to non-residents. Past this are the modern apartment blocks which actually represent a fairly successful foray into modern architecture – fortunately, as they've come to dominate Kelowna's skyline.

On Cawston Avenue and Ellis Street is the **Orchard Industry Museum**, presenting everything you need to know about fruit cultivation. Another Ellis Street venue, at the corner of Queensway Avenue, is the **Kelowna Centennial Museum**, which displays everything from the culture of the native peoples to a trading post of 1861 vintage, stocked with everything a pioneer's heart could desire. Located in the same building is the **Kelowna Art Gallery**. Bernard Street, the city's main axis, will bring you back to City Park.

East of Highway 97 there are campgrounds and smaller beaches. Turn left at the hospital and you come to **Guisachan Heritage Park & House**. Built in an East Indian colonial style, this house was once the home of the Earl and Countess of Aberdeen; the gardens they planted here are the second-largest in the province of B.C., after the famous Butchart Gardens in Victoria.

Head along Highway 97 through the city and turn off left after Orchard Park to come to **Father Pandosy's Mission**. The native peoples were already using a form of crop rotation in fruit cultivation here when Father Pandosy secured himself an option to buy and began to farm the land in 1860. He trained settlers and held Catholic masses. Today visitors can see

149

the small church, the original log cabin, and several farm buildings.

From Vernon to Three Valley Gap

Vernon, in the north of the valley, is surrounded by three lakes: **Okanagan Lake**, **Swan Lake** and **Kalamalka Lake**. Driving up from the south you pass, on the southern outskirts of town, **Polson Park**, pleasant, shady gardens which even boast a floral clock.

Vernon is proud of its history, which is well documented in the **Vernon Museum & Archives** (in the civic center). On display are clothes and everyday objects from the pioneer age; perhaps most impressive are the old photographs of the period. Some 7.5 miles (12 km) north of town is the equally interesting **O'Keefe Historic Ranch**. Members of the family lived here from 1867, when they first began breeding cattle, until 1977. Corne-

Above: Wood represents natural wealth for the region around Revelstoke.

lius O'Keefe attained considerable wealth as a "cattle baron," and fathered nine children with his first wife, and five more with his second.

Vernon is also home to the **Okanagan Springs Brewery**, one of the few small breweries to make beer in accordance with the strict purity regulations laid down in the beer center of Bavaria, Germany; Canadians, growing connoisseurs of their national brew, have come to value this purity, as well.

Some 14 miles (22 km) northeast of Vernon is **Silver Star Provincial Park**, a recreation and skiing area (Silver Star Mountain Resort) roughly 35 square miles (90 sq. km) in area. Anyone venturing further north can visit the **Cheese Factory** in **Armstrong**. There are guided tours with cheddar cheese tastings on Mondays, Thursdays and Saturdays.

From Vernon, you can also detour through **Lumby** to **Mabel Lake**. Set in a pleasant valley, the lake and its surroundings are an ideal location for walking, fishing, bathing or just relaxing. **Sica-**

mous on **Shuswap Lake** proudly refers to itself as the "houseboat capital of Canada." Visitors often take a day trip on the paddle-wheel steamer *Phoebe Ann.*

Continuing east, you pass through **Revelstoke** on your way to the Rockies. Between Sicamous and Revelstoke, the **Enchanted Forest** is a questionable combination of nature trails, fairy-tale forest, garden-gnome hideout, children's playground and mini-land. On rainy days the operators even hand out umbrellas free of charge.

Equally unusual is **Three Valley Gap**: in the 1950s the Bell family built a small motel at the east end of Lake of Three Valleys. The motel earned itself a good reputation as a stop-over and was enlarged into a resort hotel; one feature, today, are its unusual honeymoon suites. One room is decorated like a cave, for all those who wish to spend their wedding night *à la* Fred and Wilma Flintstone.

Also in Three Valley Gap is a restored **Pioneer Village**, dating from around 1880. At that time, the **Golden Wheel Saloon** with its piano player was a special attraction, as it is again today; you may feel not unlike a bit player in a Western. From Three Valley Gap, a (very bad) gravel road leads to Mabel Lake.

SIMILKAMEEN AND TULAMEEN VALLEYS

Manning Provincial Park covers some 164,710 acres (65,884 ha) of land in the Cascades mountains, encompassing high mountain regions, sub-alpine meadows and two large, wild rivers: the **Skagit**, which flows into the Pacific, and the Similkameen, which runs into the Columbia River. Sadly, most people only drive through this park as a kind of transit area on their way from Vancouver to the Okanagan Valley. Yet Manning Provincial Park offers good hiking trails, routes for adventurous back-country trail rides, mountain bike trails and whitewater

canoe routes. In contrast to the better-known Rocky Mountain parks, this is truly a paradise for real fans of the great outdoors. That said, the park has shorter, easier walks, as well; brochures for these self-guided trails are available in the **Visitors' Centre**.

Driving through the **Similkameen Valley**, you reach **Princeton** with its pretty pioneer-age facades. Anyone interested in the history of this farming and mining region should visit the **museum**, where exhibits range from old farm equipment to displays about local geological conditions.

Though the town has little to offer n the way of spectacular sights, a visitor to Princeton will soon be aware of its inhabitants' pride in their town. Then again, it does have one rarity: **Princeton Castle**, a ruin with its very own story. This "castle" was initially a cement factory, built in 1908 during a period of optimistic belief in industrial progress. Just nine years later the dream was over. Some historians believe that a lack of the necessary raw material, limestone, led to the factory's demise. Others assume that a shortage of coal hampered the factory's operations. Shortly after it closed, an individual named Mr. George Edwards arrived in town. This man soon managed to convince the ladies of his abilities as a dancer and the men of his riding skills. He lived in seclusion near the factory and nobody realized that the man who was everyone's friend was in reality the notorious train robber Bill Miner. Miner was preparing a big heist in Kamloops, which turned out to be successful. Not that the town, or the factory, stood to profit: over the years, the factory became increasingly dilapidated and took on the aspect of an Irish castle ruin.

Today the castle is overgrown; you can walk around inside and fantasize about the past. Some enterprising local businessmen took up the theme and built a restaurant in the style of a medieval castle

next door; but nobody has yet managed to make a success of it. On the "castle grounds," as it were, there's a small lake with an idyllic little campground.

For the journey to Merritt, drivers are advised to take the minor road through the **Tulameen Valley**. This winding scenic route was once a trail for prospectors and the first settlers. In 1885, **Granite City** was the third-largest town in B.C., and more than 2,000 prospectors dug here for nuggets; but the veins of gold were already depleted by the turn of the century. The fortune-seekers left; the buildings fell into ruins; and only a few foundation walls remain today.

Coalmont was a small mining community whose last pit had to close in 1940. However, the venerable **Coalmont Hotel** still attracts visitors today, thanks to its picture-perfect Wild West appearance. **Tulameen** was also a bustling town at the time of the Granite Creek gold

Above: Huge farms are the norm in the area around Kamloops.

rush, with hotels and saloons, loose women and gamblers; but today, its population is no more than 250. From Tulameen, you can continue to **Otter Lake Provincial Park**, a pretty place for picnics.

Merritt may lie at the important intersection of the **Coquihalla Highway** with Highway 97c, but it has nevertheless remained a sleepy provincial town with little to attract visitors. Its only sight is the **Coldwater Hotel** downtown, dating from 1910.

NICOLA VALLEY

North of Merritt begins the **Nicola Valley**, one of the most attractive small-scale landscapes in B.C. The region took its name from the Nicola Indians, who kept Canada in suspense for weeks in 1995 with their ranch blockade; the evening news provided a running commentary. The Nicola had blocked the entrance to the **Douglas Ranch** in protest, not wanting to accept the curtailment of their hunting rights on the ranch grounds. One of the largest cattle farms in B.C., the Douglas Ranch lies in a hilly, rough area, beginning somewhat abruptly behind the golf course in Quilchena: a territory only recommended to experienced outdoorsmen. **Quilchena** consists of an old **general store** and the charming **Quilchena Hotel**, built around the turn of the century, which has the look of an English villa, complete with a pub and dining room that wouldn't be out of place in an English country house. You can book a range of outdoor activities here, including renting a mountain bike for the gravel road to picturesque **Douglas Lake**. The nine-hole **golf course** with RV park is also popular with visitors.

Kamloops, a settlement founded by the Hudson's Bay Trading Company in 1812, is today an important crossroads and service center for a large portion of the surrounding countryside. However, Kamloops also lies in the middle of the Sushwap and Salish Indians' ancestral territories: the excellent **Secwepemec Native Heritage Park**, a faithful reconstruction of a Secwepemec Indian village, was set up on the site of a settlement 2,400 years old. More recent history is highlighted at the **Kamloops Historical Museum**, which documents the activities of the Hudson's Bay Trading Company. There are also exhibits on the age of industrialization and on Kamloops' position as the "meat capital" of B.C.; the town is a major center for cattle and sheep breeding.

Passing through irrigated orchards around **Kamloops Lake**, you come into a dry valley by **Walachin**. What looks like rotting wood at the side of the highway are in fact the remains of an ambitious plan. In 1907, the marquis of Anglesey wanted to establish an irrigated area here in order to build an English country home amidst a sea of flowers. But his plan backfired when the workers he engaged were drafted for World War I.

VALLEYS OF SOUTHERN BRITISH COLUMBIA
Area Code 604
Accommodation
RADIUM HOT SPRINGS: *BUDGET:* **Blakley's Bungalows**, tel. 347-9918, pretty bungalows located within the national park, within walking distance of the thermal baths.

GOLDEN: *MODERATE:* **Kapristo Lodge**, Box 90, tel. 344-6048, homey yet luxurious. *BUDGET:* **Columbia Valley Lodge**, Box 2669, tel. 348-2508, comfortable, nice location, good food, and a base for tours into the wetlands.

GLACIER MOUNTAIN NATIONAL PARK: *LUXURY:* **Purcell Lodge**, c/o Alpine Wilderness Adventures, Box 1829, Golden, tel. 344-2639, absolutely isolated lodge which you reach in a day's hike or by helicopter.

REVELSTOKE: *MODERATE:* **Best Western Wayside Inn**, 1901 Laforme Blvd., tel. 837-6161, pool, sauna, restaurant. **The Regent Inn**, 112th St. E, tel. 837-2107, attractively furnished smallish hotel with very good restaurant. *BUDGET:* **Canyon Motor Inn**, Trans-Canada Hwy 1 & Columbia River Bridge, tel. 837-5221.

THREE VALLEY GAP: *MODERATE:* **Three Valley Gap Motel**, Box 860 Revelstoke, tel. 837-2109, pool, restaurant, 12 mi/19 km W of Revelstoke.

INVERMERE: *MODERATE:* **Panorama Resort**, Panorama, tel. 342-6941, ideal for sportsmen.

WILMER: *B&B:* **Delphine Lodge Country Inn**, tel. 342-6851.

FAIRMONT HOT SPRINGS: *MODERATE:* **Fairmont Hot Springs Resort**, Box 10, tel. 1-800-663-4979, pools, golf course, restaurants, camping. *CAMPING:* **Timber Resort**, camping and bungalows, 4 mi/7 km S of town, tel. 345-6636.

KIMBERLY: *BUDGET:* **North Star Motel**, tel. 427-5633 or 1-800-663-5508, on the road towards Radium, nice and well-tended.

NASKUP: *CAMPING:* **Naskup Hot Springs Camping**, tel. 265-4528, lovely location on the river.

AINSWORTH HOT SPRINGS: *MODERATE:* **Ainsowth Hot Springs Resort**, Box 1268, tel. 1-800-668-1171.

NELSON: *BUDGET:* **Lord Nelson Hotel**, 616 Vernon St., tel. 352-7211, historic building with pub at the center of town. *B&B:* **Emory House**, 811 Vernon St., tel. 352-7007, romantic English cottage with water views. **Inn the Garden**, 408 Victoria St., tel. 352-3225, Victorian house with antiques and a beautiful garden.

PENTICTON: *MODERATE:* **New Penticton Inn**, 333 Martin St., tel. 492-3600, new, tastefully furnished house, very good value for money. **The Clarion Lakeside Resort**, 21 Lakeshore Dr. W, tel. 493-8221, expensive, but good, set on the shores of Okanagan Lake. **Three Gables Hotel**, 353 Main St., tel. 492-3933, lovely little place, central, with pub and restaurant. *B&B:* **Lost Moose Lodge**, tel. 490-0526, gorgeous setting; call in advance to ask about availability and directions. *CAMPING:* **Todd's Tent Town**, tel. 767-6644, .5 mi/1 km N, right on the water.

PEACHLAND: *BUDGET:* **Edgewater Inn**, 5830 Beach Ave., tel. 767-9191, tidy, down-to-earth. *CAMPING:* **Peach Orchard**, on the water.

KELOWNA: *LUXURY:* **Grand Okanagan Lakefront Resort**, 1310 Water St., tel. 763-4500, new and elegant; magnficent waterside location; lovely restaurants; a range of activities. *MODERATE:* **Hotel Eldorado**, 500 Cook Rd., tel. 763-7500, lovely place right on the water, partly furnished with antiques; good restaurant. *BUDGET:* **Misson Park Inn**, 3339 Lakeshore Rd., tel. 762-2042, lovely large rooms, terraces, not far from the beach. *CAMPING:* **West Bay Beach Resort**, Westbank, tel. 768-3004, quiet campground in a lovely setting.

SICAMOUS, the self-styled "Houseboat Capital of B.C.," is the place to go if you want to spend your vacation in a houseboat; see "Tips & Trips" for addresses.

MANNING PROVINCIAL PARK: *MODERATE:* **Manning Park Resort**, Manning Park, tel. 840-8822, hotel resort with a range of activities: hiking, camping, riding, canoeing, mountain biking, skiing, fishing.

PRINCETON: *MODERATE:* **Princeton Hotel**, 258 Bridge St, tel. 295-3355, centrally located hotel with a Western flair. *CAMPING:* **Castlepark Camping**, tel. 295-7988, campground by the romantic "factory castle."

COALMONT: *MODERATE:* **Coalmont Hotel**, tel. 295-6066, historic hotel.

NICOLA VALLEY: *MODERATE:* **Quilchena Hotel & Resort**, Quilchena, tel. 378-2611; lovely rooms furnished with antiques; riding, hiking, mountain biking, golf. *CAMPING:* **Nicola Valley RV Park**, tel. 378-2923, very well-kept, next to a golf course.

KAMLOOPS: *MODERATE:* **Coast Canadian Inn**, 339 St. Paul St., tel. 372-5201, pool, restaurant. **Days Inn**, 1285 W Trans-Canada Hwy. 1, tel. 374-5911, heated pool, jacuzzi, restaurant. **Stockmen's Hotel**, 540 Victoria St., tel. 372-2281, restaurant.

Restaurants

GOLDEN: **Big Bend Hotel**, 429 N 9th Ave., good pasta and steaks; live bands perform at "Packer's Place."

RADIUM: **The Old Salzburg Restaurant**, tel. 347-6553, café ambience, good food.

INVERMERE: **Myrtle's Restaurant**, pretty, historic house with garden, tel. 342-0281. **The Lakeside Inn**, pub and bar with terrace and lake views. **Chalet Edelweiss**, fine food in a pleasant atmosphere, tel. 342-3525.

PENTICTON: **Theo's**, 687 Main St., very good Greek place. **Earl's**, 1848 Main St., salads and pasta in the usual good form. **The Barking Parrot Bar**, 21 Lakeshore Dr. W; bar, pub and lakeside terrace. **Salty's Beach House**, 100 Lakeshore, excellent, innovative Thai and Caribbean cuisine. **Saba's**, 988 Lakeshore, Italian cuisine, trendy crowd.

SUMMERLAND: **Shaughnessy's Cove**, Sunday brunch and diverse daily specials, live music, and a great lakeside location, tel. 494-1212.

KELOWNA: **Café Safari**, 3151 Lakeshore Dr., African fare. **Mekong**, 223 Bernard Ave., tel. 763-2238, very good Vietnamese restaurant. **Williams Inn**, 526 Lawrence Ave., tel. 763-5136, charming renovated old house with fine food, featuring game.

VERNON: **The Sundowner**, 2501 53rd St., tel. 542-5142, pleasant restaurant with pasta, seafood, steaks. **The Sundowner Ranch House**, on the O'Keefe Ranch, tel. 542-2178, classic Western cooking.

SICAMOUS: **Mara Lake Inn**, comfortable and good restaurant in a lovely lakeside location, tel. 836-2126.

PRINCETON: **The Apple Tree**, 255 Vermillion Ave., tel. 295-7745; the building once belonged to the owner of BC Energy Princeton, one of the last private energy utilities in Canada. Today, a former geologist operates the restaurant, which has won a number of awards.

MERRITT: **Coldwater Hotel**, very good Tex-Mex, tel. 378-2821.

Museums

FORT STEELE: **Fort Steele, Heritage Town**, tel. 489-3351, 9:30 am-sunset, admission charged only from June-late September.

PENTICTON: **Art Gallery of the South Okanagan**, 11 Ellis St., tel. 493-2928, Tue-Fri 10 am-5 pm, Sat & Sun 1-5 pm. **Penticton Museum**, 785 Main St., open June-September daily 10 am-5 pm, other times Mon-Sat 10 am-5 pm.

KEREMEOS: **The Crisp Mill**, tel. 499-2888.

KELOWNA: **Father Pondosy's Mission**, Benvoulin Rd., Kelowna, tel. 860-8369, Easter-mid-Oct, 8 am-dusk.

Butterfly World/Parrot Island, 1190 and 1160 Stevens Rd., Kelowna, tel. 769-4408 and 769-6911, April-Oct, 10 am-4 pm.

VERNON:**Vernon Museum**, 3009 32nd Ave., tel. 542-3142, Mon-Sat 10 am-5 pm. **O'Keefe**

Ranch, 7 mi/12 km N of Vernon on Highway 97, tel. 542-7868, May-Oct 9 am-5 pm.

KAMLOOPS: **Historical Museum and Archives**, 207 Seymour St., tel. 828-3576, closed Mon; objects relating to local history.

Tips & Trips

EDGEWATER: **Edgewater Market** (signposted), Saturdays 10 am-1 pm, farmers' market with produce and homemade knickknacks. Come early before all the best things are gone.

RADIUM: **Radium Hot Springs**, open mid-May-mid-Oct. 9 am-10:30 pm, other times noon-8 pm, tel. 347-9485.

INVERMERE: **Art Exhibit**: SW of town (Westside Road/corner of Johnson Road) there's an open-air art show from mid-July to mid-August, daily noon-7 pm; for information call 342- 6341.

PENTICTON: Every year in mid-August is the week-long **Peach Festival** with sporting events, music, dance, and a parade on Saturday. At the end of August is the **Ironman Triathlon**, one of the hardest in the world. From late September to mid-October there's the popular **Okanagan Wine Festival**, with wine-tastings, wine-pressing (by foot), baking contests, seminars and dancing. Information: 861-6654, or pick up the brochure *Okanagan Wine Festivals* at the tourist office.

WINE TOURS: For detailed information about the wines of the **Okanagan Valley**, including a brochure with descriptions of each vineyard, arranged by varietal, contact the **B.C. Wine Institute**, Suite 5, 1864 Spall Rd., Kelowna, tel. 762-4887.

Tours and activities in individual wineries, as well as special gourmet events, are arranged by **B.C. Wine Trails**, Box 1077, Summerland, tel. 494-7733. In **Penticton**, among others: **Cartier Wines**, 2210 Main St., tel. 492-0621 and **Hillside Cellars**, 1350 Naramata Rd., tel. 493-4424; both offer free guided tours with wine-tastings.

SUMMERLAND: **Trout Farm**, 13405 Lakeshore Dr., tel. 494-0491, daily 8:30 am-3 pm.

VERNON: **Okanagan Springs Brewery**: enquire at 542-2337 about guided tours.

FRUIT TOURS: **Harker's Fruit Ranch**, on Highway 3, Crawston, tel. 499-2751. **Summerland Sweets**, 6202 Canyon View Drive, Summerland, tel. 494-0377. **Sun-Rype Products**, 1165 Ethel St., Kelowna, tel. 470-6417. **Appleberry Farm**, 3193 Dunster Rd., Kelowna, tel. 868-3814, Tue-Sat 10 am-5 pm, Sun 11 am-5 pm.

FOREST TOURS: **Invermere Forest District**, 625 4th St., Invermere, tel. 342-200.

BOAT RENTAL, HOUSEBOATS & SAILBOATS: **Sicamous Chamber of Commerce**, Box 346, Sicamous, tel. 836-3313, the office has a complete list of providers of houseboat vacations.

Riverside Marina, P.O. Box 862, Sicamous, tel. 836-4253, rents motorized pontoons; you can put your camper on them and ship it around. **Okanagan Boat Charters**, 291 Front St., Penticton, tel. 492-5099, motorboats and sailboats; a great way to explore the valley. **Houseboating on Shuswap Lake**, contact Shuswap Lake Tourism, Box 1670, Salmon Arm, tel. and fax 832-5200.

ORGANIZED BOAT TOURS: Animal-watching trips into the **wetlands** of the **Columbia River**: **Eco Excursions**, Box 1990, Golden, tel. 344-5060 or **Kinbasket Adventures**, Box 4137, Golden, tel. 344-6012, or **Columbia River** Wetland Tours, tel. 344-5979.

Departing from **SICAMOUS**: **tours on Shuswap Lake**, Sun 12:30 and 3 pm (two-hour trips), Tue 9:30 am-4 pm, with lunch; Thu 9:30 am-4 pm, tel. 836-2200.

HELICOPTER: **Alpine Heli Tours**, tel. 345-6116, for reservations and information, contact the Panorama Resort/Invermere, tel. 342-6941. **Canadian Helicopters**, Penticton Base, tel. 492-0637.

RAFTING on Toby Creek and the Kootenay River: **Fairmont Mountainside Villa Recreation Centre**, tel. 345-6341. **Purcell River Odysseys**, tel. 342-6941 (Panorama Resort).

MOUNTAIN BIKE RENTAL: **IGA Mall Invermere**, tel. 342-3517. **The Bike Barn**, 300 Westminster Ave. W, Penticton, tel. 492-4140.

RIDING: **Apex Mountain Resort**, tel. 492-2880, tours of one or several days on old "Gold Rush Trails," also mountain biking. **Apex Mountain Guest Ranch**, W of Penticton, Green Mountain Road, tel. 492-2454, day tours or longer excursions, Western style; excellent breeder of Norwegian ponies. **Top of the World Guest Ranch**, Box 29, Fort Steele, tel. 426-6306, marvelously situated ranch with riding, canoeing and fishing. **Mistaya Outfitting**, Hwy. 61, Silverton (S of New Denver), tel. 358-7787, day trips and longer excursions.

Shopping

FarWest is a well-known producer of Gore-tex clothing; a factory outlet sells remainders and seconds. Vernon, Highway 6, tel. 545-9048.

Tourist Information

Columbia Valley Chamber of Commerce, Box 1019, Invermere, tel. 342-2844. **Kamloops Infocentre**, 10 10th Ave., tel. 374-3377. **Kootenay Country Tourist Association**, 610 Railway St., Nelson, tel. 352-6033. Penticton Information Centre, 185 Lakeshore Dr. W, tel. 492-4103. **Tourism Association of Okanagan/Similkameen**, 1332 Water St., Kelowna, tel. 860-5999. **Manning Provincial Park**, Zone Manager, Box 3, Manning Park, tel. 840-8836, or contact the Manning Park Resort (see "Accommodation").

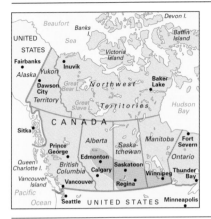

THE PRAIRIE PROVINCES

SOUTHERN MANITOBA
SASKATCHEWAN
CENTRAL ALBERTA

Knowing the meaning of names is not a Canadian strength – they're still debating the origins of the name of their own country, although critics might poitn out that this uncertainty isn't calculated to help much in the country's search for its national identity. The most likely explanation is that when, in 1535, the French explorer Jacques Cartier asked the Huron-Iroquois the name of their country they replied *Kanata,* meaning "village" or "huts." A more tongue-in-cheek explanation would have it that in 1811, the French-speaking settlers were only allowed to have one beer a day, and the cynical English settlers coined the term *A can a day*, a phrase that was later corrupted into the country's name.

It is perhaps less surprising that the origins of the names of the individual provinces are unclear. Saskatchewan probably comes from the Cree word *kisiskatchewan,* meaning "quickly flowing water." Most attractive of the various etymologies of the name Manitoba is that it is a combination of the two Cree words *Manitou Napa,*"country of the great spirit" – not a bad choice for such a wide

Preceding pages: Grain elevators – cathedrals of the prairie. Left: The West Edmonton Mall – the world's largest roofed shopping and recreation center.

open province. The Canadians call it the *big sky:* a flat strip of land stretching away to the horizon, almost humbly making way for a blue Canadian sky traversed by high, restless clouds. In Manitoba, Saskatchewan and large sections of Alberta, Europeans can only sigh and comment, with a mixture of wonder and envy, So much room...

The expression "Prairie Provinces" is somewhat misleading: the only true grass prairie here is in Grasslands National Park in southern Saskatchewan. "Prairie" has come to be used as a general term that also applies to the fields of grain stretching farther than the eye can see.

SOUTHERN MANITOBA

Winnipeg

The wheat-trading center of **Winnipeg**, capital of the province of Manitoba and the fourth-largest city in Canada, is a friendly place, compact in spite of its considerable size – some 650,000 inhabitants – multicultural and, by Canadian terms, with a long historic pedigree, to boot.

In 1738, the French trapper Pierre Gaultier de La Vérendrye arrived in Cree and Assiniboine Indian territory and set up a fur trading post (Fort Rouge, later

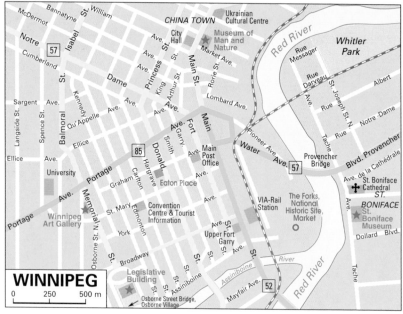

WINNIPEG
0   250   500 m

rechristened Upper Fort Garry) at the confluence of the Red and Assiniboine Rivers. For the first time, an interloper dared to challenge the monopoly of the Hudson's Bay Company. In 1763, the Treaty of Paris awarded Canada to Britain, and British fur traders from New York proceeded to set up their own trading posts, eventually joining to form the North West Company; in 1821, however, under pressure from the British government, they were assimilated into the Hudson's Bay Company. This came not a moment too soon, given the conditions of the moment. The Earl of Selkirk, a representative of the Hudson's Bay Company, had been giving land to penniless Scots and Irish since 1812, and this led to constant conflicts between the two trading organizations. And there was yet another group fighting for its rights: the Métis, people of mixed native and French blood, saw a growing threat to their traditional

Right: "Mounted" mountain bike policeman in front of St. Boniface Cathedral.

way of life. The conflict escalated on numerous occasions; the worst episode took place in 1816, when the Métis slaughtered 20 settlers. In 1870, the Company sold its territory to the Canadian Dominion. Under the leadership of Louis Riel, the Métis rose up again, with the result that they were allocated land on the Red River (see "History," p. 41).

At the confluence of the Red and Assiniboine Rivers, an area known to the Cree as *win nipi* (muddy water) is a site of great historical importance: **The Forks**. Declared a **national historic site**, this park (east of Main Street and the west bank of the Red River), covering some 55 acres (22 ha), offers an ideal first introduction to the city of Winnipeg. Within it are colorful covered markets offering all kinds of edibles and snacks; restaurants with outdoor seating; and Johnston Terminal, which houses shops and an exhibition about all of the regions of Canada. Located here, too, is the **Children's Museum**, a wonderful imaginative place that combines the didac-

tic with the entertaining and even includes a children's television studio.

A walk along the river bank leads to **Upper Fort Garry**, now somewhat hemmed in between new modern buildings and the enormous complex of Hotel Fort Garry, but in fact giving a good picture of just how tiny this early trading post really was. The **Riverwalk** continues along the Assiniboine River to the seat of local government, the **Legislative Building**, built in 1920, with its trademark dome perched atop slender columns. Two bronze bison, the province's symbol, flank the staircase in the lobby; while atop the 235-foot (72 m) dome is *Golden Boy*, a 5-ton gilded bronze statue which has become a city hallmark. He faces north, where Manitoba hopefully projects its economic future. The torch in his right hand stands for progress, while the sheaf of wheat in his left represents the cornerstone of the province's industry. On the southern bank of the Assiniboine River is the oldest park in Winnipeg, **Assiniboine Park**, with a zoo and an English garden.

Balmoral Street leads to Winnipeg's excellent **Art Gallery**, which contains contemporary Canadian art, international art from the 16th century on, an outstanding Inuit collection, photographs and porcelain. For all of its valuable art, there's nothing stuffy about this venue, which offers a range of hands-on programs (lasting anywhere from several hours to several days), films, and special events for children, all helping to make it a lively place to visit.

Portage Avenue and Kings Street bring you to the **Exchange District**, named for the **Winnipeg Commodity Exchange**, which was once the largest wheat exchange in the world. The visitors' gallery is open from 9:30 am to 1:15 pm. **Market Square**, on the corner of Kings Street and Bannatyne Avenue, is the neighborhood's lively hub, lined with bars and restaurants – although it only really bustles in summer.

There's a local saying that Manitoba has seven months of Arctic winter and five months of cold weather. Icy storms and temperatures of below -22°F (-30°C) tend to freeze Winnipeg's *joie de vivre* a bit, as locals evade the weather in the city's underground shopping arcades (Portage Avenue / corner of Main Street).

Every visitor, even those who don't like museums, should make a point of going to the ingenious **Museum of Man and Nature** (Main St./Rupert St.). The museum's realistic recreations of Manitoba's landscapes, nature and native life incorporate pictures, sounds and smells. Visitors can clamber aboard a replica of the **Nonsuch**, the sailing ship that left England in 1668 to find the Northwest Passage. The replica was built in 1970 to mark the 300th anniversary of the Hudson's Bay Company and sailed almost 14,000 miles (22,600 km) before putting down anchor for good in this museum. Equally interesting is the **Aviation Museum** at the airport, the second-largest aviation museum of its kind in Canada.

Kings Street and Rupert Avenue mark the boundaries of Winnipeg's small **Chinatown**, which, although small, has its own **cultural center** in the Dynasty Building. Entrance to this quarter is through the **China Gate** which leads from Logan Avenue to James Avenue.

Not far away, in the **Ukrainian Cultural and Educational Center** (184 Alexander Ave. East), Manitoba's Ukrainian community presents its history and culture, including folk art.

On the other side of the Red River is the French-Canadian quarter of **St. Boniface**. In 1890 the French language was banned in schools and in administrative or public capacities. Although Winnipeg has the largest French-speaking community west of Quebec, it wasn't until 1980 that bilingualism became set in a code of law. The history of the quarter can be followed in the **St. Boniface Museum**, housed in a venerable oak log

Right: Nature-watching by canoe – Oak Hammock Marsh.

building dating back to 1844 – positively antique by western Canadian standards. St. Boniface is proud of its long history: its Catholic Hospital of Grey Nurses is the oldest in Western Canada. Louis Riel, the French-Canadian who fought for the rights of the Métis, is buried in the cemetery of **St. Boniface Cathedral** (built in 1818, later destroyed and rebuilt several times). Riel was exiled after the 1870 rebellion, but returned in 1885 (as an American) to take part in a Métis uprising in Saskatchewan. He surrendered, and after a dramatic trial was hanged; but his sentence is still contested today (see "History," p. 41). **Riel House**, his birthplace in the south of the city (330 River Road) has been restored in the style of 1885, the year he was executed, and is open to the public.

Osborne Village, south of Osborne Street Bridge, is a charming shopping street and hangout for students and Bohemians.

Excursions in and around Winnipeg

Manitoba has several regions with Mennonite settlers. The Mennonites are Christians in the Calvinist tradition who fled their native countries to escape compulsory military service (see "History," p. 42). From 1874 on, Mennonites began arriving in Manitoba from Switzerland, Holland, northwestern Germany and the Ukraine; some continued their journey on as far as Mexico and Paraguay. In **Steinbach**, southeast of Winnipeg, there is a fascinating open-air museum, the **Mennonite Village Museum**, which gives insights into the life of the community. The items displayed document every aspect of Mennonite life, from an old piano to a covered children's sled. An old barn has been restored and converted into an excellent restaurant, where you can sample everything from complete Mennonite meals to smaller dishes such as borscht, a Russian-Ukrainian red beet soup.

Once a year in mid-July, the prairie town of **Morris** south of Winnipeg is the site of the second-largest rodeo in Canada: the *Manitoba Stampede*.

If you're driving north, it's worth detouring, at the intersection of River Road and Highway 410, to the missionary church of **St. Andrews**, which saw its first flowering under the Reverend James Hunter between 1855 and 1865. Hunter and his wife not only taught the Cree Indians about the Bible, but also instructed them in such practical skills as farming, spinning and weaving.

Lower Fort Garry, near Selkirk, has been beautifully restored. After an 1826 flood had wiped out the settlements of Win Nipi and Upper Fort Garry, Governor George Simpson had this new stone fort built some 19 miles (30 km) upstream. However, he failed to appreciate that peoples' lives centered around the confluence of the two rivers and that few were prepared to make the long journey north for shopping or trading; accordingly, he put the Upper Fort back into use

in 1837. And yet, thanks to the steady flow of settlers, Lower Fort Garry, local headquarters of the Hudson's Bay Company, once again became a supply center (with a boatyard, a brewery, a smithy, and a mill). In fact, it even secured itself a monopoly on trade in the area, and blocked free trade. But after 1870, this whole commercial structure fell apart; the fort became a training camp for the Royal Canadian Mounted Police, and later, in 1885/86, a lunatic asylum.

Today, the site recreates the place's heyday, the years between 1832 and 1870. In the entrance area, an exhibition with life-sized figures illustrates the hardships endured by the early pioneers. A winding path leads along the picturesque banks of the **Assiniboine River** and up to the fort; on the way, you can see the typical *York boats* that the Hudson's Bay Company used to carry heavy loads on rushing rivers from the Rockies and the Arctic to the Red River. Many of the costumed workers in the fur warehouse, the general store, the doctor's or the blacksmith's are students, who really enjoy their summer jobs because, for one thing, "you finally get a chance to learn about your own history," as one person commented.

Arrow-straight Highway 67 heads on westwards. Leading off it, the dusty track 220 forms a stark contrast to the area of wetlands it leads to: **Oak Hammock Marsh**, a stretch of land that was restored to its original natural state after most of it, like the lands that still surround it, was drained for farming. In World War II, the area was even used for test bombing. The **information center** here blends nicely into the surroundings, thanks in part to its walls of local limestone; if you look closely, you'll see that the stone is riddled with fossils. The Oak Hammock Marsh administration concentrates mainly on waterfowl. The project is jointly operated by Manitoba's government and Ducks Unlimited, a private organization whose efforts are directed at preserving waterfowl.

The center is divided into several sections. First, there's a general introductory exhibit. The first settlers referred to this region as "St. Andrews Bog" or simply "The Bog," and viewed it with a mixture of caution and respect; it seemed to exude something mystical and frightening, yet they were obliged to enter it to cut the moor grass that was their only source of heat in the winter months. In the next section, visitors can learn all they need to know about ducks and geese. Sound out one of the pleasant "interpreters" on the subject, especially if you want to know more about the snow geese who stop off here on their annual migration in late September/early October.

The final room is a must for anyone who enjoys hands-on fun. True, the area is meant for children, but not all of the painting tasks and guessing games are easy. Through touch-screen computer technology, for instance, you can "create" your own birds capable of flying. A

SOUTHERN MANITOBA

0   25   50   75 km

list posted at the entrance provides information on the scheduled events. Several times a day, for example, there are bird-watching sessions from the grass-covered roof. Another highly interesting activity is a canoe trip through the marsh area. Guests are provided with life jackets and paddles, and the guides explain the rudiments of canoeing as well as giving information on flora and fauna. The canoe glides silently through the water, an otter passes by, the wind forms ripples on the lake surface and the characteristic cry of the loons pierces the air: an experience not to be missed.

From Selkirk, Highway 9 heads up to enormous **Lake Winnipeg**. In **Winnipeg Beach Provincial Recreation Park**,

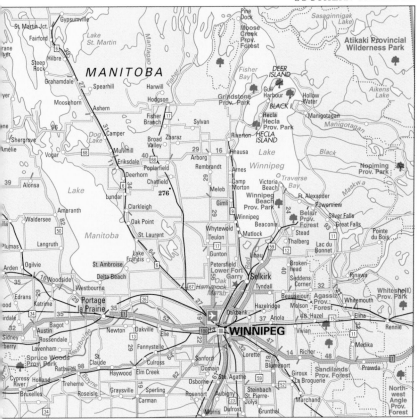

water sports enthusiasts will find everything their hearts desire, and the wind is ideally suited to windsurfing.

Resident in **Gimli** is the largest Icelandic community outside of Iceland. Between the restored harbor and the sand beach, you forget that you're not on the ocean but "only" on a lake. The feeling that you've been suddenly deposited in Scandinavia continues on **Hecla Island**, which Icelandic settlers named for an Icelandic volcano; the whole island has been declared a provincial park. In addition to its magnificent forests, the park's other attractions include a wide variety of wild animals and birds (including the bald eagle), a spectacular coastline, and the charming little town of Hecla.

West of Winnipeg

Anyone starting their journey in Winnipeg and heading west may feel that the trip confirms all of his clichés about North America: the arrow-straight Highway 1 extending in an unbroken line to the horizon, with huge trucks whizzing by and, parallel to the road, seemingly endless freight trains. **Portage la Prairie** boasts another fort that was built by de la Vérendrye, **Fort La Reine**. Today, it houses a museum, whose artifacts include the original Pullman car used by William Van Horne, one of the leading lights of the Canadian Pacific Railway.

Somewhat south of **Austin** on Route 34 is the **Manitoba Agricultural Mu-**

seum and Homesteaders Village. Here visitors can admire a comprehensive collection of working farming equipment. Some of the exhibits may look to the layman as if the farmer had left them to rot in his back yard, but in the relatively young country of Canada, anything that smacks of the past qualifies as "historic" and is therefore worth exhibiting. If you want to see **Lake Manitoba**, head for **St. Ambroise**, where there's a provincial park offering pleasant beaches and camping facilities, as well as guided bird-watching tours. One of the most extensive marsh areas in North America is nearby, close to **Delta Beach**; access, however, is very limited (contact the Research Station for information).

At **Carberry** (where there's a small gallery with works and objects from the estate of Ernest Thompson), Highway 5 turns south and leads the 20-odd miles

Above: Silent, splendid nature in Riding Mountain National Park. Right: Black bears often share the park's hiking trails.

(some 30 km) to the entrance to the forests, hills, praries, lakes and springs of **Spruce Woods Provincial Park**. There is also a strange phenomenon here: the **Spirit Sands** of Bald Head Hills. These are a large area of shifting sand dunes extending over several square miles, Ice Age relics that are gradually being taken over by vegetation. Complete with cacti, they convey a sense of desert seldom found in this northern country.

Before venturing into the park, stop off at the **information center** which provides brochures and tips on, for example, the attractive walking trails. A word of warning to those that tire easily: don't underestimate the heat in the dunes, and remember that walking on sand is fairly wearing. But Spruce Woods is also distinctive for the fact that its flora ranges from conifers through prairie flora to plants requiring large amounts of water. Unique to the region is the non-poisonous hognose snake. This ingenious creature pretends to be poisonous by puffing out its cheeks as if it had poi-

sonous fangs. If this ploy does not work, it will play dead. The northern prairie skink is a type of lizard which, in contrast to most reptiles, looks after its young. If attacked and held tight, it can cast off its tail which grows again within 15 minutes. Other park attractions include the **Devil's Punch Bowl**, a hollow 98 feet (30 m) deep filled with greenish water, or the walking trails on the other side of the river at Kiche Manitou Lake.

Riding Mountain National Park

If you're traveling north, you have a choice of several routes. In the pretty little town of **Neepwa**, with the small, crooked **Beautiful Plain Museum** housed in the former railway station, you have to decide whether to go for the classic route through Minnedosa and Erickson or opt for a more adventurous option: some 25 miles (40 km) north of Neepawa, at **Norgate**, an unpaved road leads into the park through the **East Gate**, a structure of which the National Park ad-

ministration is very proud on account of it being more than 60 years old. This route is only an option in dry weather, because some sections are quite steep (so much for the flat plains of Manitoba!), and rain can turn the whole road into a mudbath. Yet when the weather's fine, this route is one of the best ways fully to appreciate the park's scenic variety: deep, cold, blue lakes; dead trees that rise up into the sky like monuments; aspen woods; peace and quiet. You may be lucky and spot an elk or a black bear. To see the herds of bison that roam the park, though, you will need the help of a guide. After much bumping around you get to **Wasagaming**, which offers modern amenities (including an 18-hole golf course and tennis courts) yet has remained a lovely and attractive little village with all of its original charm. Its strength lies in its balance between civilization and wilderness – just 15 minutes out of town, you feel that civilization is light-years away. Wasagaming is also the site of the park's **Visitor Information**

Centre, where you can pick up a copy of the park's semiannual magazine *Bugle* containing general information and details on the park's history.

Continuing north, you again have two alternatives as to which route to take. The route through the park leads to **Dauphin**, a town with a Ukrainian feel to it, which every August hosts Canada's National Ukrainian Festival featuring much dancing, traditional costumes, and good food. Near **Roblin** is **Asessippi Village**, deserted by settlers when the railway lines bypassed the settlement. Today all that is left of the village are a few ruins on the eastern border of **Asessippi Provincial Park**.

North of Roblin is **Duck Mountains Provincial Park**, whose vegetation is similar to that of Riding Mountain. **Baldy Mountain** (2,717 feet/8,312 m) is both the park's highest mountain and Manitoba's highest elevation; there are wonder-

Above: Bright flecks of color in the prairie landscape: grain elevators.

ful views from its observation tower out over the endless forests.

The second route heads south out of Riding Mountain National Park and through the small farming communities of rural Manitoba. Since this is a region with many Ukrainian settlements, you often see the sun glinting on the golden tower of a Ukrainian church. This string of Ukrainian communities continues up as far as the region around Edmonton. At **Sandy Lake** there are two attractive churches, while a small museum tells of the arduous journey that Ukrainians took upon themselves in crossing the Atlantic and coming to the territory that is today Manitoba.

The landscape around **Rossburn** is characterized by gently rolling hills and **Birdgate River** valley is pleasant, but grain elevators form the only dominant feature of the countryside. Indeed, these enormous grain storage facilities lining the railroad tracks are arguably the most characteristic feature of this wheat-farming region.

SOUTHERN MANITOBA
Area Code 204
Accommodation
WINNIPEG: *MODERATE:* **Fort Garry Hotel**, 222 Broadway, tel. 942-8251, huge chateau-style edifice with a casino, well situated for trips to The Forks. **Norwood Hotel**, 112 Marion St., tel. 233-4475, nice, distinctive hotel in St. Boniface. **Crown Plaza**, 350 St. Mary's Ave., tel. 942-0551, good value for money, good restaurant, indoor and outdoor pools. *BUDGET:* You can rent rooms through the **university**, tel. 474-9942.
HECLA PROVINCIAL PARK: *MODERATE:* **Gull Harbour Resort**, in the north of the island, tel. 279-2041.
WASAGAMING: *MODERATE:* **The Mooswa**, Box 39, Mooswa Dr, tel. 848-2533, bungalows and motel, good food, pool. **Elkhorn Resort**, Clear Lake, tel. 848-2802, attractive resort hotel, with riding stables and small golf course, near the 18-hole course at Clear Lake.

Restaurants
WINNIPEG: **La Vieille Gare**, 630 Rue des Meurons, tel. 237-5015, top-notch French cuisine in a restored train station. **Le Beaujolais**, 131 Provencher Blvd., tel. 236-6306, fine, and expensive, French. **Alycia's**, 559 Cathedrale Ave., tel. 582-8796, Ukrainian fare in pleasant surroundings. **Branigan's at The Forks**, the best place to see and be seen, with excellent Caesar salad. **Mondetta at The Forks**, good Italian cooking. In **Chinatown**, you can find genuine, slightly down-at-heel Chinese eateries, while Italian restaurants line **Corydon Ave. Osborne Village** (Osborne St. and the side streets around it) is an "in" spot for students and bohemians, with delis, cafés, and tearooms. **The Forks**: snack bars, food market, bistros and restaurants with outdoor terraces.
NEEPAWA: **Hamilton Hotel**, Burger and Co.
WASAGAMING: **Wig Wam**, local hangout with good food. **Sportsman Park**, best cheeseburgers in the whole region.

Museums
WINNIPEG: **Arts Gallery**, 300 Memorial Blvd., tel. 786-6641, Tue-Sun 11 am-5 pm, Thu til 9 pm. **Centennial Centre**, complex with concert hall, planetarium, theater; tel. 956-1360. **Museum of Man and Nature**, 190 Rupert Ave., tel. 956-2830, planetarium; for showtimes call 943-3139. **St. Boniface Museum**, 494 Tache Ave., tel. 237-4500. **Riel House**, 330 River Rd., St. Vital, tel. 257-1783, mid-May-Labour Day daily 10 am-6 pm. **Ukrainian Cultural and Educational Center**, 184 Alexander Ave. East, tel. 942-0218, Tue-Sat 10 am-4 pm.
STEINBACH: **Mennonite Heritage Village**, tel. 326-9661, May and Sept. 10 am-5 pm; June,

July, Aug. 9 am-7 pm. **SELKIRK**: **Lower Fort Garry**, tel. 785-6050, open daily, mid-May to Labour Day, 10 am-6 pm.
OAK HAMMOCK MARSH: tel. 467-3300, May-Oct. Mon-Fri 8:30 am-8:30 pm, Sat, Sun 10 am-7 pm, Nov-April Mon-Fri 8:30 am-4:30 pm, Sat, Sun 10 am-4:30 pm.

Shopping tips
WINNIPEG: The brochure *Where Winnipeg* includes a complete list of **factory outlets**.

Tips and Trips
WINNIPEG: There's a whole range of **self-guided walking tours** through the city; for more information, check at the Tourist Centre. The **Prairie Dog Central Steam Train** (a historic train from the turn of the century) operates from June to Sept. every Sunday at 11 am and 3 pm to Grosse Island and back (36 mi/58 km), departing from CNR St. James Station. Info 832-5259. **Assiniboine Park**, 2355 Corydon Ave. W, tel. 986-2751.
Tours to the ocean port of **CHURCHILL**: A large part of Manitoba's coastline runs along Hudson's Bay. Churchill was named in 1769 for John Churchill, Duke of Marlborough, who carried out astronomical studies. The Duke was as fascinated with the **aurora borealis** (northern lights) as any modern visitor, but the main attraction today is **polar bear watching**.
Fort Prince of Wales (which you can visit by boat from Churchill), sitting in an exposed location at the mouth of the Churchill River, was built by the Hudson's Bay Company in the 18th century.
From mid-June to the end of August, you can take **whale-watching trips** from the mouth of the Churchill River into Hudson's Bay. You can reach Churchill either by plane or by train.
The train ride from Winnipeg to Churchill takes one day and two nights, and is one of the world's most spectacular railway trips: **VIA Rail**, 123 Main St, Winnipeg, tel. 949-8780 and 1-800-561-8630 (reserve well in advance! There are package arrangements including excursions and meals).
RIDING MOUNTAIN: Riding tours lasting one or several days are available in Kelwood, tel. 967-2077, or Lake Audy, tel. 848-7649. There's also a brochure describing the local **mountain bike tracks**; bike rental from the Tempo Gas Station in Wasagaming, tel. 848-2535.

Tourist Information
Winnipeg Information, Airport, tel. 774-0031. **Travel Manitoba**, 155 Carlton St,. Winnipeg, tel. 945-3777. **Tourism Winnipeg**, 320-25 Forks Market Rd., tel. 943-1970. **Spruce Woods Provincial Park**, for info about carriage rides, ski trails: tel. 834-3223 or call the Visitor's Centre at 827-2543. **Riding Mountain National Park**, tel. 848-7275.

SASKATCHEWAN

Through Yorkton to Prince Albert National Park

Gopherville, just over the Saskatchewan border on Highway 16, is less an actual village than a kind of curiosity show created out of thin air that has its own mischievous charm. "Gopher" is North American parlance for "ground squirrel," a species which lives in burrows, and visitors to Gopherville are greeted by carved likenesses of the same. The community also has the world's largest bicycle, with room for 44 people, and "Goliath," the highest swing in the world. Are you looking for a train ride, trampoline for the kids, or perhaps an hour browsing in the Santa Claus Shop? Gopherville has all these things. Perhaps one of the most curious attractions are the displays of landscapes from around the world in miniature. It's clear that some of the artists involved have never actually visited the landscapes they depicted, but that doesn't seem to bother anyone, documentation being perhaps less at issue here than diversion.

In **Yorkton**, a typical, dusty country town with a multicultural citizenry (many of them Ukrainian), the **Western Development Museum** is well worth a visit. In all there are four of these museums, each with a different theme; this one focuses on people, depicting the way that immigrants to western Canada went about their daily lives with, for example, a reconstructed pioneer home with life-sized figures. The museum is very proud of its gigantic gas tractor from the year 1916, as it is one of only two in all North America.

Passing through Ebenezer and Gorlitz on Highway 9, you come to the poplars of **Good Spirit Lake Provincial Park**. Here, seemingly in the middle of nowhere, there's a small settlement comprised of gas stations, a telephone and a

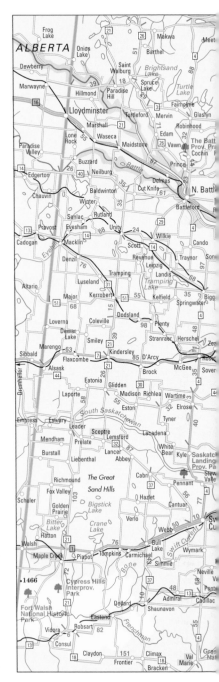

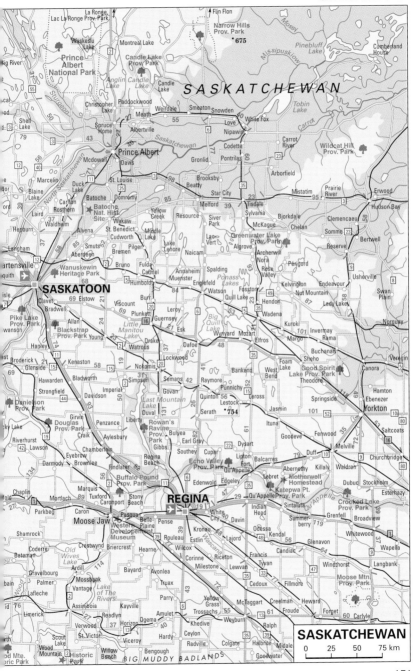

SASKATCHEWAN

0   25   50   75 km

general store, plus a highly unusual freshwater lake surrounded by sand dunes up to 16 feet (5 m) in height. **Good Spirit Lake** is especially striking in the spring, when the water is still frozen, but the dunes under the deep blue sky evoke the spirit of warmer climes.

From Buchanan it is worth taking one of several minor roads northbound which head through hilly country, "the real Saskatchewan": ranchland with cows or horses and dirt roads that disappear into the distance and give you an impression of how big the ranch they are on actually is. You are not likely to encounter many other drivers, either, unless it's a believer making for one of the region's innumerable charismatic churches, where enthusiastic reverends praise Jesus in clarion tones.

Further northwest, in **Greenwater Provincial Park**, there are stands of Norway spruce and silver aspen, and very

Above: A ground squirrel enjoys a snack in "Gopherville."

few European tourists. In **Fishermen's Cove** there's a population of crusty old fishermen; kids glued to the TV, burning with hockey fever; taciturn bear hunters; canoers; park rangers; and the local policeman. South of the park a notice points the way to **Crawford Studios**, which has an excellent exhibition of historical photographs of the region.

Highway 3 leads through **Melfort** to the little town of **Prince Albert**, the main supply center for the parks to the north. Though it has few attractions of its own, it is pleasantly located, hugging the Saskatchewan River. Prince Albert was a fur-trading post as early as 1776, and a missionary settlement from 1866 onwards. One of its claims to fame is the fact that three former Canadian Prime Ministers lived here at various times: John G. Diefenbaker, William Lyon MacKenzie King, and Sir Wilfred Laurier. **Diefenbaker's House** tells the story of that individual's life through old photographs and assorted memorabilia, while the **Historical Museum** deals with the history of the town; and its tea room, which overlooks the Saskatchewan River, is itself worth a visit. Prince Albert still relies heavily today on its timber industry. **Weyerhaeuser Pulp & Paper Mill**, one of the largest paper factories in the world, 11 miles (18 km) east of town, offers guided tours of its premises. Since the timber business has come under such sharp attack and is now subject to strict ecological restrictions, the mill operators go to great lengths to explain the complexities of this industry to outsiders. Weyerhaeuser is also an important member of the *Prince Albert Model Forest* in the National Park, along with the government, several Indian organizations and Forestry Canada.

It takes just 45 minutes to drive from Prince Albert to the national park of the same name, which is considered a highlight of western Canada. If **Prince Albert National Park** is the northernmost point on your itinerary, you can drive there along Highway 2 and return via the scenic route through the park to Tweedsmuir, or vice versa. Starting point for all activities is the tourist resort of **Waskesiu Lake**, which blends in perfectly with its surroundings. Rotating exhibitions are held in the **Nature Centre**, as well as a range of lectures organized by the park's sponsors.

In some ways the park can be compared to Riding Mountain National Park: both have extensive areas of aspen forest, and both were also set up to create jobs during the Great Depression, when men were collected in camps to build roads, lay out walking trails or construct buildings. For a dollar a day single men – men with families were turned down – were "permitted" to do what amounted to hard labor; in Riding Mountain, in fact, there were actually prisoners working out their sentence among the laborers. Grey Owl, an Englishman who posed as a member of the native tribes, was also active as a conservationist in both parks. One of the most attractive walks in the park leads to his cabin, **Beaver Lodge**, on **Lake Ajawaan** (12 miles/20 km). You can also take a boat trip across Kingsmere Lake. Staff at the tourist information center can give you more information on this and other activities, such as details on guided walks to places where you can observe the park's wild animals. Prince Albert boasts not only moose and elk but also a large caribou population; in addition, a herd of white-tailed bison grazes in the park. The pelicans which nest on **Lake Lavallée** are the second-largest colony in Canada. Also available from the information center is the publication *Wolf Country*, an interesting magazine about the park.

One factor that makes the residents of Sakatchewan particularly appealing is their infectious enthusiasm for their country. Rangers work round the clock; even when their official working day is over, they set off in search of poachers. All too often they come across the terrible sight of a bear whose paws have been cut off – bear paws being a souvenir which brings good money in parts of Asia.

Partly within, partly outside the park is **Anglin Lake**, a veritable little gem. In **Jacobson Bay**, a community of vacation homes, the Jacobson Bay Outfitters run an excellent café and a general store, rent wonderful log cabins, and organize boat and canoe trips. Several years ago a skeleton was found at Anglin Lake. First people assumed someone had been murdered, then it was discovered that the skeleton was 500 years old, and it was handed over to the National Park Authorities. They found out it that was the skeleton of a 18- to 27-year-old female Indian, who was subsequently laid to rest with all due ceremony at Anglin Lake by her people. The Jacobson Bay Outfitters were also invited to attend – something that was taken as an enormously significant gesture of trust and a step in the right

direction towards true coexistence between the native peoples and the white man.

Northern Saskatchewan

It's north of the boundaries of Prince Albert Park that you come to the kind of territory that true wilderness fanatics recognize as solitary. **Lac La Ronge Provincial Park** is a paradise for fishermen and canoeists with its thousands of wooded islands, waterfalls, and powerful rapids in the **Churchill River**, which is so wide in places that it looks more like a lake. This is an ideal location for fishing, canoeing, camping and walking. **La Ronge**, a small resort in the south of the park, is also a starting point for excursions to completely isolated "fly-in camps," which can only be reached by plane.

Above: Saskatoon, a prairie beauty. Right: Christian churches and sects vie for followers in the prairie provinces.

A particular treat for anyone seeking solitude is the route through **Candle Lake** and **Narrow Hills Provincial Park** to Flin Flon in Manitoba. Candle Lake took its name from an Indian legend about the millions of candles dancing over the lake – something explained more prosaically by scientists as escaping marsh gases that ignite. **Narrow Lake** is a popular venue for snowmobile enthusiasts in winter. On the way to Flin Flon, the road leads past endless lake systems. Apart from a few campgrounds, there is nothing much here in the way of civilization.

In and Around Saskatoon

In 1882, the Methodist priest John Lake founded **Saskatoon**. Originally, he wanted to name the settlement "Minnetonka," but then he sampled the red *mis-askwatomin* berries and found they tasted so good that he took over their name, corrupting it to Saskatoon in the process. Yet the temperance society which he had in mind didn't find a ready following in the area; by the turn of the century, the town had only 117 residents.

Regina and Saskatoon have long competed for the title of fairest city in the province. The most attractive view over Saskatoon and the venerable **Bessborough Hotel** is to be had from Saskatchewan Crescent on the other side of the river. The parks lining the Saskatchewan River are venues for mountain bikers, rollerbladers, mothers with children, and businesspeople taking their lunchbreak. Children flock to the small **Kinsmen amusement park** at the foot of **University Bridge** (Spadina Crescent/25th Street); while kids both young and old love trips on the **cruise boats** (which stops near the music pavilion in Kiwanis Park, near the Mendel Art Gallery). And all the most noteworthy buildings are strung along the river like pearls. Northernmost of them is the **Mendel Art Gallery**, mainly devoted to Canadian art, but with European works, as well; it also has a conservatory, coffee shop and museum store on the premises. Not far from the gallery, the **Ukrainian Museum** displays various objects pertaining to the lives of the Ukrainian immigrants; most interesting here are the old photographs.

On the other side of the river spreads the extensive campus of the **University of Saskatchewan**; its attractive buildings and grounds make this a worthwhile stop-off for visitors. The campus also boasts several museums and galleries which are open to the general public. The **St. Thomas More Art Gallery** displays works by local and regional artists, while the **Right Honorable John G. Diefenbaker Center** presents personal objects belonging to "Dief," who was Prime Minister from 1957-63. Finally, there's the **Little Stone Schoolhouse**, Saskatchewan's first school and also the oldest building in the city. If you like, you can take a guided tour of the campus; these depart from the **Place Riel Campus Centre**.

Walking along the university river bank, you eventually come to the **Western Development Museum** in the south of the city. The main exhibit here, *Boomtown 1910*, does a fine job of recreating that period and bringing it to life: it's a faithful reconstruction of a town street, complete with the clip-clop of horses' hooves and the hammering from the blacksmith's shop – in short, a truly "living" museum.

Though **Wanuskewin Heritage Park** is only about 3 miles (5 km) north of downtown, a few minutes in this spiritual center can make a visitor feel he is light-years away from urban life as he knows it. Conceived principally by members of native tribes, the center presents a sensitive examination of native cultures past and present, both within the museum buildings and on location at prehistoric archaeological sites. Before entering this mysterious world, visitors should make a point of seeing the 17-minute film which makes excellent use of the mystical effect of five native languages: to borrow a Ca-

175

nadianism, "it will blow you away." The intensity of the film prepares the eyes and soul for what is to follow: an intelligently thought-out museum equipped with modern touch-screen technology which the visitor can use to ask the ancestors about, for instance, the dangers of hunting bison.

A number of trails lead through the center's grounds, past various points of interest. You can see pots being formed and fired using traditional methods; while in front of a teepee, someone demonstrates the art of basket-weaving. The "path of the people" leads along the picturesque river banks to the sites of former villages or to washing-places. A palisade of tree branches marks the site of the bison hunt; the animals were driven towards the palisade, where hunters awaited with bows and arrows. Try standing behind the palisade and imagining the herd thundering towards you; you'll be tempted to take flight. This is the magic of Wanuskewin: it draws on the power of the imagination, on emotions and mysticism. Take the *medicine wheel*, an enigmatic stone circle reminiscent of Celtic stone circles: was it used by the medicine men? was it an astrological calendar? Nobody has yet been able to give a wholly satisfactory explanation, and up here, where the view extends out in every direction, you can feel chills going down your spine at this concrete evidence of a kind of primeval knowledge that seems to have been a constant in so many primitive cultures, even when there was no actual link or communication between them whatsoever.

Halfway between Prince Albert and Saskatoon, **Batoche National Historic Site** is devoted to the history of the Métis. Highway 11 is the most direct route, but those with more time to spare might opt for one of the many little ferries across

Right: A Mountie greets visitors to the RCMP Centennial Museum.

the river. The operators are happy at every customer they get, and will entertain you with local yarns, both plausible and far-fetched. This is an ideal way to get to see the extremely attractive Saskatchewan River valley.

Batoche was the center of the Métis settlement in the late 19th century, and Louis Riel chose the place after the 1885 rebellion as the location for his provisional government. For Franco-Canadians, Batoche represents their struggle for their own culture. On the grounds of the Batoche National Historic Site stand the church and presbytery of **Saint-Antoine-de-Padoue** (today an impressive museum) and the **East Village**. Interpretive trails lead to the battlefield where General Middleton and his 800 men attacked 100 natives and Métis. The audiovisual show is also highly recommended. If you're there at the end of July, you might coincide with the three-day festival called *Back to Batoche Days*.

Those that opt for the secondary road 763 rather than Highway 11 will come to **Watrous** and **Little Manitou Lake**. The Indians believed that this lake was conjured up by the great Manitou; a salt lake, it has as high a concentration of salt as the Dead Sea. In addition to the lake and its resort hotel, the **Manitou Springs Mineral Spa** complex in Manitou Beach with its three natural pools of curative water attracts thousands of visitors every year.

Another secondary route is to follow Routes 15 and 35 through pretty farming country. Stop off for tea in **Punnichy** at the **Hart House Tea Room**, which serves excellent fresh bread and homemade soup.

Regina and Surroundings

The cityscape of **Regina** is dominated by the **Wascana Centre** – not a building, but rather one of the largest city parks in the world, with a manmade lake into the bargain. Within it are the headquarters of

the provincial government, the university, several museums, and even a wildlife reserve for birds.

Wascana means "pile of bones" in the Cree language; it was the Cree term for a site on the banks of a river where they skinned their bison. Accordingly, the first white settlement in this marshy hollow, in the middle of a treeless and forlorn-looking plain, was called *Pile O'Bones*. Even then, the founding fathers aimed to make this a flourishing city, for the planned railway route completely bypassed the old capital of the Northwest Territories, Battleford, leaving it far to the north. And indeed, when the railroad arrived here in 1882 the settlement expanded rapidly. The government relocated here and the wife of the Governor General rechristened the town Regina (Latin for "queen") in honor of her mother, the British Queen Victoria. Furthermore, the North West Mounted Police also transferred their headquarters here. Veritable symbols of Canada, the "Mounties" maintained their base in

Regina until 1920, the year when they were transformed into the Royal Canadian Mounted Police (RCMP) and transfered to Ottawa. The Mounties started out as a paramilitary organization designed to bring law and order to western Canada (see "History," pp. 35-36); the need for such an organization became crystal-clear in 1873, when an uncontrolled conflict at Cypress Hills turned into a massacre in which 20 Indians were killed. Originally headquartered at Fort Walsh, near Cypress Hills, the Mounties moved nearer the railroad, to Regina, in 1882. The **RCMP Centennial Museum** here documents the history of the group with countless weapons and pieces of equipment, photos and other memorabilia; the tone ranges from informative to slightly bathetic. Even the original tobacco pouch used by Sitting Bull is here on display. The Mounties in their characteristic red jackets (*scarlets*) have inspired countless filmmakers, painters and writers; in addition to a police force, they were also "guide, philosopher, nurse and friend"

177

logy that pertain to the history of human-kind. Also on the north bank of the river is the **Science Center** (with the **Kramer Imax Theatre**), which manages to explain scientific phenomena even to people who hitherto believed themselves incapable of grasping such complex concepts; many visitors audibly regret that such methods were not incorporated into their own childhood science classes.

On the opposite side of the lake is the **Legislative Building**, a Neo-Renaissance edifice from 1912 set in an attractive garden. Courtroom, library and even art exhibitions here are open to participants in the free guided tours that are offered. South of here is the **MacKenzie Art Gallery**, one of the best art galleries in the whole of western Canada, with a balanced selection of Canadian and international art, and an excellent café-restaurant, to boot. From the end of May to the beginning of September small ferries run to **Willow Island**, a small picnic island in the lake.

rolled into one. On Mondays and Thursdays you can watch Mountie recruits parading on **Parade Square** at 1 pm, or lowering the flag at 7 pm; for Regina has remained the training center for the RCMP.

Downtown Regina – a small district bounded by Saskatchewan Drive to the north, Albert Street to the west and Broad Street to the east – is a rather quiet city center. Most of the buildings that are of interest to visitors are in the Wascana Center park, starting with the **Museum of Natural History**. More than 100 display cases, their visual impact reinforced with sound effects, are entertaining and informative introductions to local flora and fauna. *Megamuch*, the robot dinosaur, provides a link to geology and is a perfect example of the museum's accessibility; interactive games, too, are used to illustrate things about archaeology and geo-

Many roads lead to **Fort Qu'Appelle** – isolated dirt roads from the west or Highway 10 from the Yellowhead Highway. This town marks the original core of white settlement in a lovely valley with plentiful lakes, the **Qu'Appelle River Valley**. According to legend, a young man, out in his canoe seeking adventure, suddenly, miles from home, heard the voice of his bride calling him. "*Qu'appelle?*" (Who's calling me?) he cried, and turned and made for home, only to find his bride dead. Since then, it's said, people can hear his cries of lament throughout the valley.

There are a number of galleries and craft stores in the town which tend to offer authentic native craftsmanship rather than the standard mass-produced souvenirs. Take a little time to explore the valley and stop off at **Motherwell Homestead**, which has been restored. Also worth visiting are the parks around Regina and Fort Qu'Appelle – **Buffalo**

Above: Mailboxes are sometimes the only visible trace of civilization. Right: A rancher in Grasslands National Park.

Pound, **Katepwa Point, Crooked Lake** and **Echo Valley** – which provide ideal opportunities for enjoying nature and relaxing on the beach.

Along the American Border

It would be hard to find a sharper contrast than that between the pleasant Qu'Appelle Valley and the **Big Muddy Badlands** in the south, where the landscape is characterized by strange sandstone formations, steep cliffs and mysterious light: a lunar landscape with its own other-wordly beauty. It is all too easy to imagine how Butch Cassidy and his gang could have holed up here on their way from Canada to Mexico. Tourists can discover the caves used by horse thieves, walk along old smugglers' routes, and visit the hide-outs used by stagecoach robbers.

The detour to the south begins in **Moose Jaw**, whose **Western Development Museum** depicts the history of transportation in the prairie with magnifi-

cent old cars, airplanes, steamships and railroad cars. A narrow-gauge train starts its journeys from behind the museum, while the daring aerobatic pilots of Moose Jaw, the famous Snowbirds, fly their stunts on screen at the museum's in-house movie theater.

Highway 2 leads south through pleasant, rolling ranch country. After **Mossbank**, you start to see more fields of grain, and 15 miles (24 km) further south is the **Bunnyview Pet Farm**, a great attraction for kids that's a combination of petting zoo, museum and picnic site. Perhaps the most spectacular section of the journey is Highway 358 South, which heads though a completely desolate landscape of windswept grassy hills: images familiar from old Westerns. Highway 358 then becomes Highway 705, a dirt road; if you're into such adventures, you can go on through **Scout Lake** and **Willow Bunch** to the Big Muddy Badlands.

If you prefer your roads paved, you can find challenge enough on Highway 18 from **Wood Mountain** to **Fir Moun-**

tain, a veritable rollercoaster ride leading uphill and down dale. Here, in the middle of nowhere, the only signs of civilization are simple houses, such as the none-too-stately Royal Hotel in **Glentworth**.

South of the town of **Wood Mountain**, the **historic park** of the same name relates the story of the Mounties, particularly focusing on the difficult negotiations they conducted with the Sioux. In this magnificent scenic setting, history seems to flow seamlessly into the present, and the story of the native peoples' dealings with the white man takes on tangible form.

Wood Mountain is actually part of **Grasslands National Park**, but the best point of access to this scenic jewel with its golden hills is **Val Marie**. At the visitors' center on the main road you can pick up a brochure outlining a self-guided tour (by car, on dirt roads) through this new national park, which represents one of the only authentic stretches of grass prairie in Canada. Founded in 1988, the park is trying to buy up ranchland which currently lies between the park's two, separate, eastern and western sections; the plan is to extend the park by the year 2024. On these ranch areas, botanists are confronted with the problem of recreating the original vegetation, which farming has altered almost beyond recognition.

As for fauna, this extremely dry region is home to Canada's only prairie dogs. As they recycle their own bodily fluids, they require a minimum of additional liquid. These lively creatures live in burrows; within 1,000 square meters (about 1,000 square yards), they move approximately one ton of earth! *Prairie Dog Town* is a protected area within the park, south of Val Marie, where thousands of prairie dogs live together in quite a gregarious community. Another animal that feels at

Right: A puritanical community – the Hutterites.

home here is the mule deer, a kind of antelope without any close relations elsewhere in the world, which has adapted beautifully to prairie life in that it can see further than 3 miles (5 km).

The Grasslands mark the watershed between the rivers that flow into Hudson Bay and those that drain into the Gulf of Mexico. To the west is the distinctive outline of the **70-Mile Butte**, a tableland that once served as an orientation point for the Mounties on the way from Fort Walsh to Wood Mountain, as well as marking the only ford through the river.

Cypress Hills Provincial Park

Coming from Grasslands, you pass the Hutterite settlement of **Sand Lake**. The Hutterites are a religious community that emigrated to Canada from eastern Europe during the 19th century, as did the Mennonites (see p. 42). They reject military service and continue their traditional lifestyle, based on communal property and practices, within their communities; however, they have also been able to implement all of the latest agricultural machine technology, and export their products to other provinces. Their children receive instruction in the compulsory subjects from a Canadian teacher, but are not allowed contact with such modern teaching aids as TV or video. Since the communities are scattered throughout Canada, the Hutterites have taken to meeting at festivals to give young people an opportunity to find a marriage partner.

If you're driving on Highway 1, you'll pass through **Maple Creek** on the outskirts of Cypress Hills, a pretty, friendly town that would make a good setting for a film about the pioneer age. In the **Jasper Cultural and Historical Center** (Jasper Street) and the **Old Timer's Museum**, this turbulent period is depicted in photographs, documents and various other displays.

Spared by the glaciers of the last Ice Age, **Cypress Hills Provincial Park** rises up from the flat prairie like a green mirage, with elevations of up to 4,800 feet (1,468 m) and trees that the Métis mistakenly took for cypresses. Spanning the provincial border, the park extends from Saskatchewan to Alberta and consists of two sections known as *blocks*. The *Centre Block* is the smaller section with an attractive bungalow hotel, a swimming lake, campground and golf course; you can pick up a brochure at the park rangers' office by the park entrance describing a self-guided drive, the highlights of which are two observation points, the **Look Out** and the somewhat higher **Bald Butte**. From the latter, which is the *Centre Block*'s highest point at an elevation of 4,189 feet (1,281 m), you can see up to 50 miles (80 km) northwards on clear days: the Cypress Hills, after all, are the highest elevation between the Rockies and Labrador.

Gap Road links the *Centre Block* to the *West Block*, but, as it's unpaved and runs along the floor of a valley, you should only attempt it in good weather. However, it is a joy to drive along, passing through the woods, traversing a picturesque valley, and going by herds of cattle before coming to the *West Block*. Another option is to take the dirt road to Maple Creek through golden ranch country.

In the *West Block*, the road zigzags its way upwards; the block's main attraction is **Fort Walsh** and the park of the same name. The fort is an accurate reconstruction of the original fort built in 1875 for the then-fledgling North West Mounted Police, which used the building as their main headquarters from 1878-82. Perhaps the most historic element here is **Farewell's Trading Post**, a 1.5-mile (2.5 km) walk from the fort, which can also be reached by bus. Before the fort was built, cunning fur traders would come here to get skins from the Indians in exchange for cheap whisky and other worthless objects. Still, there were few serious incidents until American adventurers began

181

crossing the border and endangered the Indians' health by giving them diluted whisky cut with other liquids. One day when everyone was really drunk, a horse disappeared, and the American wolf hunters accused one of the Indians of having stolen it. The incident escalated out of control: some 20 Assiniboine Indians and one Canadian died in what became known as the Cypress Hills Massacre (1873).

Until 1883, as many as 1,000 people lived in the village by the fort, depending on how many traders were there, but once the Mounties left, things quieted down. From 1942 to 1968, the RCMP used the fort only for horse breeding and as a training camp for the traditional *Musical Ride* in Fort Macleod (see p. 97).

Today, visitors to the fort can try typical pioneer food or have a go at washing old-fashioned clothes by hand. Incidentally, the fort is also a place of refuge for animals during the hunting season: Fort Walsh is, unlike Cypress Hills Provincial Park, a "National Historic Site," which means that hunting is not allowed.

Scenes from Jurassic Park

East of Cypress Hills, the town of **Eastend** is the center of "dinomania." Since 1994 a team has been excavating the almost complete skeleton of a *Tyrannosaurus rex*, nicknamed Scotty, who roamed the earth some 65 million years ago. From Eastend, a two-hour tour by bus and on foot brings you through spectacular landscapes to the excavation site, where you can watch the paleontologists at their laborious work.

For adventurous people whose cars have good suspension, the dirt roads 633 and 738 offer impressive scenery, especially around the huge "desert" of the **Great Sand Hills**, an area of majestic, yet threatening, shifting sand dunes which you can also reach on Highways 37 and 32. From an elevation about a mile (1.5 km) west of **Sceptre**, you have a good view out over the whole.

SASKATCHEWAN
Area Code 306
Accommodation

TISDALE: *B&B*: **Barrier Chapparral**, Box 502, tel. 873-2401, ranch vacations, riding; wonderful setting, camping facilities available.

WASKESIU LAKE: *MODERATE:* **The Hawood Inn**, Box 188, tel. 663-5911, new, physically attractive wooden hotel with lovely large rooms and exclusive suites; great views over the lake. **Jacobson Bay Outfitters**, Anglin Lake, tel. 982-4418, gorgeous new log cabins with every conceivable luxury right on the lake, or cheaper rooms by the café.

BUDGET: **Mackenzie Inn, Northland Motel**, Box 5, tel. 663-5377, vacation apartments with kitchen and bath; Chad, the owner, is the pro at the Elk Ridge golf course. **Youth hostel**, Box 85, tel. 663-5450.

SASKATOON: *MODERATE:* **Delta Bessborough**, 601 Spadina Crescent E, tel. 244-5521, venerable railway hotel in chateau style; lovely location on the river. *B&B:* **Brighton House**, 1309 5th Ave. N, tel. 664-3278, charming house with Laura Ashley-style interiors; would fit right in in England or Ireland.

REGINA: *LUXURY:* **Hotel Saskatchewan Radisson Plaza**, Scarth St./Victoria Ave., tel. 522-7691, not especially striking from the outside, but gorgeously decorated within; Queen Victoria stayed here.

MODERATE: **Ramada Plaza Hotel**, 1919 Saskatchewan Dr., tel. 525-5255, very good value for money, three-story water slide.

MAPLE CREEK/CYPRESS HILLS: *MODERATE:* **Four Seasons Resort**, Box 1480, tel. 662-4477, marvelous bungalows in the woods or rooms in the hotel; indoor pool.

BUDGET: **Commercial Hotel**, Pacific Ave, Box 1959, tel. 662-2673, nothing exciting, but reasonably priced.

EASTEND: *BUDGET:* **Cypress Hotel**, Box 487, tel. 295-3505, romantic hotel from 1917 with newly-renovated rooms.

SCEPTRE: *BUDGET:* **Golden West Hotel**, Box 127, tel. 623-4200, with restaurant.

Restaurants

YORKTON: **The Gladhouse**, Western fare with steaks.

GREENWATER LAKE: **Fisherman's Cove**, shop, snacks, steaks, fish and salads.

PRINCE ALBERT: **Sizzling Buffet**, snacks and Chinese food.

SASKATOON: **Earls**, Queen St./2. Ave., one of the wittiest branches, architecturally speaking, of this very good chain. **The Granary**, 2806 8th St., great steaks, seafood, salads. **Martini's Dining Room**, 410 22th St., tel. 244-7770, on the 16th floor, with great views over the city and excellent food. **Jamieson Street Restaurant**, 305 Idylwyld Dr. N, tel. 664-9555, dine elegantly in a Victorian setting, or come in the afternoon for high tea.

REGINA: **Grekos**, 4424 Albert St., fine international cuisine. **Golf's Steak House**, 1945 Victoria Ave. **Alfredo's**, 1801 Scarth St., tel. 522-3366, Old City Hall, excellent pasta and pizza. **The Chimney Restaurant**, 2710 Montague St., tel. 584-7777, in a log cabin with open fireplace; very good steaks and spare ribs. **Great Canadian Bagel Company**, 2941 13th Ave., bagels fresh from the oven.

Museums

PRINCE ALBERT: **Historical Museum**, River St./Central Ave., and **Diefenbaker House**, 246 19th St., both open mid-May-early Sept Mon-Sat 10 am-6 pm, Sun 10 am-9 pm, tel. 764-1394.

SASKATOON: **Western Development Museum**, 2610 Lorne Ave. S, tel. 931-1910 or 1-800-363-6345, open year-round 9 am-5 pm. **Ukrainian Museum of Canada**, 910 Spadina Crescent E., tel. 244-3800, open Tue-Sat 10 am-5 pm, Sun 1-5 pm. **Mendel Art Gallery**, 950 Spadina Crescent E., tel. 975-7610. **University Visitor Centre**, tel. 966-5788. **Wanuskewin**, tel. 931-6767, open 9 am-9 pm from Victoria Day to Labour Day, other times 9 am-5 pm.

ROSTHERN: **Batoche National Historic Park**, tel. 423-6227, open July, Aug 10 am-6 pm; May, June, Sept, Oct 9 am-5 pm.

REGINA: **RCMP Centennial Museum**, Dewdney Ave. W, tel.780-5838, June-Sept 15 8 am-6:45 pm, other times 10 am-4:45 pm. **Legislative Building**, Legislative Drive, tel. 787-5357, Victoria Day-Labour Day 8 am-9 pm, other times 8 am-5 pm; in peak season there are guided tours every half-hour. **MacKenzie Art Gallery**, 3475 Albert St. S, tel. 522-4242, 11am-6 pm, Wed and Thu open until 10 pm. **Science Centre**, Winnipeg St. and Wascana Drive, tel. 791-7900; opening hours depend on schedule of events, as do those of the **Kramer IMAX Theatre**, tel. 522-4629. **Diefenbaker Homestead** in the Wascana Centre, tel. 522-3661. The house in which Diefenbaker lived as a child was transported here board by board and faithfully reconstructed. It contains memorabilia of the former Prime Minister and his family. **Regina Plains Museum**, 1801 Scarth St., tel. 780-9435; located in a former post office, the museum displays Indian, Métis and pioneer artifacts in rooms which recapture the spirit of the pioneer age.

WOOD MOUNTAIN: **Post Provincial Historic Site**, tel. 694-3664, open June-September, 10 am-noon and 1-4 pm.

MAPLE CREEK: Fort Walsh National Historic Site, tel. 662-3590 (in the fort) or 662-2645 (in Maple Creek), open late May-early October 9 am-5:30 pm.

Tips & Trips

PRINCE ALBERT: **Weyerhaeuser Pulp & Paper Mill**, 11 mi/18 km E of town on Highway 55; for information about visits to the premises, call 306/953-5194. Research station near Henribourg, 22 mi/35 km NE, tel. 306/922-8440.

PRINCE ALBERT NATIONAL PARK: Box 100, Wakesiu Lake, tel. 663-5322. **Elderhostel**: the youth hostel also hosts programs for senior citizens; tel. 791-8160 (Regina), 663-5450 (hostel). **Courses at the University of Saskatoon**, tel. 966-5552.

For several-day **hikes** with back-country **camping**, register at the park information center.

Bagwa canoe route, one of the loveliest routes in the north, leads through four lakes; brochures are available from the information center.

Bike rental at the Esso gas station on Lakeview Drive; ask about bike tours at the information center.

Canoe and boat rental through **Amisk Adventures**, tel. 982-3344, or **Jacobson Bay Outfitters**, tel. 982-4478.

SASKATOON: **W.W. Northcote River Cruises**, tel. 382-1166, June, July and August, hourly from 1-8 pm, weekends only in September. City **bike tours** are arranged by **Saskatoon Cycling Club Tours**, tel. 244-7332, and depart from the Mendel Art Gallery.

REGINA: **City tours** with **Double Decker Bus Tours**, tel. 522-3661.

A venue for **cultural events** is the **Centre of Arts**, Lakeshore Drive in Wascana Centre, tel. 565-4500; for schedule and tickets, call 525-9999. Concerts, ballets and opera are on offer; the center is home to the Regina Symphony Orchestra.

Boat tours on Wascana Lake: **Ferry Boat Tours**, tel. 525-8494. **Horse races** are held between mid-March and early August in Exhibition Park; for exact dates, call 781-9315.

EASTEND: for information about **Dinosaur tours**, call the Info Hotline, tel. 306/295-3606.

Tourist Information

Saskatchewan Tourism, 500-1900 Albert St., Regina, tel. 787-2300. **Grasslands National Park**, Val Marie, tel. 298-2257, Information office open late May-early September 8 am-4 pm; at other times, contact the Park Office between 8 am-4:30 pm for maps and tips.

Camping in the park is only permitted if you use a tent and forgo open fires; register at the Park Office. **Cypress Hills Provincial Park**, tel. 662-4411, Park Office and Nature Centre, open June-Labour Day 8 am-8 pm, other times of year until 5 pm.

CENTRAL ALBERTA

From Great Sand Hills the route continues via **Leader** to Highway 9, which heads for Drumheller. This is one of the most fascinating stretches of a journey through western Canada.

The **Dinosaur Trail** (Highway 838) is a 31-mile (50 km) loop through the **Red Deer River** valley, cutting up to 390 feet (120 m) into the prarie, where have been found a number of dinosaur skeletons up to 75 million years old. The **Red Deer River** has formed a lunar landscape, sprinkled with those sandstone pillars formed by erosion known as *hoodoos*. These eerie natural sculptures can be seen along 37-mile (60 km) long stretch of road known as Hoodoo Drive (Highway 10, eastbound). Some 15.5 miles (17 km) northwest of Drumheller, at **Horsethief Canyon**, there is a scenic overlook

Above: Class trip for a biology lesson at the Royal Tyrell Museum. Right: Alberta is a center for Russian Orthodox immigrants.

point from which you can also descend into the river valley.

Drumheller boasts a golf course, antique stores and a ski lift, but is of little interest in itself – except for dinosaur lovers, who are in sheer heaven here. Less than 4 miles (6 km) northwest of Drumheller is the **Royal Tyrell Museum of Paleontology**, which enjoys an excellent reputation the world over, in part because of its hands-on approach. The **Science Hall**, the first in the museum, is a truly pleasurable experience; visitors are encouraged to press buttons and try out things. In the **Hall of the Fossils**, the mysteries of geology come to life. One display, for example, uses slides to explain continental drift. Visitors can also observe paleontologists at work in their laboratory through a pane of glass.

Highlight of the exhibition is the **Dinosaur Hall** with its skeletons and lifesized models of various dinosaurs. Incidentally, the carnivorous dinosaur is called Albertosaurus Rex, a name that gives rise to great amusement in this

country of steak-eaters. Anyone with an artistic bent can play the computer game *Build Your Own Dinosaur*, selecting arms, legs, head, tail, and so on, on a specially-installed screen. The computer is a merciless judge, letting you know that your creation would starve because its arms are too short, or that its head is too heavy for its neck; finally, however, if you succeed, you can silence this critical voice, and the computer will inform you, *Type unknown, but it will survive!*

Should you have a truly insatiable appetite for dinosaurs, you can visit the small **Dinosaur & Fossil Museum** in Drumheller, which has some interesting information on the prehistoric history and geology of the badlands, with minerals and fossils on display; buy something for your own collection from the **Fossil Shop**; and, if you still want more of the same, venture out to the **Dinosaur Park** half a mile (1 km) west of Drumheller, where 20 dinosaur replicas are on view.

Then, southeast of Drumheller, there's **Dinosaur Provincial Park**, one of the most important paleontological sites and "dinosaur cemeteries" in the world, which has been classified a U.N. World Heritage Site. More than 100 dinosaur skeletons have been excavated here. Rangers guide visitors through sections of the park, including one site where you can still see a genuine dinosaur skeleton *in situ*. The Tyrell Museum also operates a research station here where you can observe scientists at work.

From Drumheller to Edmonton

Highway 56 heads north in a straight line to **Settler**, where it's worth stopping off for a bit. Settler is the starting point for the historic steam train **Alberta Prairie Railway**, which transports tourists through the prairie on tours lasting from 4 to 8 hours. In **Donalda**, lovers of curiosities may like to visit the rather eccentric **Donald and District Museum**, which displays 750 different oil lamps and 360 salt and pepper shakers, among other things! Further north, in **Camrose**,

185

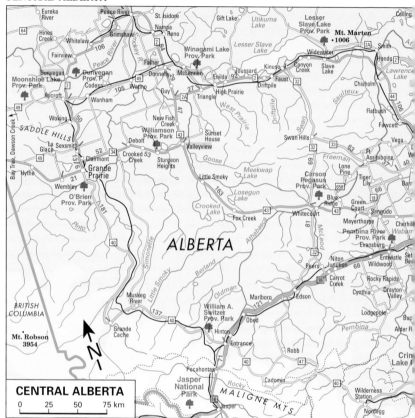

CENTRAL ALBERTA

0   25   50   75 km

there's a treat for aviation fans: at the **Albatross Littlest Airport**, you can watch model airplanes in action on miniature runways.

In nearby **Wetaskiwin**, the **Reynolds Alberta Museum** examines various forms of transport. Opened relatively recently, in 1992, the museum follows the best tradition of interactive displays, using audiovisual shows and life-sized exhibits ranging from airplanes to an entire prairie gas station.

From Camrose, Highway 834 will bring you to the **Ukrainian Heritage Village**, an open-air museum that sparks the imagination. What's offered here is living history; costumed staff, whether in the railroad station or the general store, in

the police station or in the small residential houses, bring the period between 1892 and 1930 memorably to life. A railroad official talks about stolen canvas sacks and his new gun, while a girl in a mud house is anxious to find out what the long boat journey from Europe was like. Someone else asks whether you are looking to buy land. Any tourist who plays along and, say, reports his horse missing, or goes to collect luggage from the station, will end up actually believing that he has been transported back into the time period in question.

Elk Island National Park is a smallish park and recreation area for Edmonton residents, encompassing walking trails, lakes and picnic sites. If you are

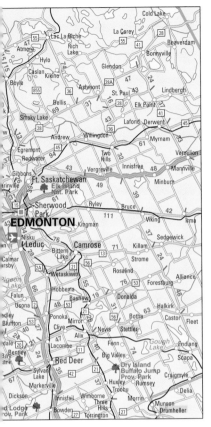

was discovered in Leduc in 1947, and today there are more than 2,000 oil and gas wells within a 99-mile (160 km) radius of the city. When this considerable wealth seems in danger of running out, the oil companies turn their eyes to the north, which has enormous supplies of oil as yet untapped. In the 1980s, the oil industry was beset with problems, pushing the local unemployment rate up to 15%; people moved to other areas, and houses stood empty. However, the city managed to weather this crisis by diversifying its industry, transforming itself into the main trade center for goods coming from the north or developed in the north; and today, it boasts a population of around 600,000.

In 1796, the North West Company and their competitors Hudson's Bay Company set up trading posts for the Cree and Blackfoot Indians on the Saskatchewan River: Fort Augustus and Fort Edmonton. The first settlers came around 1870, and soon a small community evolved. In 1897, Edmonton was the last civilized stop for prospectors caught up in Klondike gold fever on their way north and west – the *Klondike Days* in July are staged in memory of this phenomenon. In 1942, when construction started on the Alaska Highway, Edmonton was again the gateway to the frozen North.

In the days of the gold rush, the prospectors returned to town either laden with nuggets or in rags and tatters, depending on their luck. Some remained, and were joined by farmers from the Ukraine, Scandinavia, Germany, France, Poland and Hungary. It is to them and their descendants that the present-day city owes its multicultural mix. If this Canadian ideal of a multicultural society works better here than elsewhere, it might be in part because Edmonton's citizens are united by their long-standing rivalry with Calgary. At the political level, Edmonton has long since won the game: it has been Alberta's capital since 1905.

lucky, you may spot the park's main attraction, prairie bison, or even the rare wood bison.

Edmonton

Leaving behind the park's lush vegetation, you're immediately presented with a stark contrast in the form of Edmonton's oil pumps working away on either side of the Yellowhead Highway. In the east of the city, the refineries are concentrated around the 50th Street area and along highways 16a and 14. Buying gas in or around Edmonton is substantially cheaper than elsewhere; one would think gas stations had their own oil supply bubbling directly beneath the gas pump. Oil

Straddling the North Saskatchewan River, Edmonton may be Canada's fifth-largest city, but it remains pleasant and green, a sprawling place without a real center – individual taste will determine whether or not you find this an advantage. A tour of the city might begin at the **Legislature Building**, which stands in the middle of generous park grounds between 108th St. and 97th Ave.; there are daily tours offered of this Edwardian (1912) sandstone building with its imposing dome. A signposted **Heritage Trail** leads to the downtown area; in the revolving restaurant of the **Hotel Crowne Plaza** (Bellamy Hills), you have good views out over the entire city, as well as very good food. Another option is to ascend to the top of the telephone company's 33-floor headquarters, the **AGT Tower** (via MacDonald Drive), where the so-called **Vista 33** on the top storey offers a wonderful panoramic view. The

Above: The much-touted architecture of the Muttart Conservatory.

Museum of Telecommunications is also located in the same building.

Somewhat further west on Jasper Ave. is the **Aviation Hall of Fame**, whose displays include the first commercial flight simulator, models, photos, films and details about important figures in the history of Canadian aviation. The **Edmonton Art Gallery** at Sir Winston Churchill Square has a permanent exhibition of classic and contemporary art, as well as excellent rotating exhibitions.

Diagonally opposite is **City Hall**, a distinctive, some would say showy glass pyramid which has won several design awards. City Hall is a good point at which to enter the network of underground walkways known as "pedways." Given that winter temperatures in this northern clime can drop to between -22 and -40°F (-30 and -40°C), underground shopping is the only viable option.

One block further east you come to **Chinatown**, the area between 102 Ave. (where the ornate **Chinagate** marks the entrance) and 108th Ave., along 97th St., lined with Chinese restaurants and stores. Another international feature is the **Avenue of Nations**, the nickname for 107th Ave. between 95th and 116th Sts.: here are stores, snack bars and restaurants with culinary specialties from all over the world.

One of the most charming quarters in the city is **Old Strathcona**, south of the Saskatchewan River. Once the town of Strathcona, which amalgamated with Edmonton in 1912, its main center today is along 105th St. between White Ave. and 86th Ave. Magnificent old houses, street cafés, bookstores, record shops and theaters make for a special atmosphere. Guided tours of the neighborhood are also available.

Harsh winters played a considerable role in the decision to create the **West Edmonton Mall** in the west of the city. This mammoth project caused a lot of hassle for its civil and structural engineers, because the architects kept coming up with new ideas during construction work; some of the blueprints were invalid within a matter of hours. Billing itself as "the largest shopping mall in the world," the complex is a source of astonishment to Europeans; and even Americans, who are accustomed to large malls, display a grudging admiration for it. Boasting more than 800 stores, the complex also features a skating rink; the World Water Park complete with slides, "surfing beach" with waves, and artificial whitewater eddies; the amusement park "Fantasyland" with a rollercoaster; an indoor miniature golf course; an aquarium and the **Deep Sea Adventure** with submarines and dolphins. **Food Boulevards** and the restaurants in the reconstruction of New Orleans' "Bourbon Street" round out the picture.

On the south bank of the North Saskatchewan River, **Fort Edmonton Park** is the city's second main attraction. This reconstruction of the old Hudson's Bay Company fort and surrounding town offers "a stroll through history" – or a ride,

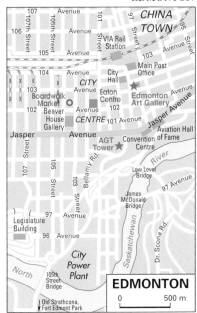

for that matter, by steam train, mail coach or vintage streetcar. The entrance area is also the railway station, and the area around it presents visitors with a picture of the town as it was around 1920. In the next section are houses dating from 1892 to 1914, a period of great upheaval during which Edmonton became the capital of Alberta. Further on, you can penetrate back to the time around 1855. Not only are the buildings reconstructed down to the last detail, but the goods on sale also reflect what was available in the pioneer age. At the end of the park stands the reconstructed fort, which evokes the rough-and-ready heyday of the Hudson's Bay Company. Various activities are held throughout the day: bread baking in the pioneer town, or old childrens' games in the fort, such as throwing woven hoops over a wooden barrel. In the "new provincial capital," smart young ladies drive by car to a garden party; nearby, there is even a séance in progress.

After exploring the fort (allow at least half a day), you might like to visit the ad-

joining **John Janzen Nature Centre**, with gardens, reptiles, an insect display and 2 miles (3.5 km) of nature trails.

In the east of the city, the impressive glass pyramidal greenhouses of the **Muttart Conservatory** present the flora of three distinct climatic zones: the tropics, subtropical desert, and a temperate zone, each in its own separate greenhouse. West of downtown is the **Provincial Museum of Alberta**, which examines the natural and cultural history of the region; displays range from a dinosaur skeleton to a trapper's equipment. A few blocks further north is the **Space and Science Museum**, which also has a planetarium and IMAX shows.

Gateways to the Far North

Driving along Highway 28, through endless suburbs, you come to **Smokey**

Above: Beloved of bird-watchers: the Kimiwan Bird Walk. Right: The famous Hotel Alaska in Dawson Creek.

Lake. The **Victoria Settlement Provincial Historic Site** transports its visitors back to the frontier days around 1890; costumed workers tell stories about the missionaries, native peoples and early farming activities. Continue north along Route 855, and after several miles you see a sign reading *Inn at the Ranch*. Following this and subsequent signs will bring you onto dirt roads and finally land you in front of a wonderful villa where two couples operate a **Bison and Wapiti Farm** and breed miniature donkeys and llamas. Given the ongoing vogue of low-fat, low-cholesterol food, tasty, naturally low-fat bison meat is in increasing demand. Anyone wishing to sample a bison steak should phone in advance.

Route 855 heads on north through an attractive wooded area, a Métis reservation. Tourist center of the so-called *Midnight Twilight Country* is the small town of **Athabasca**, picturesquely situated on the **Athabasca River**. Its tourist office, housed in an old train car, stocks brochures on a historical walking tour.

Around Athabasca there are a number of magnificent lakes. **Lawrence Lake** (northwest of town on Highway 55) has a pleasant picnic and swimming area which is directly accessible from the highway. From here to Slave Lake, the route leads through mixed woodland; the scenery already bears overtones of northern forest tundra.

Lesser Slave Lake is something of a disappointment, with a sense of oppressiveness about it. The Indian reservations and communities which surround it seem enmired in hopelessness, resignation and frustration. One such community is **Faust** on the lake's southern shore; the only real facility is a gas station, while the community center is a corrugated iron shack. Much more inviting is **Lesser Slave Lake Provincial Park**, with its attractive campground and the view from the top of 3,290-foot (1,006 m) **Marten Mountain** out over the enormous lake.

Also worth a visit is the **Kimiwan Birdwalk** in the pretty town of **McLennan**. This bird-watching center is a marshy area divided by a number of paths; explanatory notices and an *Interpretive Centre* are useful aids for novices. The center's interpreters are very helpful and manage to awaken a spark of ornithological enthusiasm in the hearts of even the most impatient. **Falher**'s claim to fame is a colossal sculpture of a bee – symbol of its self-appointed status as the *Honey Capital of Canada*.

From here, you can either continue west towards British Columbia or keep heading north. The first option brings you past **Moonshine Lake Provincial Park** which is popular with fishermen due to the lake's rich stock of salmon. You then cross the B.C. border at **Bay Tree**. Incidentally, it makes sense to tank up your vehicle here, as gas is more expensive in B.C.

The northbound route leads to **Peace River,** where at the confluence of the **Peace River**, the **Smokey River** and the

Heart River there are breathtaking views (from **Sagitawa Lookout** or **Judiah Hill**). The **Centennial Museum and Archives** acquaints you with the history of the *Mighty Peace Country*. Characteristic of this region is a milky light that still persists in the sky at 10:30 pm. Further west, in **Grimshaw**, is *Milepost 0* of the **Mackenzie Highway** (see p. 197).

Anyone smitten with the westward yearning that impelled the early explorers can follow a historic river route through the **Upper Peace Valley**. After all, the Europeans that first explored Canada generally traveled by canoe, following the course of the rivers. **Dunvegan** got its name from its Scottish founder, Archibald Norman McLeod, whose ancestors had a castle of the same name, and who thus brought a touch of his native land to this remote post of the North West Company in 1805. The **Fort** was restored and is open to the public. Just a short walk upstream, **Cathedral Rock**, looking something like a giant mushroom, towers over the river. **Dunvegan Provincial Park** is

Above: Gateway to the Far North – the Alaska Highway.

a good place to stop off and has the added benefit of a **Tea Room** (a short walk away) where you can enjoy home-baked goodies in a conservatory surrounded by flowers.

Dawson Creek is the magic word for many making for the north. Most tourists see it as the last outpost of civilization before the northern tundra begins. Note, however, that the Alaska route is one of the most-traveled vacation routes in Canada. It is 1,507 miles (2,430 km) to Fairbanks, an immense stretch of road of stunning natural beauty, and along the 1,417 miles (2,285 km) between Dawson Creek and Delta Junction there are 38 signs noting historical events and mishaps that occured during the construction of the **Alaska Highway**, built in 1942 at breakneck speed for fear of a Japanese invasion in the Northwest (see p. 203).

Mile 0 is located in Dawson Creek, and the signpost marking this spot is the town's most-photographed subject,

closely followed by the façade of the **Hotel Alaska**. A strange mood pervades the town: backpackers sit in front of the Hotel Alaska, hoping for a ride, and groups of Americans from bus tours or camper convoys stand in front of the **Station Museum**. Most people are content to photograph its exterior; a feeling of imminent departure is in the air. Yet it's worth taking a look around the museum in this former train station, because it provides a good introduction to the north. Exhibits include a winter fashion catalogue from 1950, the first snowmobile developed by the Erickson brothers, a doll-sized frontier home, and information on *cassola*, a special rape hybrid which is low in cholesterol.

The converted grain silo nearby is home to the **Dawson Creek Art Gallery**, which exhibits both local and international works. Dawson Creek also has a **Pioneer Village**, which came about thanks to the foresight of Walter Wright: he moved several buildings here, including a smithy, a schoolhouse and a trapper's log cabin.

CENTRAL ALBERTA
Area Code 403, unless otherwise specified

Accommodation
DRUMHELLER: *B&B:* **The Inn at Hartwood Manor**, tel. 823-6495, historic house with luxurious rooms and a good breakfast. *CAMPING:* **Dinosaur Trail RV Resort**, Box 1300, tel. 823-9333, W of town, not far from the Royal Tyrell Museum; nice location next to a driving range. **EDMONTON**: *LUXURY:* **Crowne Plaza**, 101 11th St./Bellamy Hills, tel. 428-6611, elegant, large rooms. *MODERATE:* **Mayfield Inn**, 16615 109th Ave., tel. 484-0821, not far from the West Edmonton Mall, good cooking. **La Bohème**, 6427 112 Ave., tel. 474-5693, historic house with romantic rooms and French restaurant. *CAMPING:* **Rainbow Valley Campground**, Whitemud Drive by Whitemud Park, tel. 434-5531. **SMOKEY LAKE**: *BUDGET:* **Plainsman Motor Inn**, Box 218, tel. 656-4040. *B&B:* **Inn at the Ranch**, Box 562, tel. 656-2474. **ATHABASCA**: *CAMPING:* **Blueberry Hills RV Park**, Box 835, tel. 675-3733, by golf course, well-tended, with walking trail. **GRAND RAPIDS**: *BUDGET:* **Four Seasons Rustic Log Cabins**, tel. 675-2521, in the north of Athabasca, isolated bungalows in the wilderness; call first for directions! **VALLEYVIEW**: *CAMPING:* **Sherk's RV Park**, Box 765, tel. 524-4949, well-tended and well-run. **MCLENNAN**: *BUDGET:* **McLennan Motor Inn**, Box 630, tel. 324-3000, clean, pleasant motel. **PEACE RIVER**: *MODERATE:* **Peace Valley Inns**, Box 6388, tel. 624-2020, clean rooms and suites, with a Smittey's Family Restaurant and an English pub. **DAWSON CREEK (B.C.)**: *MODERATE:* **Hotel Alaska**, 10209 10th St., tel. 250/782-7998, restored building from 1928.

Restaurants
DRUMHELLER: **Smittey's Family Restaurant**, home cooking. **EDMONTON**: **La Ronde**, a fine revolving restaurant in Crowne Plaza, tel. 428-6611; great Sunday brunch. **Select**, in the ManuLife Bldg., 102th St., Indonesian, tel. 429-2752. **Claude's on the River**, 197th St./Jasper Ave., gourmet food, tel. 429-2900. **Side Track Café**, 10333 112th St., tel. 421-1326, trendy spot with live music. **Cook Country Saloon**, 8010 103rd St., tel. 432-2665, country music. **SMOKEY LAKE**: **Inn at the Ranch**, Box 562, tel. 656-2474, buffalo steaks. **DAWSON CREEK (B.C.)**: **Café Alaska**, tel. 250/782-7040, good food, nice ambience. **CHARLIE LAKE**: **Red Barn**, fishermen's hangout.

Museums
DRUMHELLER: **Royal Tyrell Museum**, Box 7500, tel. 823-7707, Victoria Day-Labour Day 9 am-9 pm, other times 10 am-5 pm. **Dinosaur & Fossil Museum**, 335 1st St. E, Apr-Oct daily 10 am-5 pm,

July-Sept to 6 pm. **Dinosaur Park**, South Railroad Ave, April-Oct 9 am-on. **DINOSAUR PROVINCIAL PARK**: tel. 378-4144. **DONALDA**: **Donalda and District Museum**, 5001 Main St., tel. 883-2100, May 15-Thanksgiving Mon-Fri 9 am-5 pm, Sat, Sun 10 am-5 pm; other times Tue-Fri noon-5 pm. **WETASKIWIN**: **Reynolds Alberta Museum**, 1 mi/2 km W of Wetaskiwin, tel. 361-1351 and 1-800-661-4726, daily 9 am-5 pm. **ELK ISLAND**: **Ukrainian Heritage Village**, Yellowhead Hwy., tel. 662-3640, mid-May-Labour Day 10 am-6 pm. **EDMONTON**: **Legislature Bldg.**, 107th St., tel. 427-7362, Mar-Oct Mon-Fri 9 am-4:30 pm, Sat-Sun noon-5 pm. Nov-Mar Mon-Fri noon-4:30 pm, Sun noon-5 pm. **Fort Edmonton Park**, tel. 496-8787, late May-June Mon-Fri 10 am-4 pm, Sat/Sun to 6 pm. late June-early Sept daily 10 am-6 pm. **Art Gallery**, 2 Sir Winston Churchill Sq., tel. 422-6223, Mon-Wed 10:30 am-5 pm, Thu, Fri 10:30 am-8 pm, Sat, Sun 11 am-5 pm. **Ukrainian Museum of Canada**, 10611 110 Ave., tel. 483-5932. **DUNVEGAN**: **Fort**, tel. 835-7150, mid-May-late June 10 am-6 pm, July-Labour Day 10 am-9 pm. **DAWSON CREEK (B.C.)**: **Art Gallery**, 101 Alaska Ave, tel. 250/782-2601, June-Aug daily 9 am-noon, 1-5 pm; Sept.-May Tue-Sat 10 am-noon, 1-5 pm.

Shopping Tips
DRUMHELLER: **The Fossil Shop**, 61 Bridge St., prehistoric souvenirs. **EDMONTON**: **West Edmonton Mall & Canada Fantasyland**, tel. 444-5304 or 1-800-661-8890, shopping & recreational complex. **Old Strathcona Farmer's Market**, 83 Ave./103 St., arts & crafts, local produce, tel. 439-1844.

Tips & Trips
EDMONTON: **Neighborhood Walking Tours**, Old Strathcona, O.S. Foundation, 8331 104th St., tel. 433-5866. Late July: **Klondike Days**: parades, costumes, special events and food evoke the days of the gold rush. **Edmonton Space & Science Centre** with IMAX theater, 11211 142 St., Coronation Park, tel. 451-3344. **STETTLER**: **Railway Tours**: late May-Oct, tours of 4-8 hours 3-4 times a week, departure from corner of 47th St. and 47th Ave.; for info call 742-2811. **SLAVE LAKE**: The **Alberta North Office** has a brochure about trail rides, jet-skiing, canoeing, fishing, rafting, and hiking; Box 1518, tel. 1-800-565-3947.

Tourist Information
Dawson Creek Visitor Infocentre, 900 Alaska Ave., tel. 250/782-9595. **Drumheller Chamber of Commerce**, 60 1st Ave. W, tel. 832-2171. **Edmonton Tourism**, 9797 Jasper Ave. NW, tel. 496-8400. **Midnight Twilight Tourist Association**, 1 Sturgon Rd, St. Albert, tel. 458-5600. **Athabasca Chamber of Commerce**, tel. 675-3999. **Land of the Mighty Peace Tourist Association**, Box 6627, Peace River, tel. 624-4042.

YUKON AND THE NORTHWEST TERRITORIES

MACKENZIE HIGHWAY
ALASKA HIGHWAY
STEWART-CASSIAR HIGHWAY
CHILKOOT TRAIL / KLONDIKE
DEMPSTER HIGHWAY

The far north of Canada is a barren place. The tundra of **Yukon Territory** and the **Northwest Territories** stretches as far as the eye can see, all the way into the Arctic. Permafrost and snow storms, polar nights and icy winds make life difficult for the native peoples and the few whites who live here. Huge as these provinces are – they cover a total area of almost 1.5 million square miles (3.8 million sq. km), making them 2.5 times as big as Alaska – their attractions are not immediately apparent. But gradually the silence, the feeling of space and sublimity of the landscape work their magic in this expanse of unspoiled wilderness so overpowering that human efforts to tame it seem doomed to failure. And yet visitors to these near-empty areas – in theory, the region's 86,000 inhabitants each have 17.5 square miles (45 sq. km) at their disposal – will experience two provinces in the midst of change: the extraction of oil and natural gas, together with the timber industry, are encroaching ever more on nature. Only the edge of the Arctic still represents a barrier to human progress.

Preceding pages: The Skidoo has become a permanent feature of the endless expanse of tundra. Left: Even in summer, the tundra demands a special kind of vehicle.

MACKENZIE HIGHWAY

Driving north on the **Mackenzie Highway** takes you through Alberta's endless grain fields and dense pine woods into the barren tundra of the Northwest Territories – a drive from civilization into the wilderness. The small town of **Grimshaw** marks the official start of the route, which here leads through a landscape of farmlands, territories man has shaped himself. Lining both sides of the road are the brightly-painted grain silos characteristic of Alberta. But by the time you get to **Manning** and **High Level**, you won't find any more people working the land; and the oil men, lumberjacks, hunters and fishermen turn to look skeptically at strangers from *outside* – anyone, that is, who doesn't live and work in the Northwest Territories. Around here, you only get respect after you've made it through at least a year in the land north of the 60th parallel, which forms Alberta's northern border with the Territories or Yukon. *Sourdough*s is the joking nickname for these northerners, the word a throwback to the last century when it was used to describe anyone who was forced to survive here in the wilderness on sourdough bread.

On the Mackenzie Highway, which wasn't built until 1949, the **Government**

197

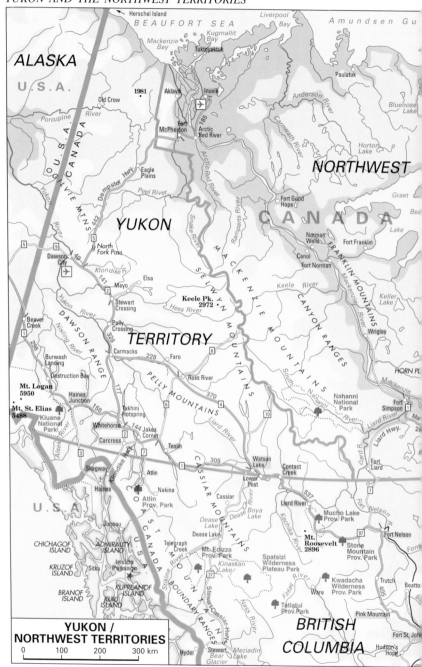

YUKON / NORTHWEST TERRITORIES

0   100   200   300 km

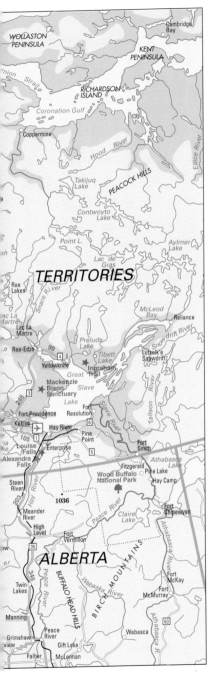

Visitor Information Centre invites travelers to stop off at the border. Anyone who still hasn't stocked up on maps is advised to do so here.

In northern Alberta, the grain farms have already given way to forest tundra, a transition zone between the agrarian land and the treeless tundra only found north of the Arctic Circle; now and again there are small birchwood forests and lakes. Long stretches of the highway also lead through dark, silent pine forests. As you drive along the ice-cold **Hay River**, the region appears lifeless; you hardly even spot an animal from the car window, even though forest tundra is a unique habitat. This highly-developed and highly-sensitive ecosystem has, in the Northwest Territories, unfortunately already suffered due to oil and logging activities.

Traveling north, it is worth stopping at **Alexandra Falls** where the Hay River plunges down some 108 feet (33 m). A little further upstream is **Louise Falls**, near which one can camp and hike.

Along Highway 5, you can turn off southeast shortly before the township of Hay River to get to **Wood Buffalo National Park**, which was founded back in 1922. This is the largest national park in Canada and one of the largest in the world; extending over an area of some 17,472 square miles (44,800 sq. km), it is even larger than the country of Denmark. The native Chipewyan and Cree tribes live here as they have for centuries, from fishing and hunting in the national park. One of the park's special attractions it its herd of wood bison, the last large herd in Canada, which has found refuge here and from which the park takes its name. Other types of bison were brought here from other areas, but have since fallen victim to epidemics; now, new herds are being resettled here. In addition to the 6,000-odd bison, the park's other main residents are waterfowl, which live on and around the inaccessible watercourses that meander through the park. Among these birds are the rare whooping crane, as well as various kinds of screech owl, terns, and the extremely rare rhino pelican.

Fort Smith lies at the end of Highway 5, on **Slave River**. This old trading post of the Hudson's Bay Company marks the entrance to the park. Slave River, usually a very calm river, suddenly shows its wild side at Fort Smith in a perilous stretch of whitewater which, to commemorate the many lives it has claimed, has been christened "Rapids of the Drowned."

Between June and mid-September, when temperatures can rise as high as 75 or 80°F (25°C), it is especially worth exploring the park's waterways. Granted, the mosquitoes are almost unbearable at this time of year, but anyone equipped with the appropriate protective headgear and insect spray will survive the plague. However, visitors are advised not to embark on longer river trips without a knowledgeable guide. Some of the best places to put your canoe or boat in the water are at Fort Smith, **Hay Camp**, **Pine Lake** and **Fort Chipewyan**, Alberta's oldest settlement at the end of Highway 5 (make sure to ask in Fort Smith about current road conditions). This Indian village nestles between **Claire Lake** in the west and **Athabasca Lake** in the east. Also highly recommended are canoe trips on the **Athabasca River** and the **Peace River**.

There are only three official campgrounds in the park, in **Fort Smith**, in **Pine Lake** and at **Dore Lake**, but camping in other areas is also permitted. Having said that, camping away from a site is not recommended for fearful *tot-inas*, the local designation for white tourists: at twilight, the incessant buzzing of mos-

quitoes together with the raucous cries of water birds can be somewhat off-putting for the uninitiated.

If you prefer shoe leather to water transportation or car travel, there are a great many hiking trails here waiting to be explored. Your chances of spotting a stray bison, a caribou, elk, grizzly or even a wolf are much greater if you are moving on foot. One aid to orientation, in addition to maps, are the nine **fire observation towers** scattered throughout the park. In winter, the park is an ideal venue for cross-country skiing.

Great Slave Lake

Continuing along Highway 5 in a northwesterly direction, you'll pass through Hay River and along the western shore of **Great Slave Lake** on to the final destination of Yellowknife on the lake's northern shore.

In the fishing town of **Hay River**, a former settlement of the Hudson's Bay Company, most of the residents today are members of native tribes. A small island across from town is home to the Dene reservation, inhabited by some 250 Indians. Past Enterprise, the next stop on the Mackenzie Highway is **Kakiska**, where you can camp close to the lake of the same name and a small Indian settlement. A free ferry service runs to **Fort Providence** across the **Mackenzie River**, the longest river in Canada. From here, Highway 3 runs along one edge of the **Mackenzie Bison Sanctuary**, where with a bit of luck, and from a safe distance, you may be able to spot a bison or two.

To the north of the lake, the scenery changes noticeably. Now the road leads through rocky gorges, over moors and into birch woods. South of the lake, by contrast, the Ice Age left behind broad expanses of sand, such as the ones that you encounter in Wood Buffalo National Park.

Right: Rivers and striking mountain peaks are dominant features of the North (here, the Athabasca River).

Detour to Yellowknife

From here to Yellowknife, the only settlement is **Rae-Edzo**, which, with 2,000 residents, is the largest settlement of the Dene Indians in Canada.

Yellowknife, boasting around 16,000 inhabitants – two-thirds of the province's entire population – is the capital of the Northwest Territories. Like Yukon Territory, the Territories are directly subordinate to the government in Ottawa. True, since the institution of the Territorial Council in 1975 the province has more autonomy than it used to, but no other region of Canada is as dependent on state help as it is. And there's another whole dimension to the battle for autonomy in places such as Yellowknife or Inuvik: the question of the rights of the native peoples. For years, the Dene and the Inuit (as the Eskimos are called in their own language) have fought for their right to independence and autonomy, and have now been promised just that: at the turn of the millenium, in the year 1999, more than two-thirds of the Northwest Territories will be granted political autonomy. This region is already known by the name *Nunavut*, Inuit for "our land." Part of the region will be made over directly to the native population, including mining rights and a share in any profits generated by mineral resources. Moreover, *Inuktiku* is to become the region's second official language, in addition to English.

But at the moment, *Nunavut* seems little more than a distant hope: in places like Yellowknife, a conspicuous number of people suffer from the effects of alcoholism and unemployment, or, even more, from the loss of a sense of cultural identity. Of the 22,000 Inuit living in Canada today (see p. 230), some two-thirds live in the coastal areas of the Territories. They look back on a long history. After the Dene, who are thought to have lived in the sub-Arctic for some 40,000 years, the Inuit were, some 4,000 to 8,000 years ago, the second large nomadic people to choose the region of the Arctic Circle as

their home. Much has changed since then. Most of the Inuit have settled down, abandoning their nomadic existence. Rather than hunting caribou or seals, many of them work in stores or as government employees.

Yellowknife itself is a young town: it wasn't founded until 1934, although the Slavey Indians, whose copper knives gave the settlement its name, had been living here for thousands of years. But Yellowknife owes its founding not to copper, but to gold, which wasn't discovered here until as relatively late as the 1930s. All that remains of the gold rush today are a few ramshackle wooden houses in the **Old Town**. Three years ago, the town's fortunes improved when rich lodes of diamonds were discovered further north. Drinking water, on the other hand, is scarce, and is still brought in by tanker.

Above: The Inuit are members of the "First People." Right: Real polar bears are not cuddly!

Worth visiting in this somewhat unattractive town is the **Prince of Wales Northern Heritage Center**, a rather unwieldy name for an excellent natural history museum. Anyone who has not yet been lucky enough to catch sight of a polar bear or a bald eagle can admire the animals here – albeit stuffed and mounted in display cases. There are also displays on all the native peoples of the region and their arts and crafts.

Yellowknife is a settlement in the middle of nowhere: the edge of town is a boundary between civilization and unrelenting wilderness. To venture into it without too much real risk, try the 43-mile (70 km) **Ingraham Trail** (go east from 48th Street along Highway 4) which runs to **Tibbett Lake**. From the dirt road running parallel to the **Cameron River** you can stop off one of the lakes for fishing or a boat trip; at the height of summer, you can even swim. Especially interesting for canoeists are **Reid Lake** and **Pensive Lake**. There are camping facilities at **Prelude Lake** and Reid Lake;

while a charming 2-mile (3 km) trail leads walkers around **Madeline Lake**.

Further West on the Mackenzie Highway

Highway 3 leads back to the Mackenzie Highway which heads on a further 372 miles (600 km) northwest, following the course of the **Mackenzie River**. However, the 136-mile (220 km) stretch of unpaved gravel road up to Wrigley makes for a somewhat boring drive. The river, which freezes over completely at times, is at 1,116 miles (1,800 km) the longest in Canada. The Indians refer to it as *Deh Cho*, which translates approximately as "big river." Its "white" name commemorates the legendary Alexander Mackenzie, who explored the river in 1789 – one of many white explorers who, after the early 17th century, began to venture into the unexplored regions of the Arctic in search of the ever-elusive Northwest Passage and untapped mineral resources.

Fort Simpson is a departure point for *flightseeing* trips to **Nahanni National Park**, which is not accessible by road. Unchallenged highlight of this park are **Virginia Falls**, where the **South Nahanni River** plunges some 294 feet (90 m). Experienced whitewater rafters can explore the river for some 124 miles (200 km) starting in **Nahanni Butte** (approach from the **Liard Highway**). In **Fort Liard**, you can also get Nahanni flights; following the Liard Highway south from here will ultimately bring you to the Alaska Highway.

ALASKA HIGHWAY

Dawson Creek (see p. 192) is proud of the fact that it marks "mile 0" of the 1,451-mile (2,340 km) Alaska Highway. **Fort St. John** is at mile 47 of this famous thoroughfare. It's hardly an attractive town; visitors will look in vain for a compact city center or any really noteworthy buildings. Yet the town does contain the eminently worthwhile **North Peace Mu-**

seum Complex and the **Peace Gallery North**. The museum displays prehistoric finds, including a replica of the skeleton of a bear 10,500 years old, and objects illustrating daily life in the frontier days, such as a trapper's cabin and one-room hospital. If you're looking for a novel place to get married, consider the tiny chapel on the museum grounds. Entertainment, meanwhile, is furnished by the theater *Doin's at the Derricks*, also within the museum complex. The pleasant little art gallery exhibits local artists and presents interesting slide shows on traveling in the area.

Fort Nelson is an old Hudson's Bay Company trading post, mainly frequented today by lumberjacks and oil men. Though the scenery between Fort St. John and Fort Nelson is charming, the real highlights of the route are yet to come: **Stone Mountain Provincial Park** and **Muncho Lake Provincial Park**. Here, the highway heads through the majestic landscape of the Rocky Mountains, reaching its highest point in the Stone Mountains: 4,235 feet (1,295 m). At such heights the weather is unpredictable; even in summer, it is not unusual to be caught in sudden snowfalls, although this doesn't greatly trouble the region's denizens, grizzly bears and bighorn sheep. In clement weather, you can take a pleasant walk around **Summit Lake**. The view of the valleys in the north is breathtaking, while the narrow ribbon of the Alaska Highway disappears into the wilderness.

654 feet deep (200 m), the bright blue waters of **Muncho Lake** are, alas, too cold for swimming. Still, the presence of two campgrounds and several relatively easy walking trails in the vicinity might make you consider staying a while. The sheer quiet of the place, surrounded by mountains 6,540 feet (2,000 m) high, is

Right: 25,000 souvenirs of home – the tin signs at Watson Lake Signposts.

itself overwhelming. And even in these chill northern temperatures, no one has to forgo the pleasures of outdoor swimming: the sulfur springs in the **Liard River** reach temperatures of as much as 140°F (60 °C).

Contact Creek is noteworthy for history buffs: it was here, in 1942, that the Canadian and American construction crews working on the Alaska Highway met up, having made their way steadily through the wilderness. Just after you pass **Lower Post**, you finally enter Yukon territory.

The Alaska Highway, running the 1,641 miles (2,647 km) between Dawson Creek and Fairbanks, was originally built for military reasons: the U.S. army wanted a better route into Alaska, fearing the Japanese would attack the area due to its strategic importance in World War II. Looking back, one can say that this dusty gravel road has had a much greater impact on the north of Canada than even the gold rush did in its day: without it, oil and gas corporations, timber companies and other modern gold-diggers would have had a much harder time penetrating into the territory.

Today, the Alaska Highway, together with the other two major routes, is both the gateway to the north and, for the "sourdoughs," an important link to civilization. Yet in winter, when the highway often becomes impassable, some hardened Northerners welcome the return of their wonted total isolation with a certain degree of satisfaction.

A reflection of the isolation and loneliness the road construction workers experienced is preserved in the legendary **Watson Lake Signposts** at the northern end of **Watson Lake**. Initially a construction worker named Carl L. Lindley set up a signpost here for his hometown of Danville, Illinois. Since then, more than 25,000 people – most of them tourists – have followed his example and nailed their own town's name onto the

wooden posts. Watson Lake itself is a major traffic junction, but has little to offer in the way of sights. Moreover, the Alaska Highway's winding route westwards through the border region between Yukon and British Columbia does not make for a particularly interesting drive.

At **Jakes Corner**, where the Alaska Highway turns decisively northward, make a detour down on Atlin Road (Highway 7) to **Atlin Provincial Park**. The scenery around the southern shores of Atlin Lake was shaped by the last Ice Age: this is a rough but charming mountain landscape with glaciers and alpine vegetation. The village of **Atlin** was founded almost 100 years ago and was, despite its remote northern location, used as a retreat for rest cures. Visitors should take a look at the lovingly assembled displays in the **museum** of local history and the paddle-wheel steamer *S.S. Tarahne*. You can make the drive back along Atlin Road and then up the Alaska Highway to Whitehorse in around two hours.

Whitehorse

The site of a former settlement of tents and log cabins which served as a trading center for those making for the Klondike has today swollen to a town of 25,000 inhabitants which has nonetheless managed to retain something of its original pioneering spirit. Though **Whitehorse** is the largest town in Yukon territory, it is a rather unexciting place that seems fated to remain a transit stop rather than a destination in its own right. Once, it was prospectors who passed through; today, it's hikers, drawn by the area's beautiful landscape, or canoers and rafters eager to paddle down the Yukon. Whitehorse experienced a brief flowering during the construction of the Alaska Highway, but after it was completed, the town quickly reverted to its former status.

The paddle-wheel steamer *S.S. Klondike*, beached on the banks of the Yukon River (South Access Road), is a reminder of the town's great past. This was the last and largest sternwheel riverboat to operate on the river between Whitehorse and Dawson City. More testimony to the wild days of the gold rush is preserved in the **Macbride Museum**. The same topic is examined from a different angle in the **Old Log Church Museum**: the exhibits tell of the hard time missionaries had trying to convert natives and prospectors alike.

Even though Whitehorse was once notorious for its rapids, this was the first navigable stretch of the Yukon River. Today, anyone looking at the slow-flowing Yukon from the dam of **Schwatka Lake**, a few miles southwest of town, will find it hard to imagine the perils of yesteryear. The dam was built at the end of the 1950s and tamed the Whitehorse Rapids; a walking trail along the east bank of the Yukon brings you to the dam and its salmon ladders. Beyond this manmade lake, the Yukon has carved its way through **Miles Canyon**, a spot where many adventurers met with their death. Today, heading north by canoe or boat from Whitehorse is no longer a dangerous undertaking. Numerous stores in town rent or sell the equipment necessary for a 5- to 6-day tour downstream along a stretch of this 1,975 mile (3,185 km) long Yukon River, one of the longest in North America.

Kluane National Park

As you continue west on the Alaska Highway, turn off in **Haines Junction** to detour over to **Kluane National Park**, which combines mountain ranges, glaciers and mountain lakes. Kluane (pronounced *klu-ah-nee*) is an old Tutchone word meaning "place of many fish." For many years the eastern region of the **St. Elias Mountains** (the highest mountain range in Canada) was considered a spe-

Right: Bear Glacier is one of the characteristic valley glaciers, miles long, of Northern Canada.

cial tip for hard-core adventurers: for the park was not opened until 1976, and the area remained undeveloped for a long time. Everyone, therefore, had to conquer Kluane on his or her own, without such amenities as campgrounds, paved roads or marked walking trails.

Then as now, such efforts were rewarded with breathtaking views of Canada's highest mountains: **Mt. Logan** (19,456 feet/5,950 m) and **Mt. St. Elias** (17,946 feet/5,488 m). The last Ice Age also left its mark here – with valley glaciers up to 62 miles (100 km) long, Kluane National Park has the world's largest glacial area outside the Arctic proper.

The ranger's offices at **Haines Junction** and **Sheep Mountain** have maps, issue permits and provide useful tips for visitors. A number of walks start from here, such as the 2.5-mile (4 km) **Dezdeash River Loop Trail** or the 12-mile (19 km) **Auriol Trail**, on which you should count on spending one night in the wilderness. Anyone in good physical condition and with the right equipment can take on the five-day **Cottonwood Trail**, 53 miles (85 km) long, which leads you from the park's only developed campground at **Kathleen Lake** to **Dezadeash Lodge**. On the route itself there are only a few very rudimentary campsites; basically, you're thrown back on your own resources for a few days. **Slims River Trail** offers the most scenic hike, past deserted gold mines and to within a short distance of the **Kaskawulsh Glacier**, the only accessible glacier in the park. This 15.5-mile (25 km) trail is not for anyone who's afraid of getting his feet wet, as you have to wade through several streams along the way.

STEWART-CASSIAR HIGHWAY

The 457-mile (737 km) **Stewart-Cassiar Highway** (Highway 37), leading from **New Hazelton** in B.C. to intersect

with the Alaska Highway west of Watson Lake, is another highly attractive route into the far north. Apart from logging trucks, this road is not very busy; nor is it entirely paved, and should therefore be avoided by anyone overly concerned with his car's bodywork.

From **New Hazelton** (see p. 128), the road leads north to **Meziadin Lake**, from where you can swing over into Alaska on the well-paved Highway 37a. This route takes you past ice-blue glaciers up to spectacular **Bear Glacier**, which thrusts into a mountain lake and, especially in summer, sends large chunks of ice crashing into the water. The two dull little settlements of **Stewart** and **Hyder**, in Alaska, are only to be recommended as overnight stopovers if you don't feel like driving back to the Cassiar Highway on the same day.

Farther north, past **Kinaskan Lake**, the highway leads between **Mt. Edziza Provincial Park** to the west and **Spatsizi Plateau Wilderness Park** to the east. Both of these conservation areas are of interest mainly to experienced mountain-climbers and hikers, as they are hardly accessible by car. Around **Mt. Edziza**, volcanic eruptions in days long gone by have left behind fantastic lava fields. After passing **Dease Lake** and **Boya Lake**, you reach the Alaska Highway at Watson Lake.

CHILKOOT TRAIL AND KLONDIKE HIGHWAY

Today, you can easily and comfortably reach the northern part of western Canada along one of three large highways. In the late 19th century, however, prospectors had to take a very different route, starting with the boat journey along the **Northern Inside Passage**. Today, you can follow in their footsteps on the 36-hour boat journey from **Prince Rupert** through the Alaska Panhandle up to Haines and Skagway, past icebergs and cliffs, through a fascinating world that only awakens from its frozen sleep and blossoms into bright, brief life for a few weeks every summer. Stopovers are no problem; you can leave the car ferry at a number of places, and board the next one the following day.

It was in **Haines**, Alaska that prospectors who planned to brave the long Dalton Trail to the gold fields of the Klondike prepared themselves for the long trek ahead. The old prospectors' settlement of Dyea, near Skagway, has all but disappeared, but in **Skagway** itself, you could feel that you've stepped into the year 1898. Only 700 people live here today, but at the peak of the Klondike gold rush, from 1897 to 1900, almost 30,000 people milled through the town. The small tent town quickly developed into a real settlement where saloons and equipment stores, in particular, flourished. Starting at the old **Whitepass and Yukon Railroad Depot** on the southern outskirts of town and continuing along **Broadway Street**, you can still see many buildings from the town's boom period. There is the **Red Onion Saloon**, for example, an old bar and brothel, or the impressive **Arctic Brotherhood Hall**, where, behind the imposing driftwood façade, the first brotherhood of prospectors held its secret meetings around the turn of the century.

For more information on this as well as other interesting tales from this period, visit the **Trail of '98 Museum** in the **City Hall**. One exhibit that particularly evokes the spirit of the times is a blood-spotted tie that belonged to Soapy Smith, a hoodlum whose gang scared the wits out of the community in 1898. Sheriff Frank Reid bravely agreed to a duel with Soapy Smith in which both men died. It is ironic that the two former enemies are now both resting in peace in the **Gold Rush Cemetery** northeast of the town. The townsfolk set up a fancy tombstone for Frank Reid, their local hero, whereas

Right: Former prospectors' route, today a hiking trail: the Chilkoot Trail.

Soapy Smith's grave is graced merely with a simple wooden cross.

Soapy Smith had set his sights on other prospectors' gold nuggets, presumably finding stealing infinitely preferable to the arduous trek along the perilous and steep **Chilkoot Trail**, or the longer White Pass Trail, which was also suitable for pack mules. However, if you want to get a taste of the travails of prospectors of the past, are fit enough and have the proper equipment, you might consider tackling this 33-mile (53 km) mountain pass. There's a payoff: the Chilkoot Trail is considered one of the most beautiful trekking tours Alaska has to offer. It generally takes from three to five days to complete.

Starting point for the Chilkoot Pass trail is **Dyea**, 8 miles (13 km) northwest of Skagway; the initial stretch leads through densely-wooded, damp mountain country. It's after this part that the going starts to get tough: the gradient is up to 30%, and the trail ascends to an elevation of 3,728 feet (1,140 m), where even in high summer sunny weather can quickly yield to ice and snowstorms. The edge of the trail is lined with abandoned equipment, garbage, the bones of horses, and wagon wheels, all evidence of the struggles of the often poorly-equipped gold seekers. Today, at least, there are shelters on the route. The first ascent to the Chilkoot Pass was originally known as *The Golden Stair* because the men had carved steps into the ice.

Note that this pass marks the border between the U.S. and Canada, and make sure that you register at the park information center in Skagway before you depart. There's a limit on the number of hikers allowed into Canada on a given day, and if you show up unannounced, you could well be sent back the way you came.

In **Bennett**, at the end of the trail, you can take a boat across Bennett Lake to **Carcross**, which is also accessible by bus

from the Klondike Highway. Carcross used to lie on the migratory route of caribou herds, which have since disappeared. What remains to the town is a rather dubious tourist attraction: **Carcross Desert** (1.2 miles/2 km north of town), billed as the smallest desert in the world, which is actually nothing more than the sandy bottom of a prehistoric glacial lake.

Opened relatively recently, in 1979, the **Klondike Highway**, running the 444 miles (716 km) from Skagway via Whitehorse to Dawson City, more or less follows the route to the gold fields on the Klondike River which more than 30,000 gold-seekers traveled in the gold rush year of 1898 alone. However, these early prospectors traveled by boat along the Yukon River, a dangerous undertaking given the river's perilous rapids.

Dawson City – the Dream of Gold

Once a small and unremarkable settlement at the confluence of the Klondike and Yukon rivers, Dawson City consisted of a few humble wooden huts until gold rush fever hit the town between 1897 and 1899, bringing in a flood of thousands of fortune-seekers drawn by what were supposedly the richest gold fields, southeast of town. Despite its unwelcoming location just 149 miles (240 km) south of the Arctic Circle, Dawson City not only flourished but also earned itself the reputation of a hotbed of vice in the Far North. Most of the gold-seekers were on the payrolls of entrepreneurs or other fortune-hunters who had had the good fortune to strike it lucky sooner. They squandered their measly wages in the saloons or gambling dens, and it was hardly surprising that such illustrious and hardbaked men as *Skokum Jim, Swiftwater Bill* or *The Evaporated Kid* turned up here and terrorized the area.

With the end of the gold rush, Dawson City's fortunes went rapidly downhill, and the town is a quiet backwater today. With just 1,500 inhabitants the town, more than a century after its founding, has come full circle: only in the summer

209

does it see an influx of visitors, who arrive bearing cameras and gold pans. Even so, Dawson City, unlike many other gold rush towns, has managed to retain its original character: hardly any other town in Canada conveys such an authentic sense of the days of the gold rush.

If you want to seek gold for yourself, you can either contact **Gold City Tours** on Front Street or travel 8 miles (13 km) south of town to **Bear Creek**, where you can pan for gold under the watchful eyes of a park official. Take note, with all private "claims," that unaccompanied tourists are not particularly welcome on the gold fields, as they are still worked by professionals: around Dawson City alone such finds generate several million dollars a year. And yet, this precious metal – like lead, copper and silver – is at once a blessing and something of a curse to the

Above: On the gold rush trail – tourists panning for gold. Right: On the pleasure trail – Gertie's Gambling Hall, Canada's only legal casino.

poor Yukon Territory: depending for its economic survival on a few precious metals, the Territory sees its fortunes rise and fall with world market prices, and when world prices sink, people in the Yukon feel it. During the recession at the beginning of the 1980s, almost all the mines in the Yukon area – working some 40% of all Canada's metal ores – were forced to close down, pushing the unemployment rate up to 18%, twice its normal level, for several years.

A visit to the small **Dawson City Museum** (5th Ave. & Church St.) provides insight into the prospectors' daily lives. As well as a replica of a hut, various pieces of trapping equipment and dogsleds, the museum relates the history of the Athabascan tribes.

This area, between 2nd and 3rd Avenues, was originally the town's center for the world's oldest profession. Today, however, those in search of loud, coarse entertainment have to make do with a visit to the **Palace Grand Theatre** (corner of 2nd Ave. and King St.). This

plush, kitschy theater still presents the now-legendary *Gaslight Follies*, consisting of a range of dance numbers and variety sketches that could truly have originated in the gold rush period: fast-paced and none too refined. The theater is a faithful replica of the original, 1899 edifice, restored as part of a 1960s program in the course of which Canada Parks renovated the entire downtown area. In **Diamond Tooth Gertie's Gambling Hall** (corner of 4th Ave. and Queen St.) you can still try your hand at roulette, blackjack and poker in Canada's only legal gambling casino.

Those prospectors who weren't interested in gambling could take their gains to the post office (corner of 3rd Avenue and King Street) to be sent home. Still in operation, the **Old Post Office** looks just as it did 100 years ago, though its most famous clerk is no longer on duty: Robert W. Service used to count nuggets here by day and write poems by night. His log cabin is located on the town's southeastern outskirts (Hanson St./8th Ave). Ser-

vice did not come to Dawson City till 1909 and was therefore only familiar with the real gold rush through stories, although that didn't stop him from immemorializing the period in humorous poems such as *The Cremation of Sam McGee*. Author Jack London, by contrast, experienced the gold rush first hand: he lived near here for a year in 1898. His log cabin was moved to 8th Avenue, south of Fifth Street, and today presents daily readings from his works, such as *The Call of the Wild* or the much-anthologized short story "To Build a Fire."

DEMPSTER HIGHWAY

Barren yet majestic, the endless expanse of silent landscape stretches inscrutably before the modern traveler just as it did in the days of Jack London. The **Dempster Highway** is the only public highway on the North American continent that crosses the Arctic Circle. Driving the 484 miles (780 km) from Dawson

City to the north brings you through wild, uninhabited regions of the subarctic tundra as far as Inuvik on the Mackenzie River delta. If you're going to tackle this road, make sure to ask about weather conditions at **Dempster Corner** (25 miles/40 km east of Dawson City), the highway's official starting point, and fill up your vehicle (taking along a spare gas can or two) before setting out. Bear in mind that it's another 226 miles (364 km) to the next gas station – with auto repair shop – at the Eagle Plains Hotel.

The Dempster Highway has cut a swathe through the habitat of both man and beast: the road runs through the old settlement areas and pastureland of the Gwich'in and Inuit peoples. At first, the route leads through the broad plain before the Ogilvie Mountains which can just be seen in the distance: this is a monotonous drive through moss-covered tundra with lakes and dark coniferous forests. If you are lucky you might spot

Above: The Mackenzie River Delta.

the odd prairie hen or mountain sheep.

Because of the great view, you should pause at the **North Fork Pass** (4,218 feet/1,290 m) in the Ogilvie Mountains before taking a break at the **Eagle Plains Hotel**. After crossing the **Richardson Mountains**, put your watches forward one hour: you've crossed into the Mountain Time zone of the Northwest Territories. Just before Fort McPherson, a free ferry bears you across the Peel River. **Fort McPherson**, a small, old fur-trading post with gas station and café, is mainly inhabited today by Locheux Indians, whose art and artisan work can be purchased here at reasonable prices.

Some 62 miles (100 km) ahead of Inuvik, another free ferry crosses the **Mackenzie River**, near the small Indian settlement of **Arctic Red River**. From here, you continue northward to the small community of **Inuvik** (3,400 inhabitants). Though the name (meaning "place of the people") is Indian in origin, the settlement was actually built from scratch as a supply center in 1955. There is not much of interest among the simple flat-roofed buildings, constructed to withstand a nine-month winter, except for the igloo-shaped Catholic church of **Our Lady of Victory**, which contains an interesting Stations of the Cross by Inuit painter Mona Trasher. House and pipes here are mounted on stilts to protect them from the permafrost, which can extend down to depths of 980 feet (300 m); only in the height of summer does the upper surface thaw for a few weeks, making for a muddy mess.

The period between May 24 and July 24 – the time of the midnight sun – is a time for lively celebrations. During this time the community, mainly Inuit and Dene Indians, makes up for everything they have missed in nine months of darkness. Kickoff to the celebrations is **Midnight Madness**, which marks the summer solstice. In July, the town hosts the **Arctic Northern Games**, and the same month sees a celebration of ethnic arts and crafts, the **Great Northern Art Festival**. Then, **Delta Daze** takes place before the winter sets in; from December 6 to January 6, the area is plunged in the darkness of the long polar night.

Summer is the best time to explore the fauna of the **Mackenzie River Delta**; numerous operators offer boat, canoe and plane trips from Inuvik to the surrounding area. In July and August, you can see the schools of beluga and Greenland whales, especially in **Kugmallit Bay** around **Tuktoyaktuk**, 87 miles (140 km) northeast of Inuvik. In spring and fall, migratory birds flock to the area before returning to their Arctic breeding grounds or setting off for the south.

A flight to **Aklavik** or **Herschel Island** gives you a bird's-eye view of this wonderful unspoiled delta. However, in **Beaufort Sea** there are huge reserves of oil and natural gas. To date, these have only been tapped sparingly, due to the high costs of extraction and transport. But for how much longer?

YUKON AND THE NORTHWEST TERRITORIES

Area code 867, unless specified otherwise

Accommodation

DAWSON CITY: *MODERATE:* **Downtown Hotel**, 2nd/Queen Sts., tel. 993-5346, centrally located, nice Western-style interior. **Eldorado Hotel**, 3rd Ave./Princess St., tel. 993-5451. **Westmark Inn**, 5th/Harper Sts., tel. 993-5542. *CAMPING:* **Gold Rush Campground**, 5th Ave./York St., tel. 993-5247 (only for campers and mobile homes). **Guggie Ville**, Klondike Highway, tel. 993-5008.

FORT NELSON: *MODERATE:* **Coach House Inn**, tel. 250/774-3911, simple, clean rooms. **Provincial Hotel**, Box 690, at the southern end of Fort Nelson, tel. 250/774-6901.
BUDGET: **Pioneer Motel Ltd.**, MP 300, Alaska Hwy. near Fort Nelson, tel. 250/774-6459.
CAMPING: **Western Campground**, Fort Nelson, tel. 250/774-2340.

FORT ST. JOHN: *MODERATE:* **Pioneer Inn**, 9830 100th Ave., tel. 604/787-0521, centrally located, airport pick-up service, swimming nearby, pub and restaurant.
BUDGET: **Coachman Inn**, 8540 Alaska Highway, tel. 250/787-0651, tidy hotel with restaurant.
CAMPING: **Beatton Provincial Park**, tel. 250/787-3407, camping right on the lake. **Charlie Lake Provincial Park**, tel. 250/787-3407, attractive spot in an aspen woods on the lake.

FORT SIMPSON: *MODERATE:* **Maroda Motel**, Box 67, tel. 695-2602. **Nahanni Inn**, Box 248, tel. 695-2201.

FORT SMITH: *BUDGET:* **Pinecrest Hotel**, tel. 872-2320. *B&B:* **Lehmann's B&B**, 36 Polar Cresc., PO Box 12, Fort Smith, NT X0E 0P0, tel. 872-4239. *CAMPING:* **Queen Elizabeth Campground**, on the Slave River, nr Fort Smith.

FORT PROVIDENCE: *MODERATE:* **Big River Motel**, tel. 699-4301, well-equipped hotel with grocery store, gas station and garage.

HAINES: *CAMPING:* **Port Chilkoot Camper Park**, Box 473, at the Halsingland Hotel, tel. 907/766-2755.

HAINES JUNCTION: *MODERATE:* **Kluane Park Inn**, Box 5400, tel. 634-2261.
CAMPING: **Kathleen Lake Campground**, on Haines Rd., 17 mi/27 km S of town, tel. 634-2251, well-kempt campground on the edge of the wilderness of the national park. **Kluane R.V. Campground**, on the Alaska Hwy., tel. 634-2709, very good, moden campground near the national park.

INUVIK: *MODERATE:* **Eskimo Inn**, PO Box 1740, tel. 777-2801. *CAMPING:* **Chuk Park**, Airport Rd./Dempster Hwy.

MUNCHO LAKE: *MODERATE:* **Highland Glen Lodge**, Mile 462, tel. 250/776-3481, motel and campground, gas station, good food, bakery; a real "service station" on your way into the wild.

NORTH STAR: *MODERATE:* **Sunny Valley Lodge**, PO Box 137, tel. 836-2603, wilderness lodge in comfortable log cabin style; proprietors organize guided tours and events; very good and ample food.

PINK MOUNTAIN: *BUDGET:* **Mae's Kitchen**: tel. 250/772-3215, motel, gas, garage, and even excellent homemade baked goods.

SKAGWAY: *MODERATE:* **Golden North Hotel**, 3rd Ave./Broadway, Box 343, AK 99840, tel. 907/ 983-2451, oldest hotel in Alaska; wonderfully restored interior. **Gold Rush Lodge**, 6th Ave./Alaska St., tel. 907/983-2831.

CAMPING: **Dyea Camping Area**, on Dyea Rd., 9 mi/15 km NW of Skagway, right near the start of the Chilkoot Trail, tel. 983-2921 (also suitable for RVs). **Pullen Creek RV Park**, 15th/State, tel. 907/983-2768.

RAE-EDZO: *MODERATE:* **Jeik'o Motel**, Box 10, tel. 392-6182, small, clean motel.

WATSON LAKE: *MODERATE:* **Watson Lake Hotel**, Box 370, tel. 536-7781. *CAMPING:* **Camp Ground Services**, PO Box 345, tel. 536-7448.

WHITEHORSE: *LUXURY:* **Westmark Whitehorse**, 2nd Ave./Wood St., PO Box 4250, tel. 668-4700, comfortable little hotel with wood-paneled rooms. *MODERATE:* **River View Hotel**, 102 Wood St., tel. 667-7801, some rooms with views over the Yukon. **The Bonanza Inn**, 4109 4th Ave., tel. 668-4545.

BUDGET: **Baker's B&B**, 84 11th Ave., tel. 663-2308, nice B&B with a very personal touch.

CAMPING: **Robert Service Campground**, Robert Service Way (South Access Road), tel. 668-3721. **Sourdough Park**, 2nd Ave., tel. 668-7938. Both sites clean and very well equipped.

WOOD BUFFALO NATIONAL PARK: **Kettle Point**, on the south shore of Pine Lake. **Pine Lake Campground**, also on Pine Lake.

YELLOWKNIFE: *LUXURY:* **Explorer Hotel**, 48th St., tel. 873-3531, the best and one of the most expensive hotels in northern Canada; wonderful views of the city; attractively appointed rooms. *MODERATE:* **Prelude Lake Lodge**, PO Box 596, (on the Ingraham Trail), tel. 920-4654, log cabin complex. *BUDGET:* **YWCA**, 5004 54th St., tel. 920-2777. *B&B:* **Blue Raven Guest House**, 37b Otto Dr., tel. 873-6328, small, attractive B&B.

Restaurants

DAWSON CITY: **Nancy's**, Front/Princess Sts., tel. 993-5633. House specialty is the formidable "Gold-digger's Breakfast."

FORT ST. JOHN: **Buster's**, 9720 100th St., tel 250/785-0770, good steaks.

HAINES: **Bamboo Room**, 2nd Ave./Main St., tel. 907/766-2800, very good breakfasts.

INUVIK: **Peppermill Restaurant**, 228 Mackenzie Rd., tel. 777-2999, very good fish dishes and caribou steaks.

SKAGWAY: **Corner Café**, 4th/State Sts., tel. 907/983-2155. **Prospector's Sourdough Restaurant**, Broadway/3rd St., tel. 907/983-2291.

WHITEHORSE: **Panda's**, 212 Main St., tel. 667-2632, fine dining (priced accordingly); decorated with Klondike memorabilia. **Cellar Dining Room**, Edgewater Hotel, 101 Main St., tel. 667-2572, rather down-to-earth restaurant with tasty fish dishes and good steaks.

YELLOWKNIFE: **Our Place**, 50th Ave./50th St., tel. 920-265, restaurant specializing in caribou. **The Wildcat Cafe**, Willey Rd. (in the old town), tel. 873-8850, log cabin restaurant; the gold-rush flavor is enhanced by the colorful if dubious clientele. **The Lunch Box**, Yellowknife Centre Mall; hangout of Yellowknife's "business crowd"; reasonable prices.

Museums

DAWSON CITY: **Dawson City Museum**, 5th Ave., tel. 993-5291. **Jack London's Cabin**, 8th Ave., daily readings of London's works at 1 pm, May to Sept, tel. 993-5575 (Klondike Visitor Association). **Diamond Tooth Gertie's**, 4th St./Queen St., tel. 993-5575 (Klondike Visitor Association) and the **Palace Grand Theatre**, King St., tel. 993-6217; shows only between May and September.

TESLIN: **George Johnson Museum**, tel. 390-2571 (open only from May to September).

WHITEHORSE: **MacBride Museum**, First Ave./Wood St., tel. 667-2709. **Old Log Church**, Elliott St./Third Ave., tel. 668-2555. **S.S. Klondike**, South Access Rd./2nd Ave., tel. 667-4511. **The Yukon Berlinga Interpretive Centre**, Alaska Highway, tel. 667-5340; opened in 1997, this museum is devoted to the exploration and founding of Alaska and the Yukon. **Yukon Transportation Museum**, at the Airport Whitehorse/Alaska Hwy., tel. 668-4792, vintage airplanes and locomotives.

Tips & Trips

ATLIN: **Indian River Ranch**, PO Box 360H, tel. 250/651-7550. Boat excursions on Atlin Lake. **Summit Air**, Jamie Tait, Box 134, tel. 250/651-7600, glacier excursions; wildlife "safaris" from the air.

DAWSON CITY: **Gold City Tours**, Front St. (opposite the *S.S. Keno*), tel. 993-5175, guided tours panning for gold. **Yukon Lou**, Front St., tel. 993-5175, boat tours on the Yukon. Free guided **city tours** depart several times a day from the **Commissioner's Residence** on southern 1st Avenue.

INUVIK: **Arctic Wings and Western Arctic Nature Tours**, PO Box 1530, by the Igloo Church, tel. 777-3300, flights in the area around Inuvik, boat trips to Herschel Island, and whale-watching tours. **Midnight Express Tours**, PO Box 2720, tel. 777-2104, boat tours through the Mackenzie River delta. *FERRIES TO ALASKA:* **Alaska Marine Highway**, Box 25535, Juneau, Alaska, tel. 1-800-642-0066, depart several times a week from Prince Rupert between April and late September. Sample prices: one adult, $124; a camper, from $341 to $656, depending on length; car, $286.

SKAGWAY TOURS: **Frontier Excursions**, tel. 907/983-2512, hiking tours of the area. **Skagway White Pass Tours**, tel. 907/98-2244, trekking on White Pass Trail. Both agencies are in Skagway. The **White Pass & Yukon Railway** runs historic steam trains from Skagway to Fraser, 28 mi/45 km away. tel. 1-800-478-7373 (Canada) or 1-800-343-7373 (USA).

TOURS AROUND WHITEHORSE: **Atlas Travel**, Westmark Whitehorse Hotel, 2288 2nd Ave., tel. 667-7823, tours through the Yukon Wildlife Reserve and river rafting at reasonable prices. **Guided Nature Walks**, tel. 668-5678, free walking tours in summer with lectures on history, geology, flora and fauna. **Northern Outdoors**, 208a Main St., tel. 667-4074, well-run hiking shop; various tour and trip offers are posted here, as well. **Prospect Yukon**, 2159 2nd Ave., tel. 667-4837, canoe and hiking trips through the surrounding wilderness. **M.V. Schwatka-Yukon River Cruises**, Box 4001, tel. 668-4716, offers boat trips through Miles Canyon. **Takhini Hot Springs**, Klondike Hwy., 18 mi/29 km NW of Whitehorse, tel. 633-2706, popular thermal springs.

FLIGHTS TO NAHANNI N. P.: **Dhe Cho Air**, Fort Liard, tel. 770-4103, seaplane flights to Nahanni National Park, especially Virginia Falls. **Wolverine Air**, PO Box 316, Fort Simpson, NT, X0E 0N0, tel. 695-2263. Flights of several hours around the national park.

TOURS IN THE YELLOWKNIFE AREA: **Eskimo Dog Research Foundation**, Bowspringer Kennels, 101 Kam Lake Rd., tel. 873-4252, breeders of rare huskies. **Ndilo Cultural Indian Village**, on Latham Island, Yellowknife, tel. 873-2869, presents Indian culture and crafts. **Prince of Wales Northern Heritage Centre**, on Frame Lake, tel. 873-7551, history and anecdotes about the exploration and settlement of the far North. **Overlander Sports**, 5103 51st St., Yellowknife, tel. 873-2474, rents out camping equipment. **Prelude Lake Lodge**, 20 mi/32 km E of Yellowknife, on the Ingraham Trail, rents out boats, tel. 920-4654. **Raven Tours**, PO Box 2435, in the Yellowknife Inn,

Franklin Ave., tel. 873-4776, city tours and guided day trips into the surrounding countryside. **Sail North**, PO Box 2497, tel. 873-8019. Propellor plane excursions around Great Slave Lake. **The Sportsman**, 5118 50th/52nd Sts., tel. 873-2911, boat and canoe rental. **Tundra Camps**, Box 1470EX, tel. 920-4263. Hunting expeditions on dogsleds (only in the spring and fall).

Tourist Information

Haines Visitors Information Center, 2nd Ave./ Williard St., tel. 907/776-2234.

Klondike Gold Rush National Historic Park Visitor Center, 2nd St./Broadway, Skagway, tel. 907/983-2921.

Skagway C&V Bureau, Arctic Brotherhood Building, Skagway, tel. 907/983-2854.

Whitehorse City Information Centre, 302 Steele St./3rd Ave., Whitehorse, tel. 667-7545.

Whitehorse V&R Centre, Alaska Hwy. and Whitehorse Airport, tel. 667-2915.

Haines Junction Visitor Centre, Logan St., Haines Junction, tel. 634-2251.

Kluane National Park Reserve, Box 5495, Haines Junction, tel. 634-7250.

Northwest Territories Visitor Centre, Front/ King Sts., Dawson City, tel. 993-5175.

Visitor Reception Centre, Dawson City, Front/King Sts., tel. 993-5566.

Nahanni National Park, Box 348, Fort Simpson, NT, X0E 0N0, tel. 695-3151.

Arctic Hotline, tel. 1-800-661-0788 or 587-2054. Books rooms free of charge, gives information about weather conditions, etc. **Fort Smith Reception Centre**, 126 McDougal Rd., tel. 872-2878.

Hay River Visitor Information Centre, Mackenzie Hwy./McBryan Dr., tel. 874-3180.

Wood Buffalo National Park, Box 750, Fort Smith, NT, X0E 0P0, tel. 872-7900 and 872-7962.

Yellowknife Chamber of Commerce, 4807 49th St., Yellowknife, tel. 920-4944.

In Dawson Creek or Fort St. John you can pick up the brochure *Alaska Highway – A Mile by Mile Guide*, which gives comprehensive information about noteworthy sights all along the route.

Note

If you plan to enter Canada through **Chilkoot** or along the **White Pass Trail**, you have to notify Canadian customs officials ahead of time (tel. 821-4111).

Before driving on the northern highways, make sure that you're well informed about road and weather conditions, gas stations, campgrounds and accommodations. Make sure you've got an extra can of gas, tools, enough emergency provisions for 48 hours and – even in summer – warm clothing that will withstand an Arctic climate!

SKI THE POWDER!

People like Sandy Best, the manager of the Lake Louise ski resort, are the an orthopedist's nightmare. Despite an artificial knee and numerous sports injuries (not from skiing), Sandy doesn't hold with careful, deliberate skiing; for her, all that counts on the slopes are S-T-M – translated for the rest of us, that's "steep, trees and moguls." She prefers giddyingly steep slopes mined with moguls as high as a man, or shortcuts that weave between tightly-grouped trees into clouds of new powder snow.

The much-touted *champagne powder* really does exist; in fact, Canadians take it for granted: "Ice is something crystal clear that belongs in a drink, not on the slopes." While Europeans don't have the same climatic advantages, and could

Preceding pages: Inuit woman ice fishing. Above and right (Grouse Mountain and Lake Louise): Which way to the champagne powder?

never replicate these skiing conditions, they could still learn a lot from the Canadians with regard to pleasant service. No pushing in line here: friendly staff gently guides skiers into the right position, always with a pleasant word or phrase. There are kleenex dispensers at some valley lift stations – no need for anyone with a runny nose to take off his gloves or dig in her pockets. And the restaurants feature nets on the back of the chairs and grids under the seats to put your ski goggles and gear so that you actually have room on the table for food – and even carafes filled with ice water.

Beware of the following Canadian phenomenon: if, when you look in the mirror after a long day of skiing, your reflection tells you that you have aged by 15 years, don't despair; it doesn't mean you're turning into a mummy. The extremely cold, dry air parches your skin and etches wrinkles into it, and the only cure is a good skin cream and lots and lots of liquids. The ever-present ice water, which may seen strange when outdoor temperatures are -22°F (-30°C), is there for good reason. Still, not everyone here is a health fanatic, one distinctive difference between the Canadians and their American neighbors. You can enjoy an extremely rare steak in a "lumberjack"-sized serving without anyone raising an eyebrow.

It seems that the mentality of the tough pioneer or burly logger has survived in some Canadians to this day. They are hard-core skiers. Late sleepers will not find much encouragement for their behavior, even though the relatively low elevation in comparison with American ski resorts means that you tend to sleep more soundly here. If you get up in the morning to find the breakfast room empty at 8 am, don't make the mistake of thinking that everyone else is still asleep; in fact, you're late, and they're all long gone! Tourists who follow their lead are the many Japanese who flock here; an all-in-

clusive week of skiing in Canada costs them a lot less than skiing amid the huge crowds back home in Nippon.

The Canadians are superb at developing their ski areas in an intelligent and sensible manner. None of the ski lifts sit directly atop a mountain peak; and the lift supports are camouflaged in various shades of green so that in summer hikers could almost believe themselves in virgin mountain territory. At **Lake Louise**, for example, 11 lifts are sufficient for 50 slopes; in the Alps, the ratio tends to be weighted in the opposite direction. If there's any negative side to the winter fun, it's the fact that the lifts are almost exclusively chair lifts, some of them without ski rests or even a safety bar.

Each lift gives access to a range of slopes of various degrees of difficulty; you can choose which one you feel like or feel up to at the moment. No matter the choice, everyone meets up again at the bottom – where, however, no one has to wait for long to get back up the mountain. Lake Louise has even introduced a

money-back guarantee: if you have to wait more than 10 minutes for a lift, you get your money back, and if you still haven't gotten into the swing of skiing after two hours, you can exchange your pass for a free one valid the following day. No reason is necessary; sometimes you're just not in the mood. This, however, doesn't happen very often, since, despite the below-freezing temperatures, skiing in Canada's Rockies can become addictive. Because of the dry air, it doesn't seem any colder than 15°F (-10°C) would in a humid area.

However, humidity is something you'll find in **Whistler**; Sandy's succinct, joking observation is, "Here it's better, there it's wetter." This is true to a certain extent, because Whistler is only 12 miles (20 km) from the Pacific as the crow flies, and at lower altitudes the snow often gets heavy and sticky. Nonetheless, Whistler remains a dream location for ski buffs, albeit of quite a different character than Lake Louise. Whistler is a hopping resort – although mercifully unlike the concrete silo complexes that you often find in French ski getaways – with nightlife, aprés ski and plenty of action. Whistler in fact consists of two separate ski regions: **Blackcomb** and **Whistler Mountain**. Although you only need one pass to ski both of them, the economic competition between the two spurs each of them continually to introduce improvements for its customers. Not long ago, Blackcomb opened the Excalibur, a high-speed chair lift that zooms ski freaks farther up the mountain at breathtaking speed, while the **Glacier Express** set a new record, carrying passengers from 2,300 to 6,500 feet (700 - 2,000 m) in less than 23 minutes, up to a glacier wonderland of such vast dimensions that the Alps look like foothills in comparison. When the Horstmann Glacier is bathed in late afternoon light, with the sharp contours of the Rockies silhouetted against the Canada-blue sky, Canada fans swear that these are the most beautiful mountains on Earth. If you get up early enough, you can be the first skiier to shoot down the fresh powder snow of the slope dubbed "Highway No. 86." The frozen trees reflect the early sun like giant heads of cauliflower, with masses of virgin snow all around. Once a week, Whistler has a special offer: before the lifts begin their regular service, the gondola takes particularly avid skiers up to the Panorama Restaurant at the top for breakfast – ham and eggs or pancakes with maple syrup. As the saying goes, the early bird catches the worm.

Lake Louise and Whistler are also the resorts best-known abroad; by now, you can book a whole range of vacation ski packages, including flight from your own country, ski pass and accommodation, for surprisingly reasonable prices. Many of the top-of-the-line luxury hotels, such as those of the CP chain, offer rooms in

Right: Heli-skiing in B.C. – one should live it up once in a while…

winter at fairly low prices, as well; in the summer, the rate is often more than twice as much. Other resorts are also relatively well-known in Europe: **Mystic Ridge & Norquay**, located about 15 minutes from Banff, is a small area suitable for a day's skiing. Most of the ski trails through the trees at Norquay are extremely cold, which means that the snow is fantastically dry. **Sunshine**, located 25 minutes from Banff, is a mid-sized area with easy to moderate skiing set in particularly delightful scenery. **Marmot Basin**, the region around Jasper, is especially enjoyable for expert skiiers: it's shaped like a large bowl, with the easy and moderate slopes nestled in the center part at the bottom. The "bowl's" edge, by contrast, offers plenty of challenge: demanding mogul slopes below Marmot Peak and Caribou Ridge as well as fabulous downhill runs – to be used, however, only when there's no danger of avalanches.

In addition, Canada still has a lot of resorts that are mainly or completely unknown in Europe. **Smithers** calls itself B.C.'s best-kept secret; and it's true that these 18 runs below Hudson Bay Mountain are really only known to locals – to people, that is, living between Prince George and Prince Rupert. Most of the runs at Smithers are classified as moderately difficult. There's also an excellent and comprehensive program for children and adolescents, with a range of camps for kids and various ski school programs. In addition, anyone less than 8 or more than 65 years old skis for free.

If you are traveling from the north to the southern part of British Columbia, three resorts in **Columbia Valley** could spice up your winter weekend. The **Panorama Ski Resort** near Invermere boasts the second-highest vertical ascent in North America: more than 4,500 feet (1,400 m). Panorama is also a center for helicopter skiing. **Kimberley**, the pseudo-Bavarian village, has a ski resort boasting the longest floodlit slope in

North America, while the **Fernie Snow Valley** is a area that emphasizes aprés ski, good hotels and restaurants.

There are also fabulous snow conditions in the wine region of the **Okanagan Valley**. An abundance of powder snow in December is followed by long periods of clear, cold wintry days. In winter as in summer, this valley is one of the most climatically blessed spots in Canada. And three other areas all offer a difference in elevation of more than 1,900 feet (600 m) with between 30 and 40 slopes; their ski trails are not especially long, but delightful for tree-skiing between pines and spruce whose branches are thickly powdered with sugary snow. **Apex Alpine Village** can be reached from Penticton; **Big White**, from Kelowna; and the charming western-style **Silver Star Mountain Resort**, from Vernon.

Vancouver has its own special attractions in winter – not so much fabulous skiing as sheer variety. You can sail or stroll through a museum in the morning and then ski **Grouse Mountain**, not far from downtown, in the afternoon; the slopes are illuminated until 11:00 pm. Or you can take the wintry ferry crossing to Nanaimo and continue from there to the Campbell River and on to **Mount Washington**: for **Vancouver Island** also offers crisp slopes, as well as bars with ocean views for aprés-ski cocktails.

In the next few years, Peter Stumböck, who has been actively marketing Canada for years, will join forces with Nancy Green and the Japanese firm Nippon Cable to expand the **Todd Mountain** ski region. Located 32 miles (53 km) northeast of Kamloops, the area consists of 46 runs between 4,000 and 6,500 feet (1,200-2,000 m) in elevation. The Japanese have already invested $40 million. Hitherto, Canadian ski areas have suffered from the fact that skiers are forced to rely on their cars; none of the ski slopes start directly from the "front door." But the new Sun Peak Lodge at Todd Mountain will be only about 50 yards (50 m) or so from the lift – Canada's first "on-the-mountain" resort!

221

A FISHERMAN'S PARADISE

Every year, in late spring, the towns of British Columbia and the Yukon seem utterly deserted. The cause: salmon fever. Anyone capable of holding a rod has gone off to the river. For it's now, at the beginning of May, that the first salmon return to the rivers to spawn.

King Salmon is the Canadians' respectful designation for the largest of all the salmon species. The name certainly is fitting, since this leviathan fish is 3 feet long (1 m) and weighs 65 pounds (30 kg). And that's only the average. The biggest king salmon ever caught in Canada weighed in at more than 100 pounds (50 kg). Such a catch is, of course, the dream of every fisherman.

King salmon travel upstream along almost the entire northwest coast of North America, from northern California all the

Above: Trout fisherman. Right: Five different species of salmon swim in B.C.'s rivers – all you have to do is catch them…

way up to Alaska. But British Columbia also offers ideal conditions for salmon fishing, and the chances of hooking one of these noble fish here are quite good. Around 50% of the entire salmon population travels upstream through only 15 river systems; accordingly, the number of fish in those rivers and streams is quite high.

The Skeena River, which flows into the Pacific at Prince Rupert, is probably the best location for salmon fishing. Fishermen from all over the world, but mostly North Americans and Germans, flock to the Skeena between May and August to catch the king of the salmon.

A little later in the year, beginning in July, the second-largest salmon variety makes its appearance. While clearly smaller than the king salmon, the *silver salmon* still reaches an average weight of 11 pounds (5 kg), and 22-pound (10 kg) fish are not at all unusual. Around the same time, three other smaller salmon species make their way upstream: the *pink salmon*, the *red salmon* and the *chum salmon*.

Fishing season peaks in July and August, when all five varieties of salmon are milling about in the rivers of British Columbia.

During this time, fishing lodges are totally booked out all over the country. Most fishing lodges consist of a large main building with a restaurant, bar and tackle shop, surrounded by "huts" for the guests. These huts run the gamut from plain to princely, depending on the price category; but don't take the word "hut" too literally, since the furnishings and appointments generally leave nothing to be desired.

In addition, most fishing lodges also offer guide services. Groups of 2 to 4 guests are appointed a fishing guide who leads them to the best fishing spots and makes sure that salmon fishermen are spared the ignominy of returning empty-handed.

Well, with all those fish jumping around, catching a salmon might not seem like all that much of a problem. However, nature doesn't make it too easy for the anglers: for salmon, although they're great feeders in the sea, don't eat much during their migration through the rivers. In fact, it's a mystery why they do strike at bait from time to time; perhaps the hunting instinct breaks through for a second, or maybe they see the bait as a bothersome distraction and want to dispose of it. But one thing remains sure: once an angler has caught salmon fever, he'll never get rid of it.

Curious? Then come with me on an imaginary trip to a Canadian salmon river. You're the fisherman, I'm the guide.

Tips for Spin Fishermen

Most salmon are caught by spin fishing – fishing with man-made lures, or blinkers, rather than actual edible bait. First and most important rule in salmon fishing is that the lure has to be kept as close to the river bottom as possible.

Obviously, this means that the lure often gets caught on rocks or hung up on pieces of sunken wood. In that case, there's only one thing to do: cut the line and start over. You have to count on going through at least 3 or 4 blinkers per day. Fortunately, these spoon-shaped lures made of tin are not very expensive in Canada; nonetheless, you go through some 10 to 15 dollars in an average fishing day. But as soon as you've hooked your first salmon and are playing it in, all thoughts of money will be put aside.

A few tips about the color of blinkers: early in the season, in May and June, you should use silver, silver-green or silver-blue lures. Perhaps, looking through the water, the salmon mistakes this wobbling, shiny tin bauble for one of the herring that formed his dietary staple in the ocean. Later in the season, you should go over to flashy colors – as humans do with their fall fashions – such as red, orange or yellow.

223

Action on the Bottom

Another common and very effective method of spin fishing is to use a so-called Tyrolean "hölzl" or plug, originally a piece of wood, but now a piece of plastic tubing which is weighted on the underside and has an eyelet for attachment to the main line. The advantage of this method is that this elongated weight doesn't get snared between the rocks, but happily bobbles above the bottom – right where the salmon are.

Attaching one is very simple. Pull the main fishing line through the eyelet of the plug, and tie on a swivel. This prevents the leader from rotating and makes it easier to change lures. Attach the leader, about 1.5 yards (150 cm) long, to the swivel and you're set. Wait, something's missing: the lure. Try a streamer, a wet fly made from feathers and animal hair to

Above: If you follow the pro's tips on salmon fishing to the letter, you may need a very large icebox.

resemble a minnow, which you can buy at any tackle store in Canada. A real classic is the orange-yellow pattern known as the Mickey Finn. Just ask the sales clerk which streamers the salmon are going for at the moment, and they'll be glad to advise you.

The shopkeeper will certainly be able to dig up a box of artificial salmon eggs somewhere. Don't stop at buying just a couple, but give these a real chance, as well; it could pay off. By the way, real salmon eggs in a gauze bag are such good bait that they are forbidden in many rivers. But you should keep them in mind in case you find a river where this bait is permitted...

Step by Step

The technique is the almost the same for both types of spin casting. Cast your lure upstream and wait a little, to give it a chance to sink to the bottom. If you're using a blinker, reel in the line very slowly. If you're using a plug, hold the rod high and let the lure gently arc over to the bank; shortly before it actually reaches the shore, bring it out again with a series of sharp tugging motions. Especially in strong currents, the salmon hang out close to the shore.

Before you cast again, let me tell you a very important salmon rule. It goes like this: two steps, one throw. Okay, I know, you're on vacation and don't want to be bound to any hard and fast rules. Still, you have to take a step between casts.

I'll be happy to explain why. On their migration to their spawning grounds, the salmon have to overcome rapids or jump up waterfalls. Because of this, they often take a well-deserved break and rest motionless at the bottom. If the fish doesn't move, and you remain pinned to one place on the shore, you can forget about your plans for a delicious salmon steak dinner. So, don't forget: cast, take two steps, and cast again. That's the way to hook a salmon.

Salmon Rest Stops

Now that you know a bit about how to catch salmon, the question remains: how do you go about finding a good place to fish? Well, the best places are always the spots where the salmon collect to rest and regroup.

Take a close look at your river. Find a place where the river gets narrower and the current is stronger. Fine. Downstream from here, the water is calmer and deeper. There are almost always fish in this spot. You can also try casting upstream from these sections of rapids, for the salmon pause after their exertions to gather new strength to continue their journey.

The same rules apply to waterfalls. Unfortunately, however, these spots are usually overrun with locals, and the fish know all the lures all too well, probably down to the catalogue number and exact price.

Trout

Even if you're suffering from salmon fever, you shouldn't forget that western Canada has a lot more to offer. Whether you're in British Columbia, Yukon Territory or Alberta, you'll hardly find a stream or lake without its population of trout or char. And salmon season is the absolutely best time to angle for these delicious and contentious fish undisturbed – all the other sport fishermen, after all, are out fishing for salmon! Here, you can find rainbow trout, cutthroat trout and a variety imported from Germany, the brown trout, as well as two varieties of char, the Dolly Varden and brook trout. So you can see there's quite a variety.

Trout and char are gourmets. They go after the salmon eggs that are swept away by the current and drift downstream. Even in brooks where there are no migrating salmon, salmon eggs are excellent bait. You can use the same rigging as you would for salmon; just use a slightly thinner line and somewhat smaller salmon eggs.

Small spoon lures and spinners are also very effective. Spinners are lures with a small metal blade revolving around a fine wire shank, producing an alluring ripple effect; with these, it's especially easy to catch yourself a nice dinner.

Incidentally, you don't find trout and char only in brooks and rivers. There are also plenty of them in the country's many lakes, along with pike, bass, whitefish, giant char and members of the cod family.

So, if you ever travel to western Canada, there are two things you shouldn't forget: your rod and reel.

After all, nothing perks up a campground menu as much as a filet of fresh fish you've caught yourself grilled over the campfire – not only does it taste good, but it serves to impress everyone around you.

GOLF BETWEEN WILDERNESS AND SNACK BARS

As you take your clubs from your golf bag at the **Clear Lake Golf Course** in Riding National Park in Manitoba, the early summer sun sparkles off the last of the ice floes. On the shore – so perfect it borders on kitsch – a moose is posing with her calf. In the foreground, on the 9th tee, someone is doubled over with laughter. It's Ian, the club manager, who between giggles manages to splutter out that a raven has just stolen his ball from the fairway. One reason this is especially funny is that Ian is wearing the club T-shirt, which is emblazoned with the slogan *You are entering the Raven Zone*.

European golfers are dumbfounded, tongue-tied by their ideas of proper golf etiquette: braying with laughter on a golf course? But golfing in Canada is an eminently democratic sport. It doesn't matter where you're from or what you're wearing, and makes no difference if the dollars for your green fee come out of a designer bag or the pocket of your battered sweatpants. The money, after all, is the same color wherever it's kept.

The **Waskesiu Golf Course** in Prince Albert National Park, in the north of Saskatchewan, is comparable with Riding Mountain in some respects. Both parks owe their existance to job-creation programs during the Great Depression, when unemployed men were collected and housed in camps while they constructed roads and buildings. This beautiful golf course is a product of the extraordinary course designer Stanley Thompson, who left a signature with the "Lobstick Tree," standing about 360 feet (110 m) beyond the first tee. According to an Indian legend, the tree has always been a point of orientation, and its ancient spiritual

Right: Relaxed is the catchword when golfing in Banff – surrounded by magnificent scenery.

powers must have given it a certain magnetism: golf balls are drawn to its branches, which they strike regularly only to bounce off in all directions.

And while the ravens are the only uninvited guests on the Riding Mountain course, beware of other even more troublesome interlopers in Prince Albert. Often enough, when someone is on his way to retrieve a ball hit into the woods, his conversation dies on his lips and he stares – at something that stares right back. For black bears just love this terrain.

In **Banff**, on the other hand, it's wapitis who observe your game. Entire herds graze on the fairways; after all, this cultivated grass tastes much better than those hard-to-reach natural varieties in the forest. Stanley Thompson always considered the natural surroundings when designing a golf course. He practically mirrored the gigantic Rock Mountain peaks in his fairways and opened up views gorgeous beyond even an artist's wildest dreams. The Banff course cost more than a million dollars to lay out in 1927, making it the most expensive golf course of its time. Yet the money was well invested, for not only is the location superb, but players have great excuses for bad shots: distracted by roaming elk and some of the most majestic scenery on Earth, one can easily make a few ricochet shots!

Golf magazines have often placed the equally spectacular **Jasper Park Lodge** golf course at the top of their list of greatest courses. In addition to the gorgeous landscape, there's a kind of mirage that appears after the 8th hole. Here, there's a line of parked golf carts, and the golfers, their game temporarily forgotten, lean up against a wooden hut and drip ketchup on their golf shirts. Canada's most elegant club is graced with an ordinary snack bar.

The Columbia Valley boasts some of the most beautiful courses in British Columbia, including excellent golf academies and even golf schools for beginners. Golfing magazines cite the driving

range and practice areas at **The Springs at Radium** course as among the best in North America. Experienced golfers practice on 18-hole championship courses, each with its own character and breathtaking panoramas. **The Springs**, designed by Les Furber, hugs the course of the Columbia River. Water obstacles at the 8th, 9th, and 10th holes are tricky, and the par 3 holes are a true challenge – particularly the 14th, which after the par 5 on the 13th can create a kind of mental block.

The **Fernie Golf and Country Club** captivates many because of its location at the foot of Three Sisters Peaks, and drives many others to despair with its devilish sand traps.

Trickle Creek, also a Les Furber product, is a very complex course: the first several holes give golfers a false sense of security which is challenged with the tricky section on the back nine. The par 5 17th hole is often compared to the notorious 17th hole at St. Andrew's.

Canada is good golfing country; and beginners, in particular, can profit from the casual approach to the game, practicing on par 3 courses (practically every little town has one) or pretty 9-hole ones without the pressure of other golfers breathing down their necks or sneering at their lack of experience or handicap. In Canada, you can take 20 strokes if you need to – the main thing is to have fun.

Among the many less-known courses is the **Blueberry Hill Golf Course** in **Athabasca**, which just expanded to 18 holes in 1995; its beautifully placed, tricky greens lie on the sloping banks of the Athabasca River. The **Nicola Valley Golf Course**, also little-known, lies in Quilchena, in the golden hills of the Nicola Valley. Its beautiful long fairways would be quite easy to play if it weren't for the creek that zigzags through the course. Both courses share an additional Canadian feature: there are neat, clean campgrounds directly adjacent to them (Blueberry Hills RV Park, Nicola Valley RV Park), where golf bags are leaned up against RVs and old golf hands trade notes on birdies and eagles.

227

WINE FROM THE OKANAGAN VALLEY

A few years ago it was still customary for B.C.'s vintners to buy their grapes, or even their grape juice, in Chile or California and then bottle it back home – which justified use of the misleading label "Made in British Columbia." Canada's wine-growers managed to avoid the topic of local wine production for a long time. But when the first "ecologically minded" young people arrived from California, Australia and Germany and began to cultivate small vineyards and bottle wine from a single variety of grape, it represented a revolution in miniature which roused the Canadian vintners from their complacent lethargy.

The newcomers initiated the quality designation *VQA* to distinguish their product from those less pure. Voices of

Above: Founded in 1972, Gray Monk is one of the most successful wine producers around Okanagan Lake.

gloom and doom echoed throughout the valley, for the old-timers prophesied to the young "upstarts" that Canadians could never be turned into wine connoisseurs, much less persuaded to pay 10 dollars for a bottle of wine.

Ironically, it was a small private brewery which ultimately showed the way to fine local wine. The Okanagan Springs Brewery proved tremendously successful with its beers, produced in accordance with the Bavarian Purity Law, using only pure water, hops and barley. Canadian taste buds recognized the difference. It was the brewery's owner who encouraged his son to try his hand at producing quality wines. The son, being a good son, listened to his father and went to Germany, where he studied wine-making and worked for quite some time. Today, Eric von Krosigk produces some of the best wines in the valley.

Von Krosigk made the LeComte Estate one of the leading cellars in the valley: "You can't imagine the things we've concocted here: dandelion, rhubarb, anything that had any kind of flavor, and then a helluva lot of sugar.Our cognac was a mixture of raisins and a chemistry kit."

When he got home, Eric had his work cut out for him trying to explain his ideas to his colleagues; on the other hand, the Canadian spirit, a sense of "Let's just try," came to his aid. His foreman Albert, a real handyman, welded the stainless steel tanks himself and fiddled around with new irrigation systems long enough to perfect them. Irrigation is of prime importance in this valley: with only 10 inches (260 mm) of precipitation a year and 3 bone-dry summer months, sprinkler systems are indispensable.

But the valley's absolutely reliable microclimate is a very positive factor. There are crisp winters and a short spring; most of the rain falls in June, and then there's nothing but sun until the first frosts hit in mid- to late October. "It is, of course, sensational for the picking season – we can practically decide ourselves how ripe we want the grapes to be," says Eric. Anything that hasn't been picked before the first frost will become *Eiswein*, a sweet wine made from grapes which have been exposed to frost: a rare luxury in Europe, but a standard product of this valley.

LeComte's specialty and best seller are his neutral Gewürztraminers, which grow on more than 22 acres (9 ha) and create a wine that complements the freshness of West Coast cuisine. By now, they have even managed to go beyond the "Okanagan export threshhold." Just a few years ago, "export" meant that a wine was sold to neighboring Alberta; today, however, LeComte's wines can be found in London and at international wine fairs. Red wine, too, is on the way; LeComte is planting Cabernet Savignon and Merlot grapes in his southernmost areas.

Adolf Kruger, whose Wild Goose Vineyards produce excellent wines, warns of too much red wine euphoria: in 1985, he lost 2,000 vines to a cold snap.

Kruger is very experienced in the well-established Maréchal Foch, a wine that is greatly underestimated. Wine ripened in oak barrels acquires a complex taste; Adolf Kruger uses 53-gallon American-made barrels (200 lit.) that were actually designed for the aging of whiskey.

"Organic" wine has also been around in the valley for quite some time: interesting, for instance, are the vineyards of Hainle, the "Pope" of great dry white wines. Since 1993, Hainle has been able to claim the appellation "100% organic" – a controlled designation awarded by the Similkameen Okanagan Organic Producers Association (S.O.O.P.A.). The Hainle family's Riesling is crisp and lively with an especially fruity touch, and the Chardonnays have a notable character.

Quails Gate Estate's Rieslings, too, are known all over the world. The Chasselas, known as an eating grape in France, produces a soft, full-bodied wine slightly reminiscent of Swiss Fendant. The N.V. Harvest White, a harmonious blend of Riesling, Sylvaner and other choice grapes, has surprised even critical wine drinkers. Quails also produces "organic" wine, originally out of financial necessity: artificial fertilizer proved just too expensive!

For wine fans, there are many routes through the Okanagan Valley: brochures outline drives from vineyard to vineyard, and the B.C. Wine Institute provides detailed information (see p. 155.)

The wineries described here represent only a fraction of the producers; the prize-winning Gehringer Brothers, among many others, are worth a little detour. You will not only be rewarded with excellent wine, but also breathtaking countryside – and naturally with that unmistakably Canadian flair. Where else in the world are bears the most-feared natural disaster during the harvest? These intelligent animals don't bother eating grapes off the vine, but prefer to eat right from the tub full of picked grapes, simply removing the lid and helping themselves.

THE INUIT – SURVIVAL ON THE EDGE OF A SEA OF ICE

In the autumn of 1994, Inuit hunters from Igloolik killed a Greenland whale for the first time in years, and divided up the meat between their communities in the Canadian Arctic. Not long afterwards, they were taken to court. Although the Inuit, in principle, agree with the strict conservation laws for whales and generally cooperate with the environmental protection agency, they are still striving for exceptions to be made for their hunters. Paul Quass, the former president of Tungavik Inc., the organization responsible for the land rights of the Inuit, defended the whalers: "I was told that the whale had offered itself to the hunters as a present because it knew how much the older members of the tribe had been longing for whale meat. The

Above: When they both grow up, they can go dogsledding together. Right: Inuit art of wood and walrus ivory.

Igloolik hunters did what they learned as children – obeyed their elders." The Inuit believed that, in this case, their very culture was on trial; moreover, the verdict that was reached was a product of the legal system of that very social order which was itself ultimately responsible for the extermination of the whales in the first place. It seems to be a sign of our times that people are more interested in protecting the rights of animals than those of human beings.

Compared to many native peoples, the Inuit are relative "newcomers" who came from Asia 6,000 years ago and occupied the northern edge of the continent and the Arctic archipelago. The Dorset Eskimos (ca. 1000 BC), who mainly lived on caribou, were driven out by the Thule Eskimos, who then spread out from Alaska to Greenland. With their boats and harpoons, the Thule had an enormous "technological advantage" and were thus better able to hunt seals and whales. The present-day Inuit are descendants of these Thule people, and it's Thule culture that the modern industrialized world has to thank for many things they've adopted from the Inuit, such as the familiar parka, anorak and kayak.

Most important weapon of the Thule Inuit was the harpoon, which consisted of the shaft, the head, and a long line attached to a float or buoy made of hide, which last caused the harpooned animal to tire out. Hunting was a joint effort: there had to be an armed hunter sitting by every hole in the ice where a seal might come up for air. The Thule Inuit diet consisted mainly of seal and other ocean mammals. The women used the *ulo*, a type of chopping knife, in their daily work.

Although there were a wide range of different Indian cultures, Inuit culture was relatively uniform in terms of its spiritual beliefs, largely because the barren environment led people to focus on absolute necessities. For this reason, the

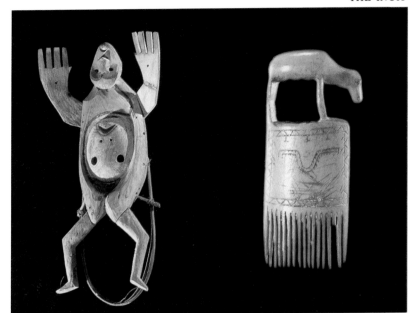

Inuit didn't really have a sense of art as such until well into this century. Even their perfectionism in fashioning clothes, such as the *mukluks* (boots) made of seal fur, was born of the necessity of imitating nature with a minimum of materials. Uniformity is also evident in the language, *Inuktitut*, which is understood from Siberia to Greenland, and is even written in Latin letters as well as in a variation of Cree syllabic writing.

Although most of the Inuit converted to Christianity in the 19th century, in recent years there has been a noticeable return to traditional beliefs which survived in the underground. A central motif of Inuit religious beliefs is the myth of Sedna, the deity of game. If the hunt is unsuccessful, it is because Sedna's hair is unkempt or dirty. The *angakok* (shaman) must put himself into a trance and travel to Sedna on the bottom of the sea to rearrange her hair. In recognition for his service, Sedna releases the animals from her care. The *angakok*, performing various spiritual rituals such as healing the sick,

is a common motif in contemporary Inuit arts and crafts.

The Inuit have a complex concept of the soul, which they believe inherent in everything, includng river rapids, a stone, or the animal they are hunting. Calming these *Inua* and respecting the taboos and rituals associated with them was traditionally an important spiritual process that was thought to ensure survival when there was no other means available. The tradition of miniature walrus ivory carvings rests on this belief; the carvings, originally amulets, represented the *Inua*.

From the arrival of the Europeans in the 19th century to the beginning of the 20th century, whaling gave the Inuit new opportunities for trade, which brought new materials (metals) and tools (such as pots) to the Arctic. With the decline of whaling, European whalers tried to supplement their dwindling incomes by trading furs and thus encouraged the Inuit to begin trap hunting. From 1910 to 1945, hunting for furs was the most important source of income for the Inuit. Since the

middle of the century, however, it has played only a secondary role, while the Inuit depend primarily on government subsidies for their existence.

The rapid change in the culture is based on two factors: first, the introduction of the rifle, and second, the area's incorporation into the world market, both in terms of export and the import of goods. The rifle made it more efficient to hunt sea animals from land than from the ice, and enabled fewer hunters to cover more hunting territory. The traditional hunting and storage cooperatives dissolved; many Inuit were drawn to the trading posts where they could trade their catch for food and equipment. This, however, created more dependencies: the Inuit became dependent not only on the cycles of economic development, but also on the natural cycles of the animals

Above: Learning to build igloos in a storm isn't just an art – it can be a question of life and death. Right: Seal and whale meat are no longer the only elements in the Inuit diet.

they were hunting, which force a rotation of four years, for example, with the polar fox hunt. Caught up in the exigencies of supply and demand, it proved impossible to survive economically: for world prices began to decline appreciably after World War II, falling steadily until they reached a new low as a result of the animal protection campaigns beginning in the 1970s.

The new, unfamiliar lifestyle brought new health problems, as well. Unhygienic living conditions in the trading posts led to a high rate of infection; in addition, the Inuit were often improperly nourished or simply undernourished as a result of adopting a new, leaner and therefore unsuitable diet. As a result, recent years have seen alarming spreads of TB, influenza and children's diseases, which cost many Inuit their lives, since it wasn't until the 1950s that an effective medical system started to be implemented.

Even though the Inuit have long since traded their igloos and summer tents for wooden houses and get around in air-

planes and snowmobiles instead of komatik sleds, hunting remains an integral part of the family's income for approximately 60% of the Inuit, and still serves as a criterion for the establishment of the social hierarchy. Before the white man arrived, the Inuit didn't have any social organization beyond the family unit; only successful hunting alone determined the social status of an *Inuk* (singular of Inuit). Unlike European hunters, the Inuit don't allow anything of their catch to go to waste. A European import embargo on seal skins means that seal skins have become almost impossible to sell. Visitors to the Northwest Territories can count on being asked about the latest activities of Greenpeace activists, Prince Charles or Brigitte Bardot.

In Canada, there are about 30,000 Inuit living in more than 60 communities, most of which are located on the sea, since only there can an adequate natural food supply be found. The Inuit are a very young people; more than half the population is under 15 years of age.

Thanks to state subsidies, an active arts and crafts movement has developed over the past few decades. In developing their modern style, the Inuit reach back to their roots, drawing on archaeological finds of the Pre-Dorset culture for motif and inspiration. The materials used are traditional: soapstone and walrus ivory, even whale bone and driftwood. The sculptures, which hearken back to Cubism, stand in sharp contrast, in terms of their color, to the modern, colorful Inuit graphics and textile products, which have helped to introduce new techniques and stylistic principles. Popular collectors' items, Inuit soapstone sculptures and other works of art are the most important Inuit export products in the Arctic.

Since everything that can be produced in the Arctic can also be manufactured more cheaply somewhere else, unemployment presents the most urgent problem. Almost every Inuit receives some form of government aid. It wasn't until unemployment became widespread that violence, alcohol and drug abuse became

233

an unfortunate part of daily life. Most of the Inuit who do have steady jobs work in administrative positions or in national service organizations.

Because of their traditionally isolated lifestyle, the Inuit had no real chance or occasion to develop a sense of ethnic identity until a few decades ago. Political organizations did not appear until after World War II. The Inuit Tapirisat (or brotherhood) of Canada, founded in 1971, is considered the most important special interest group. Unlike some of the other Indian tribes, the Inuit had not, until quite recently, concluded any land representation deals with the British Crown; the far north, after all, wasn't really considered a region with a glowing economic future. Not until 1984 was the Inuvialuit Agreement signed, a treaty for the area around Inuvik in the Makenzie District of the NWT, since with the start of

offshore oil extraction in the region it was suddenly important to spell everything out as far as territorial rights were concerned. After tough negotiations with Ottawa in 1992, the inhabitants of the central and eastern Arctic regions also reached a similar agreement.

By 1999, part of the NWT is to be officially ceded to the Inuit, to be administered by the Inuit themselves under the name *Nunavut* ("our land"). This new territory, comprising 20% of Canada and encompassing 741,000 square miles (1,9 m sq. km), will be inhabited by 22,000 people, 18,000 of them Inuit. Iqualit (Frobisher Bay), in the south of Baffin Island, is to become the seat of government. One problem is that only a few Inuit have had a kind of education that equips them to deal with complicated administrative structures.

Another step in the creation of Nunavut are payments amounting to more than 1.1 billion Canadian dollars, which will be paid to the Inuit in return for ceding the majority of their territorial rights to

Above: Modern igloos on Bathurst Inlet/NWT. Right: The Inuit drum dance hearkens back to shamanistic rituals.

the Canadian government. The federal government in Ottawa expects that new jobs will be created in Nunavut, and hopes that investors will be interested in the area's wealth of natural resources. Yet apart from the technical difficulties of mining in a permafrost region, the Inuit themselves could be a hindrance for the exploitation of natural resources. Since they form the majority of the population, they can themselves decide their country's fortunes, and their decisions aren't always based on economic advantage. The Inuit at Baker Lake, for example, despite 80% unemployment, turned down a German uranium company that wanted to open a uranium mine on permafrost in their region. The Inuit were especially outraged that a caribou calving area had been chosen as the site of the new mining town.

The young Inuit remain skeptical about their elders' hopes for Nunavut. Many believe that solving social problems should take priority over administrative autonomy, and hold the generation of the successful Inuit politicians responsible for the fact that, as of yet, so many of these social problems remain unsolved. An increasing number of young people grow up without any connection to the culture of their ancestors, drawn instead to the glitter of Hollywood which, traveling to the Arctic via television and video in the long polar nights, has created a generation of TV junkies with wishes that no one can fulfill. "Even when it's 20 below (-30°C), there are young people trying to dress like Michael Jackson in California," said Jose Kusugak from Tungavik Inc. "This is a concern; we've had a lot of facial frostbite cases lately." Many young people dream of leaving home to study or find jobs in the south. Through watching television and occasioinal travel, they believe themselves sufficiently acquainted with life in the outside world. That their chances of establishing themselves in large cities are slim is demonstrated through the sad example of too many of their cousins on Indian reservations in the United States.

235

URANIUM MINING IN SASKATCHEWAN

Prejudice against Indians? No, he doesn't have any, says the taxi driver in Saskatoon, and adds, immediately contradicting himself, "but they're lazy and spend their money on alcohol right away." He points to an idle character lounging nearby. "Why don't they stay up north? After all, they could work in the mines."

The mines: the El Dorado of the uranium industry all around the geological formation of the Athabasca Basin. Just as was the case with the legendary gold country, the uranium region in the northern reaches of Saskatchewan is extremely difficult to get to. The airplane is the main form of transportation; and some settlements have no road links at all with the outside world.

The two facets of Saskatchewan are best seen from the air. The south is dominated by the right angle, which runs through its cities and tidily organizes its endless wheat fields – territory mapped out with surveying equipment. Beyond the town of Prince Albert, however, begins the untamed expanse of the sub-Arctic north: dark forests and swamps sprinkled with countless lakes. Pilots of the little "SaskAir" planes use the roads below them for orientation.

Far in the north, the lakes balloon into huge bodies of water: Athabasca Lake, Reindeer Lake, Wollaston Lake. From the air, you can see the unsightly wounds the hand of man has gashed into the landscape: gaping holes, monstrous ditches. Uranium is being extracted here, the fuel for nuclear power plants. Open-pit mining is on the surface for all to see. But there is also mining under Wollaston Lake; the tunnels extend for miles beneath the earth. Visible traces above ground are the *tailings*, the storage basins and piles of refuse created in the manufacture of *yellow cake*, as uranium in its raw form is called.

There are about 30,000 northerners living in these wide open spaces, scattered over 117,000 square miles (300,000 sq. km) of land. Most of them are members of the Cree and Dene tribes. What do they think about uranium mining on their land? How does uranium affect their lives?

Take Wollaston Post. Houses, schools, churches, a supermarket and a police station huddle around Wollaston Lake's Welcome Bay. This is home to approximately 1,000 Indians and a handful of whites. There is hardly any work. A few Indians work at the supermarket, and a repair shop for Skidoos, or snowmobiles, employs a few more. Most of them have to live on welfare – not a happy development for a community that for millennia was self-sufficient as hunters, fishermen and gatherers. Food has to be flown in; only during the short summer months, when the lake is free from ice, does a ferry run the 25 miles (40 km) across the lake to the dock on the western shore, where Highway 105 passes by.

A few old-timers, trappers their whole lives long, are sitting around in the community center telling hunting stories, like trappers all over the world. But their stories are sad, and tinged with a sense of threatening doom. They tell of animals they have found losing their hair around the uranium mines, and other sick animals they've encountered. "We can't prove that these phenomena are caused by radiation from the mines and tailings," says Ed, one of the younger ones. "We've caught badly deformed fish in this lake. But there's no money for the necessary tests. Not once has anyone ever taken any measurements of the radiation in this area."

Right: Uranium mining in northern Saskatchewan – caught between questions of economic advantage, environmental issues and Indian rights.

Ed used to work in the mines himself. Now he belongs to a small group of environmentalists who are working against uranium mining with very limited resources. They're up against large Canadian- or French-owned companies; German uranium companies are also involved. Cluff Lake, Key Lake, Collin's Bay are the names of the mines; more are due to arrive in the next few years. There are also discussions about a disposal site in Saskatchewan for radioactive waste.

Ed and his colleagues have often tried to talk to the mine operators about their environmental concerns. There was the accident in the Key Lake mine, for example, when some 500,000 gallons (2 million lit.) of polluted water flowed into Wollaston Lake. The manager talked his way out of the problem by claiming to have no knowledge of his predecessor's files. "That's these guys' specialty: they always claim they don't know any details," Ed says bitterly. "They know exactly what they're doing," say environmentalists in Saskatoon, administrative hub of the uranium industry. Uranium mining is the first link in a deadly nuclear chain. The leached rock in the tailings still contains up to 85% of its original radioactivity. Wind spreads radioactive dust over wide areas, and radioactive material seeps into the groundwater and travels through rivers and lakes for thousands of miles. The poisonous chemicals used in the production of uranium destroy fauna and flora, and make their way through the food chain into the human body. And the Saskatoon taxi driver's advice about jobs in the mines? In that regard, the promises of mine operators are largely empty. Barely ten people from Wollaston Post work in the mines. And they don't want to hear about health hazards. You have to take what you can get here. And anyone who flies south from here for any reason may be lulled into a false sense of reassurance by the fact that, as the airplane travels south, those ugly holes quickly disappear, to be replaced by the orderly wheat fields of southern Saskatchewan.

HISTORIC RAILWAY HOTELS

The Canadian Pacific Railway had high-flying plans. Vice-president William Cornelius van Horne recognized the potential for tourism as early as the 19th century. "Since we can't export the land," he said, "we'll just have to import tourists." In 1886, the company built its first hotel, **Mount Stephen House**, in Field – just one year after the financial backer and businessman Donald A. Smith (later Lord Strathcona), Stanford Fleming and Cornelius van Horne, positioned at Eagle Pass in cutaway coats and top hats, called out "All aboard for the Pacific!" announcing the completion of their transcontinental railway project. The Banff Springs Hotel opened in 1888, and Chateau Lake Louise in 1890.

No other hotel chain in the world can boast hotels which have become sights in their own right to such a degree as the establishments of the Canadian Pacific. They are true landmarks, symbols of the cities they stand in. Not only do they have stories to tell, but they are a piece of history in themselves.

The clicking and clattering of the heating in some of the rooms at the **Banff Springs Hotel** gives you an idea of how much money and effort are required to restore and modernize such old buildings without lessening their historic charm. Modeled on a 16th-century chateau in the Loire valley, this fairy-tale palace in the Rockies originally boasted two wings and five stories; In 1903, another wing and two towers were added. In the year 1911, 22,000 people stayed in the palace, at a cost of $3.50 a night: in those days, that was an astronomically high number of guests for such a princely price. In 1911, the architect William Painter began transforming the Loire castle into a Scottish seat of nobility – or at least his impression thereof. He had hardly completed his work when a fire destroyed it in 1926. The hotel reopened in 1928, and it has been an attraction ever since – especially as a place of pilgrimage for Japanese tour groups and a popular getaway for honeymooners. At the turn of the century, Horne dreamed of someday creating a "luxurious oasis in the wilderness, a first-rate bathing resort." The latter was realized as well, though on a more modest scale, but with the Great Depression it became a superfluous cost factor and had to be shut down. In 1992, the hotel was officially designated a historic site; and finally, in 1995, a new spa complex (solus par aqua) was opened on a scale that would have made even Horne's head spin. It represents the renaissance of large traditional spa bathhouses, with pools and steam baths faced in marble, waterfalls, a fireplace, lounges and galleries.

Should you see a suitcase mysteriously moving around the hotel's long corridors by itself, don't fear: it's just the ghost of Sam McAuley, the former bellhop, who once swore never to leave these premises.

Chateau Lake Louise, at the foot of the Victoria Glacier, is quite different in character from the Banff Springs Hotel. Despite the fact that from the outside it appears to be a huge, defiant castle, it remains quiet and less busy as soon as the awe-struck day-trippers have departed. Anyone who has stayed even once at this hotel and watched, from his window, the spectacle of the sun rising over the glacier, will fall in love with the place, in spite of its bombast.

In fact, this splendid edifice opened as a small wooden chalet able to accommodate 12 guests. It waas soon bursting at the seams, however; two new Tudor-style wings were added, and in 1912-13, the first stone section was built. The wooden structures were victims of a fire in 1924, whereupon it was decided to construct an eight-story brick building. The guest list of the chateau reads like a

Right: The Banff Springs Hotel, a "historic site," is a sight in itself.

Who's Who of the aristocracy, politics and the entertainment industry: the Prince of Wales stayed here in 1919, John Barrymore in 1928, Admiral Lord Louis Mountbatten in 1943, King Hussein of Jordan in 1989 and the King and Queen of Denmark in 1991. From Prince Rainer of Monaco to Alfred Hitchcock, Elizabeth II to Cary Grant, Clint Eastwood to Bing Crosby – all, in their day, had high tea here, a tradition today's visitors can still enjoy in the Lakeview Lounge.

High tea is also a byword at the **Empress Hotel** in Victoria, which upholds English traditions and customs in the midst of opulent Victorian splendor. The **Hotel Vancouver** is also one of its city's landmarks; it was even Vancouver's tallest building when it was completed in 1939. The **Hotel MacDonald** in Edmonton was built in 1915 by the Grand Trunk Railway Company; the CP group took it over in 1988 and painstakingly restored it. Most desirable rooms are the suites in the turrets. **The Palliser**, built in 1814, is a Calgary institution: during the annual Calgary Stampede, it hosts some elite events for the chosen few – a big honor in this horse- and cowboy-loving city.

In addition to the venerable old buildings, there are new hotels vying for similar "classic" status: **Waterfront Centre** in Vancouver, **Chateau Whistler** and the **Lodge at Kananaskis**.

Canadian Pacific Hotels & Resorts also owns the most beautiful hotel resort in western Canada: the **Jasper Park Lodge**. Luxury bungalows line the shore of Lac Beauvert, on the site where Jack and Fred Brewster first pitched tents for guests in 1915, and later felled trees and built small wooden houses with their own hands. The Canadian National Railway Company bought them out, recognized the magic of this location, and retained the bungalow style. So photogenic is the Jasper Park Lodge that it's served as the setting for several movies: *The Emperor Waltz*, starring Bing Crosby and Joan Fontaine, in 1949, and, in 1953, *River of no Return*, with Marilyn Monroe, and *The Far Country*, with James Stewart.

239

PREPARING FOR YOUR TRIP

Climate / When to Go

In Canada, summers are dry and, by European standards, warm rather than hot: average temperatures in July and August are between 75°F and 85°F (25°-30°C). In the northern reaches of the country, winters are extremely cold, with temperatures of as low as -40°F/C: in 1989/90, the mercury sank down to -58°F (-50°C) below zero. The nearer you are to the Arctic Circle, the longer winter is likely to last.

Because of the mountain chains running north to south, there are, of course, exceptions: cold Arctic air flows down as far as the United States, while hot tropical air from the Gulf of Mexico can create heat waves in Central Canada. Often, hurricanes sweep across the country, bringing days of rain in their wake that lead to flooding. Tornados are less frequent, but still a remote possibility. One specialty of Alberta is the chinook, a wind that raises temperatures by as much as 65°F (20°C) within a single hour.

B.C.'s coast has the most balanced climate, with mild winters and relatively temperate summers; however, this region gets a lot of rain. The prairie provinces, by contrast, are known for their climatic extremes: temperatures in winter often fall to -40°F/C, while in summer they can get up to 85°F (30°C) and above.

April and early May are not ideal times to visit western Canada. There's still snow on the ground in places, nothing is flowering yet, and the tourist attractions are still closed. The period from mid-May to the end of June sees the awakening of the tourist year. In the Rockies, there's sometimes snow on the ground until the end of June, inhibiting access to many high-altitude attractions. Lake Louise is the most wintry spot in the Rockies: it's still winter here in late May, while around Jasper spring is already underway.

July and August are high season, and the main attractions are flooded with tourists. September and early Oktober burst into the warm rich shades of fall foliage, blanketing the mountains with color. Late October sees the return of winter, and is therefore not an ideal time to travel. Real winter in Canada, however, is an unforgettable experience, even if you don't ski. Temperatures of around -22°F (-30°C) are actually easier to bear in the dry climate of the mountains than they would be in more humid regions.

And a word about **mosquitos**, which are at their worst from June to around mid-August. The only hope is a family-sized bottle of an insect repellent such as *Off* or *Cutter's*.

Clothing

Canadians are generally informal, and leisure wear is the most sensible equipment for vacationers. Two important accessories in a country geared toward outdoor activity, where people spend plenty of time outside, are a good, warm, wind- and waterproof jacket and a sturdy pair of shoes. In expensive restaurants, however, you'll be expected to appear in appropriate garb.

Medical Coverage

Canada's state medical insurance covers absolutely no medical or hospital costs for foreign tourists. Before your trip, therefore, you should probably take out a travel medical insurance policy that will cover you for the duration of your stay.

Money

Canadian dollars (Can$) are divided much like American ones. Coins appear in the following denominations: 1c (penny), 5c (nickel), 10c (dime), 25c (quarter), 50c (half dollar), $1 (loonie), $2. Bills appear in denominations of $5, 10, 20, 50 and 100. Canada, like the States, is credit-card friendly: Visa and

Mastercard are accepted virtually everywhere, and American Express is useful at hotels, car rental agencies and airlines. If you lose your card: American Express: tel. 1-800-268 9855; Visa: tel. 604/654 3210; Mastercard: tel. 604/684 4571. **Traveler's Checks** are generally accepted, but Eurochecks are not.

Getting There

Vancouver has Western Canada's largest international airport, but there's also international service to Calgary, Edmonton, and Regina, among others. From the United States, there's direct service to Canada from more than 20 cities.

The two Canadian airlines, Air Canada and Canadian Airlines, offer a range of international flights. **Air Canada** has the largest selection of direct flights from the U.K., with flights from Heathrow, Manchester and Glasgow to Vancouver, Calgary, Edmonton, and Winnipeg, among others. Its toll-free number in the U.S. and Canada is 1-800-776-3000; for information in Britain, call 0181/759-2636 or 0345/181313.

Canadian Airlines (a partner of **Qantas** and **Lufthansa**, among others), also flies from Heathrow to Calgary, Edmonton, and Vancouver. Together with Qantas, the airline also operates flights from Sydney to Vancouver. In the U.S. and Canada, call 1-800-426-7000; in Britain, call 0181/667-0666 or 0345/ 616767; in Australia, call 02/299-7843; in New Zealand, call 09/3090-3620.

British Air, KLM, Northwest and United are among the other airlines offering direct international service from the U.S and U.K. to Western Canada; United also runs direct flights to Vancouver from Sydney and Auckland.

Another option is to fly to the U.S. and then travel to Canada by **train**: from Seattle, for example, to Vancouver. For details and pricing, call Amtrak at 1-800-872-7245 (toll-free, in the U.S.A. and Canada).

Entering the Country

A valid passport is sufficient for anyone who wishes to enter the country. U.S. citizens can get away with some other form of identification. Tourists cannot remain in Canada for longer than six months.

TRAVELING IN CANADA

By Plane

Air Canada and **Canadian Airlines** provide service for longer domestic routes, while small airlines run short flights and service islands and the less accessible regions of the far North. **Air Canada**, Place Air Canada, Blvd. Dorchester Quest 500, Montreal, tel. 514/422-5000 and at the airline's city offices.

By Train

VIA Rail is the Canadian railway line. Trains are an attractive means of transportation in Canada, especially with the *Canrailpass* or the *Youth Canrailpass*. Info: **VIA Rail**, La Gauchetière Ouest 935, Montreal, tel. 1-800-663-8238 or 1-800-561-8630. The **sightseeing train** *Canadian* runs year-round from Toronto to Vancouver; the trip takes three days (departures from Toronto Tue, Thu and Sat; leaves Vancouver Mon, Thu and Sat). Reserve well in advance. For information on other sightseeing trains – through the Rockies, or from Winnipeg to Churchill – check the "Guideposts" at the end of the individual chapters.

By Bus

Greyhound and a number of smaller bus lines serve even remote areas. You can save a lot of money by investing in an *Across Canada Ticket*, which is issued in several variations for different lengths of time. For imformation, contact **Greyhound Lines Canada**, SW 877 Greyhound Way, Calgary, tel. 403/265-9111, tel. throughout Canada 1-800-661-8747. **Red Arrow**, tel. 403/424-3339. Bus lines, however, operate to very few of the national parks. The company **Brewster's** organizes excursions to some main attractions; there's an information line in Calgary at 403/221-8242 or 1-800-661-1152.

By Car

All measurements of distance are given according to the metric system. The speed limit on expressways is 62 m.p.h (100 km/h); on four-lane divided highways, you can go up to 68 m.p.h. (110 km/h) in places. On two-lane highways, you can go 55 m.p.h. (90 km/h) or 50 m.p.h. (80 km/h); on smaller secondary highways, 50 m.p.h. (80 km/h); and within town limits, 20-30 m.p.h. (30-50 km/h).

Seatbelts are required. If the road is clear, you are allowed to turn right on a red light. You may not pass a schoolbus with its blinkers on, even if you're traveling in the opposite direction.

Canada is a great country for drivers. Traffic jams are virtually unknown, except during rush hour in Greater Vancouver, Calgary and some places on Vancouver Island.

Road conditions are generally good, although some of the smaller secondary highways may be less well-tended. Some roads are unpaved dirt or gravel roads, but these are generally no problem in dry weather. Check at a gas station or tourist office about road conditions, and if you do run into rain, note that your car will emerge in dire need of a wash. The required insurance at many car rental companies doesn't cover any damages incurred on these roads. Drive carefully, therefore, and pull well over if you see a truck coming; stones thrown up by a passing truck have been the downfall of many a windshield. Some rental car companies, and almost all firms that rent campers, prohibit the renter from driving on unpaved roads at all; read carefully through the contract before you plan your route. Note, too, that many foreign visitors underestimate the distances; 30 miles (50 km) on a dirt road can feel like a journey around the world.

Roads are generally well signposted; it's important to have a road map that shows the numbered highways. All intersections are indicated several hundred yards in advance with *Junction (JCT)* signs.

Gas stations on the main expressways are open until midnight; in cities, generally until 9-10 pm; and in smaller towns often only until 7 pm. Most gas stations will accept credit cards; still, it's best to have enough cash with you to cover the cost of a tank of gas if you need it.

In case of a **breakdown**, the CAA will help anyone who's a member of an automobile club, tel. 1-800-336-4357. Non-members should call 613/820-1400 (general information: CAA, 999 W Broadway Ave., Vancouver, tel. 604/733-6660).

Car Rental: Many travelers reserve their cars before they've even left on their trip; you can sometimes get special rates, have more time to figure out what you need, and save time when you have a car waiting for you when you arrive. Reservation numbers: **Avis**: 1-800-331-1212 (U.S./Canada), 01645/123456 (U.K.); **Hertz**: 1-800-654-3131 (U.S./Canada), 01345/555888 (U.K.); **Budget** 1-800-527-0700 (U.S./Canada), 0800/181181 (U.K.).

The question, often, is whether you want a car or a camper. If you don't rent your car until you get to Canada, you'll find car rental agencies at all the airports; prices range from $30 to $100 a day, depending on make and car rental company. At smaller firms with low rates, make sure to check the kilometer allowance; if it's quite low, you could end up paying more at the end of the day than you would at an ostensibly more expensive agency. One-way-rentals can get extremely expensive, which is a great problem for anyone who wants to drive across the country: if you rent a car in Winnipeg and return it in Vancouver, you may pay more for the return transfer than for your entire outbound trip! It's thus a good idea to plan out a round-trip itinerary, unless you're going by camper between Calgary and Vancouver.

A trip with a small rental car and overnight accommodation in motels or B&Bs will cost you less than renting a camper or trailer. Renting a 2-person camper (a pick-up truck with a camper unit in the bed) will save you hotel costs, but probably balance that out through the price of gas: these "gas-guzzlers" can use 6-8 gallons of gas in 60-70 miles (20-25 l in 100 km). A rented camper should not be more than two years old; these vehicles wear out quickly. You should always take out full insurance, and check carefully what this policy covers and what it doesn't (read the fine print). One agency with vehicles in good condition is **Cruise Canada**, not far from the airports in Vancouver, Calgary and and the ferry terminal: 7731 Vantage Way, Delta, B.C. V4G 1A6, tel. 604/946-5775. You can rent a camper in Vancouver and return it in Calgary, or vice versa. VW campers use less gas; furthermore, they're tougher. You can rent a "Volkswagen California" from **Westcoach Mountain Campers**, 9173 Shaugnessy St., Vancouver, B.C., V6P 6R9, tel. 604/325 -2594.

For **motorcycle rental**, contact **Cruise Canada** or **The Great Canadian Mortor Corp**, Box 239, Revelstoke, BC, V0E 2S0, tel. 604/837-6500.

PRACTICAL TIPS FROM A TO Z

Accommodation

Hotels and Motels: Western Canada has a good range of hotels and motels in every price class. The price categories in this book approximately follow these guidelines (prices per person per night): *LUXURY*, more than $70; *MODERATE,* $40-70; *BUDGET:* less than $40. "Budget" denotes simply a price category; the rooms may well be attractive and well-equipped.

Canadian prices are quoted by room, not by person. If a double room in a motel room costs $50, that means $25 a person. Often, large and expensive-looking hotels of the better-known chains offer good weekend or package rates, so don't let the appearance of luxury scare you away. In Manitoba and Saskatchewan, especially, room prices of more than $100 are rare, and you can get rooms in excellent hotels for much less than that.

B&B – Bed&Breakfast: B&Bs are often located on farms and ranches or in quiet residential areas. You can find listings for **Alberta** in the *Alberta Accomodation Guide;* for **B.C.**, offices that arrange B&B accommodation are listed in the guide *British Columbia Accomodation.* Further information from **B.C. Bed &Breakfast**, Box 593, 810 West Broadway, Vancouver, tel. 604/298-8815. In **Saskatchewan**: *Saskatchewan Accomodation Country Vacation* for farms and B&Bs; there's also the brochure *Country Vacation*, which you can order from Box 428, Gull Lake. In **Manitoba**: **B&B of Manitoba**, 93 Healy St., Winnipeg. A bible for B&B fans is *The Canadian Bed&Breakfast Guide* by Gerda Pantel (Penguin Books).

Camping: In Canada there's a distinction between private campgrounds and those operated by national or provincial parks.

The national park campgrounds are captivating for their location; campsites are generally located in the middle of the wilderness. A warden will generally come along to collect the camping fee ($12-15 per site); in other cases, one registers oneself and slips a prepared and pre-paid envelope into the park mailbox. These campgrounds don't usually have showers, only toilets with sinks. *RV*

Parks are campgrounds for motor homes, campers and trailers; they won't have any room for tents unless the sign explicitly states *Camping & RV. Full hook-up* means that electricity, gas and water are available at each individual site; there are also facilities with half hook-ups or spots with no such connections whatsoever.

Youth hostels: There are listings in the International Youth Hostel Handbook, Vol. 2. For additional information, contact Hostelling International (in **Canada**: 613/237-7884 or 1-800-663-5777; in the **U.S.**: 202/783-6161); the Youth Hostel Association in **England** (0171/836-1036), or the **Australian** Youth Hostel Association (02/565-1325).

Houseboats: These are popular on the lakes of British Columbia, especially on Shuswap Lake, and on the Lake of the Woods (on the border between Manitoba/Ontario). In high season, you have to make your reservations well in advance, but if you're traveling off peak season you'll have no trouble getting a boat on the spot. Information about **Shuswap Lake**: Shuswap Houseboat Association, P.O. Box 962, Kamloops, B.C., V2C 6H1. Information about **Lake of the Woods**: Ontario's Sunset Country Travel Association, 102 Main St., Box 647 M, Kenora, Ontario.

Banks

Canadian banks accept any standard travelers' checks, as well, in most cases, as Euro/Mastercard and VISA. Make sure you have your passport with you when conducting business at a bank. Banks are generally open Mon-Fri 9 am-2 pm, sometimes until 4 pm.

Customs

Bringing meat or plants into the country is strictly prohibited. You are allowed to bring in 200 cigarettes, 50 cigars, 1 liter of wine, and presents of up to $40 in value. You can bring in or take out as much hard currency as you like. If you

want to bring in a hunting weapon, you should consult a travel agency for details before your departure.

Discounts

Canada offers a range of discounts for senior citizens (over 65 years of age). In addition, there are also rebates for young people between 13 and 21, or for anyone holding an international student ID. Children under 12 can almost always sleep in their parents' rooms free of charge; some establishments shift this age limit up or down. In friendly Canada, it's always worth your while to ask about possible discounts.

Eating and Drinking

Many travelers labor under the false impression that food in Canada consists largely of your standard American fast food fare. Yet while every city does have its ring of fast food chains, this is far from being all that Canada's kitchens have to offer.

Among the better restaurant chains are *Earls* (striking buildings, friendly staff, with salads, pasta, steaks and wine), *The Keg* (salads, steaks and spare ribs), *Smitty's* or *The White Spot* (a family restaurant with a large menu). *Alberta Beef* is famous for its excellent steaks. Following a current trend throughout North America, the large cities are developing a real coffee culture, thanks to the prevalence of *Starbucks* coffee shops, a chain that started in Washington State (U.S.A.).

Because of the country's broad ethnic variety, you find good ethnic restaurants even in the smaller cities. As you approach the Pacific coast, seafood and West Coast cuisine start to dominate the menu: the latter is characterized by a use of Asian ingredients, creatively combined, with lots of salad and fish.

In an elegant restaurant, you should count on spending $50-100 for two; in a smaller, family restaurant, two people can eat and drink their fill for around

$30-40. Europeans, note that restaurant guests are expected to wait to be seated by a host or hostess.

For snacks or picnic supplies, you can stop off at a deli for a range of sandwiches, baked goods, snacks and beverages. No one should leave North America without sampling a bagel, a kind of doughnut-shaped bread roll, originally a Jewish staple, now a ubiquitous base for sandwiches in a range of varieties. In the cities, you find more and more bakeries which produce respectable breads vastly preferable to the spongy packaged kinds prevalent in the supermarkets.

In B.C., Saskatchewan, the Northwest Territories, and Yukon, the legal drinking age is 19; in Manitoba and Alberta, it's 18. You can only buy alcohol in a liquor store, generally not in a supermarket; and only licensed restaurants are allowed to serve it (some will allow you to bring your own if you do it discreetly).

Electricity

Canada's electrical voltage is 110 volts/60 hertz. Anyone coming from Europe should make sure that his electronic appliances can be switched from 220 V to 110 V. Nor will European plugs fit into the sockets, necessitating an adapter; if you're travelling in a camper, you'll need several of these. Travelers from the United States, however, will have no trouble.

Emergency Calls

The emergency number for emergencies of any kind is 911. If the line is busy, call the operator (0) and ask him or her to connect you.

Forest Fires

Open fires in any area other than the fireplaces in the national parks is absolutely prohibited.

In case of a forest fire, immediately dial "0" to contact the telephone operator for help.

Handicapped Travelers

Canada generally has quite good handicapped facilities; certainly better than those in Europe. Hotels, restaurants, and most cities in general, as well as the national parks, are laid out with disabled people and wheelchair access in mind. Many of the main sights in the national parks are wheelchair accessible.

For information, contact the **Canadian Paraplegic Association**, 825 Sherbrook St, Winnipeg, R3A 1M5, tel. 204/786 4753, or SW Marine Dr, Vancouver, V6P 5Y7, tel. 604/3243611.

For information on facilitites for the deaf, contact **Western Institute for the Deaf**, 2125 W. 7th Ave, Vancouver, V6K 1X9, tel. 604/ 7367391.

Holidays

New Year (January 1). Good Friday. Easter Monday. Victoria Day (Monday before May 25; beginning of the main travel season). Canada Day (July 1; celbrated with parties, parades, and cultural events). Provincial Holiday (first Monday in August). Labour Day (first Monday in Sept, end of the main travel season). Thanksgiving (second Monday in October; note that Canadian Thanksgiving is earlier than American Thanksgiving). Christmas Day (December 25). Boxing Day (December 26).

Medical Information

When visiting a doctor, you should have a credit card or proof of sufficient funds with you (it makes sense to take out travel medical insurance). In an emergency, you can go to the emergency room of the nearest hospital. In the national parks, the rangers can provide assistance. Medications can be purchased, and prescriptions filled, in the pharmacy section of any local drug store or supermarket.

National Parks

In most of Canada's **National Parks,** you have to pay an entrance fee when you drive into the park ($4-5 a day per person, or $28-$35 a year per person; the yearly ticket is good for entry into any of the 11 national parks in Canada). Near the entrance you'll find a Visitor Centre, where you can pick up maps and other information free of charge. Here, too, you can see short films or exhibits about the park and its history, its flora and fauna. The park wardens are also glad to oblige with tips and additional information.

Before the national parks were founded, there were often settlements in the region, which is why you still come across little communities within a national park's borders. National parks have strict regulations about building: the town has to fit into the landscape, such as, for example, Waskesiu in Prince Albert National Park. Banff, the only proper town in a national park, has been issued with an order prohibiting new construction altogether.

One excellent reference work is the *Parks Guide to National and Historic Sites in Western and Northern Canada*, which you can get in the individual parks.

Entry to the **Provincial Parks** is free of charge – overnight stays, however, are not. Here, you can indulge in activities which are forbidden in the National Parks: riding, for instance, on motorbikes, trikes, snowmobiles or motorboats.

Both national parks and provincial parks are ideal for camping and hiking. Take note that however photogenic a bear may seem to you, these are not suitable for petting – keep a safe distance. If you go camping overnight in a national park, keep all foodstuffs in your car, rather than in or by your tent. If you're on a canoe or hiking trip, seal foodstuffs, cosmetics and garbage so that no odor escapes, and suspend it, preferably between two trees, at least twelve feet above ground, or take advantage of the stands that are sometimes put out for this purpose. If neither of these is possible, store

it in your tent, as far as possible from the windward side, and sealed firmly. If you want to round out your diet with freshly-caught fish, clean your catch by the water and throw all waste back into the water. Cook as far as you can from your tent. And make sure to check with the park warden what else you should watch out for.

Sports

Fishing: *Equipment for salmon fishing:* a heavy rod, some 10 ft/3 m long; casting weights of 40-80 g; large reel with at least 650 ft/200 m of line; line .35 to .50. *Equipment for trout and char:* mid-sized spin rod, 8-9 ft/2.4-2.7 m long, casting weights of 20-40 g; mid-sized stationary reel with at least 490 ft/150 m of line; line .22 to .30. **Tip for backpackers**: Two-piece rods will hold you up. Much better are telescoping rods (cheap) or four-piece rods (more expensive), which you can easily store in a plastic tube at the side of your backpack.

Golf: You can find listings of golf courses in the individual provinces in *B.C. Outdoor & Adventure Vacations*, at the end of the *Alberta Accomodation & Visitor's Guide*, in the *Manitoba Explorer's Guide* and in the *Saskatchewan Vacation Book* and *Saskatchewan Outdoor Adventure*. You can pick up golfing equipment for a good price at local branches of *Nevada Bob's*, such as the ones in Winnipeg, Abbotsville.

Canoeing, Whitewater Rafting: Agencies and rental outlets are listed in the "Guideposts" at the end of each chapter. The Tourism Office of B.C. offers a brochure called *Outdoor and Adventure Vacations* which contains a list of addresses.

Hiking: Canada is a paradise for hikers who are in good shape and have adequate equipment. You can opt for longer hiking trails, which generally lead through national or provincial parks, or the easier, shorter nature trails.

Backpackers eager to set out on hikes of several days must register in advance with the park warden at the park's visitor center and pick up a permit (free of charge). The hiking trails often lead through real wilderness; be prepared to wade through brooks, follow poorly-marked paths, and pitch your tent in the middle of nowhere, regardless of wind and weather.

Street and Road Markings

Many of the roads that run in straight lines through the vast Canadian provinces have no names, but only numbers. Take note, in towns, of whether you're looking for a street (St.), road (Rd.), avenue (Ave.), boulevard (Blvd.), or drive (Dr.). Note, too, whether the street address you're looking for is followed by an ordinal (S, SW, SE; N, NW, NE). Otherwise, you run the risk of going badly astray: the difference between 3rd St. SE and 3rd St. NW could well amount to several miles!

Taxes

Foreigners can have the GST (Goods and Service Tax) on any major purchases refunded by filling out the required form at the airport Customs Office; you can also generally pick the form up at the Travel Info Centres (for information, call 613/991-3346 or 1-800-668-4748).

Telephone

You can find a telephone even in the remotest, wildest corner of Canada, but the system of different long-distance companies can make phoning a test of your patience. Local calls are still easy, and can be made with a 25-cent coin; but long-distance calls, even to the next town, are difficult to negotiate from a public phone, since you have to keep feeding in coins almost faster than you're speaking. If you have the operator connect you (dial "0"), you can hear what the first minute of the call is going to cost

you. Incidentally, the fact that you're calling within the same area code doesn't necessarily mean you're making a local call; if you're calling from Prince George to Quesnel, for example, both of which towns have the area code 250, it's officially a long-distance call, so you have to dial the area code first, even though it's the same as the one you're calling from.

There are telephone cards, but note that some of them are restricted to a single long-distance company and will only be usable from pay phones hooked up to that company's long-distance service; some, however, can be used from any public phone. Collect calls, where the charges are reversed, are also an option. If you're calling from a private home, you can ask the operator to call you back after you've finished and tell you how much the call cost so you can reimburse your hosts.

Area codes: 403 for Alberta, 604 for Greater Vancouver, 250 for British Columbia, 204 for Manitoba, 867 for the Northwest Territories (Yellowknife), 306 for Sakatchewan, 867 for Yukon (Whitehorse). The country code for Canada is the same as that for the U.S.: 1.

Numbers beginning with 1-800 are toll-free numbers, which are free of charge, sometimes difficult to reach, and cannot be dialled from outside North America. Phone numbers given in this book generally include the three-digit area code and the standard seven-digit phone number; you have to dial 1 before the area code for long-distance service.

Time

Canada's western provinces extend over three different time zones. Manitoba and the eastern half of Saskatchewan are on Central Time; the rest of Saskatchewan, Alberta and northeastern B.C. are on Mountain Time, an hour earlier; and the section of British Columbia west of the Rockies is on Pacific Time, an hour earlier than that. These time zones are identical to those in the corresponding areas of the United States. Daylight Savings Time comes into effect on the first Sunday in April and lasts until the last Sunday in October.

North America doesn't operate on a 24-hour clock; morning hours are designated with *am* (*ante meridiem*), and afternoon ones with *pm* (*post meridiem*).

Tipping
Wages in the service sector in Canada are relatively low. Restaurant personnel, especially, depend on their income from tips; 15% is the norm. Taxi drivers get 10-15%, chambermaids, $1 per day.

Tourist Alert
This is a travel call which is broadcast over the radio, posted in tourist centers or published in the paper. If you see or hear your name, immediately contact the next police station of the RCMP.

Tourist Information
In the individual provinces, nearly every small village has its own Tourist Information, Travel Info or Visitor's Centre; addresses are given in the "Guideposts" at the end of each chapter. For the main tourist offices of the individual provinces, see "Addresses," following.

ADDRESSES

Canadian Embassies Abroad
Australia: Level 5, Quay West, 111 Harrington St., Sydney, NSW 2000, tel. 02/2316522.

United Kingdom: Macdonald House, 1 Grosvenor Square, London W1X OAB, tel. 0171/258-6600.

United States: 501 Pennsylvania Avenue NW, Washington, DC 20001, tel. 202/682-1740. 1251 Avenue of the Americas, New York, NY 10020, tel. 212/5961600.

Embassies and Consulates in Canada
Australian Consulate: Suite 502, World Trade Centre, 999 Canada Pl., Vancouver, B.C., V6C 4E1, tel. 604/684-1177, fax 604/684-1856.

British Consulate: 1111 Melville St., Suite 800, Vancouver, B.C., V6E 3V6, tel. 604/683-4421, fax 604/681-0693.

Embassy of Ireland (only one office in Canada): 130 Albert St., Suite 1105, Ottowa, ON, K1P 5G4, tel. 613/233-6281, fax 613/233-5835.

New Zealand Consulate General: 888 Dunsmuir St., Suite 1200, Vancouver, B.C., V6C 3K4, tel. 604/684-7388, fax 604/684-7333.

United States Consulate: 1095 West Pender St., Vancouver, B.C., V6E 2M6, tel. 604/685-4311.

United States Consulate: 615 MacLeod Trail SE, Suite 1000, Calgary, Alberta, T2G 4T8, tel. 403/266-8962.

Provincial Tourist Offices
Alberta Economic Development and Tourism, Commerce Place, 10155 102nd St., Edmonton, AB T5J 4L6, tel. 403/427-4321 or 1-800-661-8888.

Tourism British Columbia, Parliament Bldgs., 1117 Wharf St., Victoria, B.C. V8V 1X4, tel. 250/387-1642 or 1-800-663-6000.

Travel Manitoba, 155 Carlton St., Winnipeg, MB R3C 3H8, tel. 204/945-3777 or 1-800-665-0400.

Northwest Territories Tourism, P.O. Box 1320, Yellowknife, NWT X1A 2L9, tel. 403/837-7200 or 1-800-661-0788.

Tourism Saskatchewan Authority, 1900 Albert St., Suite 500, Regina, SK S4P 4L9, tel. 306/787-2300 or 1-800-667-7191.

Tourism Yukon, P.O. Box 2703, Whitehorse, YT Y1A 2C6, tel. 403/ 667-5340.

AUTHORS

Nicola Förg is a freelance journalist and author who holds a degree in German and geology and has written several travel guides, including the *Nelles Guide Ireland*. She has explored Canada's less-traveled byways on foot, mountain bike, and horseback. She wrote the chapters "Vancouver," "The Canadian Rockies," "The Prairie Provinces," "Valleys of Southern B.C.," and the features on golf, skiing, wine, and railway hotels.

Katrin Habermann, a freelance journalist, wrote the chapter on history.

Arno Bindl has traveled many times through Canada's Rocky Mountains and explored the back country on extensive mountain hikes. He is the co-author of "The Canadian Rockies."

Astrid Filzek-Schwab, a journalist, studied art history, archaeology and history. She wrote the chapter on "Vancouver Island."

Jürgen Scheunemann, a freelance journalist, lived for a period in Seattle, during which time he traveled extensively through the Canadian Northwest. He is author of the chapter on "Yukon and the Northwest Territories."

Michael Werner is an editor of *Blinker*, Europe's largest fishing magazine. He knows Canada's fishing grounds intimately from many trips there, and wrote the feature about fishing.

Bernhard Mogge is a freelance journalist in Cologne who has been focusing for years on the topics of native peoples and human rights. He wrote the feature "Uranium Mining."

Dionys Zink studied geography and German and is a member of the Big Mountain Actions Group, which supports the native peoples of North America. He has written articles about the natives and environmental protection in Canada. His contribution to this book is the feature on the Inuit.

Marie-Luise Tolkmit has been traveling to Canada, New Zealand and Australia for years. She updated this book during her last trip to Canada in the fall and winter of 1997/98.

PHOTOGRAPHERS

Explore the World

AVAIBLABLE TITLES

Afghanistan 1 : 1 500 000
Australia 1 : 4 000 000
Bangkok - *Greater Bangkok,
Bangkok City* 1 : 75 000 / 1 : 15 000
Burma → *Myanmar*
Caribbean Islands 1 *Bermuda,
Bahamas, Greater Antilles*
1 : 2 500 000
Caribbean Islands 2 *Lesser Antilles*
1 : 2 500 000
Central America 1 : 1 750 000
Colombia - Ecuador 1 : 2 500 000
Crete - Kreta 1 : 200 000
China 1 - *Northeastern*
1 : 1 500 000
China 2 - *Northern* 1 : 1 500 000
China 3 - *Central* 1 : 1 500 000
China 4 - *Southern* 1 : 1 500 000
Dominican Republic - Haiti
1 : 600 000
Egypt 1 : 2 500 000 / 1 : 750 000
Hawaiian Islands
1 : 330 000 / 1 : 125 000
Hawaiian Islands 1 *Kauai*
1 : 125 000
Hawaiian Islands 2 *Honolulu*
- Oahu 1 : 125 000
Hawaiian Islands 3 *Maui - Molokai*
- Lanai 1 : 125 000

Hawaiian Islands 4 *Hawaii, The
Big Island* 1 : 330 000 / 1 : 125 000
Himalaya 1 : 1 500 000
Hong Kong 1 : 22 500
Indian Subcontinent 1 : 4 000 000
India 1 - *Northern* 1 : 1 500 000
India 2 - *Western* 1 : 1 500 000
India 3 - *Eastern* 1 : 1 500 000
India 4 - *Southern* 1 : 1 500 000
India 5 - *Northeastern - Bangladesh*
1 : 1 500 000
Indonesia 1 : 4 000 000
Indonesia 1 *Sumatra* 1 : 1 500 000
Indonesia 2 *Java + Nusa Tenggara*
1 : 1 500 000
Indonesia 3 *Bali* 1 : 180 000
Indonesia 4 *Kalimantan*
1 : 1 500 000
Indonesia 5 *Java + Bali* 1 : 650 000
Indonesia 6 *Sulawesi* 1 : 1 500 000
Indonesia 7 *Irian Jaya + Maluku*
1 : 1 500 000
Jakarta 1 : 22 500
Japan 1 : 1 500 000
Kenya 1 : 1 100 000
Korea 1 : 1 500 000
Malaysia 1 : 1 500 000
West Malaysia 1 : 650 000
Manila 1 : 17 500

Mexico 1 : 2 500 000
Myanmar (Burma) 1 : 1 500 000
Nepal 1 : 500 000 / 1 : 1 500 000
Trekking Map *Khumbu Himal /
Solu Khumbu* 1 : 75 000
New Zealand 1 : 1 250 000
Pakistan 1 : 1 500 000
Peru - Ecuador 1 : 2 500 000
Philippines 1 : 1 500 000
Singapore 1 : 22 500
Southeast Asia 1 : 4 000 000
Sri Lanka 1 : 450 000
Tanzania - Rwanda, Burundi
1 : 1 500 000
Thailand 1 : 1 500 000
Taiwan 1 : 400 000
Uganda 1 : 700 000
Venezuela - Guyana, Suriname,
French Guiana 1 : 2 500 000
Vietnam, Laos, Cambodia
1 : 1 500 000

FORTHCOMING

South Pacific Islands 1 : 13 000 000
Trekking Map *Kathmandu Valley /
Helambu, Langtang* 1 : 75 000

Nelles Maps in european top quality!
Relief mapping, kilometer charts and tourist attractions.
Always up-to-date!

Explore the World

NELLES GUIDES

AVAILABLE TITLES

Australia
Bali / Lombok
Berlin and Potsdam
Brittany
California
  Las Vegas, Reno,
  Baja California
Cambodia / Laos
Canada
  Ontario, Québec,
  Atlantic Provinces
Canada
  Pacific Coast, the Rockies,
  Prairie Provinces, and
  the Territories
Caribbean
  The Greater Antilles,
  Bermuda, Bahamas
Caribbean
  The Lesser Antilles
China – Hong Kong
Corsica
Crete
Croatia – Adriatic Coast
Cyprus
Egypt
Florida
Greece – The Mainland

Hawai'i
Hungary
India
  Northern, Northeastern
  and Central India
India – Southern India
Indonesia
  Sumatra, Java, Bali,
  Lombok, Sulawesi
Ireland
Israel - with Excursions
  to Jordan
Kenya
London, England and
  Wales
Malaysia
Mexico
Morocco
Moscow / St Petersburg
Munich
  Excursions to Castels,
  Lakes & Mountains
Nepal
New York – City and State
New Zealand
Norway
Paris
Philippines
Portugal
Prague / Czech Republic

Provence
Rome
Scotland
South Africa
South Pacific Islands
Spain – Pyrenees, Atlantic
  Coast, Central Spain
Spain
  Mediterranean Coast,
  Southern Spain,
  Balearic Islands
Sri Lanka
Syria – Lebanon
Tanzania
Thailand
Turkey
Tuscany
U.S.A.
  The East, Midwest and
  South
U.S.A.
  The West, Rockies and
  Texas
Vietnam

FORTHCOMING

Brazil
Myanmar (Burma)

Nelles Guides – authorative, informed and informative.
Always up-to-date, extensivley illustrated, and with first-rate relief maps.
256 pages, appr. 150 color photos, appr. 25 maps